York

MERCIA

WESSEX

Canterbury

FRISIANS

Bremen

SAXONY

Paderborn

RHINE R.

LIPPE R.

Cologne
(THE
COLONY)

MEUSE R.

Aix

Prüm

Ingelheim

Mainz

Worms

EAST FRANKS

Corbeny

SEINE R.

Reims

St. Denis

Thionville

Strassburg

BRITTANY

WEST FRANKS

LOIRE R.

Orléans

Tours

Poitiers

BURGUNDIANS

St. Maurice

Geneva L.

MT. OF JOVE

MT. CENIS

AQUITAINE

GARONNE R.

RHONE R.

PROVENCE

GASCONS

RONCESVALLES

Pampalona

Toulouse

Narbona

Marseilles

ASTURIAS

EBRO R.

Saragossa

Barcelona

Tortosa

EMIR OF
CÓRDOBA

palacios

The Middle

— Frontier of Empire

◯ Border Regions

⚥ Monastery or Mission

🏰 City or Town

⟩⟨ Mountain Pass

THE
ORTHMEN   SCANDIA

BALTIC SLAVS
WILTZI

The EMPIRE OF CHARLEMAGNE
800 - 814 A. D.

ODER R.

S L A V I C   P E O P L E S

WENDS
SORBS

BOHEMIANS

Ratisbon

VARIA

A V A R S

Salzburg

DANUBE R.

AVARS

CARINTHIA

DRAVE R.

Fruili

Aquileia

ISTRIA

SAVE R.
CROATS

DANUBE R.

BULGARS

Rialto

PO R.

Ravenna

Rimini

SERBS

Spoleto

S L A V S

Rome

Mt. Cassino

Benevento

VOLTURNO R.

Naples

CHARLEMAGNE

Books by Harold Lamb

BIOGRAPHICAL NARRATIVES

> *Charlemagne: The Legend and the Man*
> *Theodora and the Emperor*
> *Suleiman the Magnificent*
> *Genghis Khan*
> *Nur Mahal*
> *Omar Khayyam: A Life*
> *Alexander of Macedon: The Journey to World's End*

NOVEL

> *A Garden to the Eastward*

HISTORICAL NARRATIVES

> *New Found World: How North America Was Discovered and Explored*
> *The Earth Shakers: Tamerlane and The March of the Barbarians*
> *The Crusades: Iron Men and Saints and The Flame of Islam*
> *The March of Muscovy: Ivan the Terrible and The Growth of the Russian Empire*
> *The City and the Tsar: Peter the Great and The Move to the West (1648–1762)*

FOR OLDER CHILDREN

> *Durandel*
> *White Falcon*
> *Kirdy: The Road Out of the World*

"In old tales they tell us many wonders of heroes . . .
"Now here you shall read of the strife of brave men."

THE NIBELUNGENLIED

CHARLEMAGNE

The Legend and the Man

By HAROLD LAMB

DOUBLEDAY & COMPANY, INC.

Garden City, New York

Library of Congress Catalog Card Number 54–5368

FOREWORD

His NAME WAS CHARLES. Generations after he died, people remembered him as a great man, Charles the Great, and they pronounced this as *Charlemagne*.

The name, besides being unusual, came to stand for something remarkable. *Charlemagne*, unlike most other kings, seemed to belong not to one nation but to all the nations of western, Christian Europe. This may be because, toward the end of his life, he managed to unite those peoples in a single Christian community. By so doing he gave them hope.

Civilization in his time and area of the earth was dying out. With the last Roman legions, science, law, and ordered life—the mechanism that sustains us today—were draining away from these barbaric peoples of the Atlantic seaboard. They were our ancestors. Some of them, like the Visigoths and Lombards, had drifted in to the disintegrating Roman Empire and had preserved memories as well as some luxuries of the vanishing civilization. But the Franks, the people of Charlemagne, came too late upon the scene.

They found a wilderness ruled by force, in which they settled between the river Loire and the Rhine, troubled by visions of the Witches' Sabbath and the advent of the Evil One bestriding the forests of nights. They had some hope from the foretelling of missioners like the Irish Columban, of the salvation of their souls, or the possible second coming of Jesus Christ to earth.

Foreword

The Franks were men of sufficient physical force, being Germanic tribal folk, of warrior traditions—knowing the saga of the hero Beowulf who pulled an arm from the monster Grendel that could not be harmed by any weapon—and they survived bodily in their forest clearings. But they were land-bound and isolated in their corner of Europe by the pressure of the more barbaric Slavs and horse nomads of the east. They were cut off, further, by the sea from the surviving city of Greek-Roman culture, Constantinople. Across that sea was sweeping another culture, of Islam, Arab-led, antagonistic to them. In the deep darkness of the seventh century, their world seemed to be entering its last age, and many believed it would end abruptly in the year 1000 of the Lord.

More menacing than physical danger was the slow decay of minds, the failure of writing, the breakup of the universal Latin language into varied vernaculars, and the loss of ideals. The natives who survived in Roman Gaul were losing their ancient skills, while the Franks, their masters, had no understanding of a civilized state wherein an emperor governed all human beings by law. They gave their loyalty to elected tribal kings; one of these, Dagobert, pulled together his disintegrating nation; a warrior leader, Charles the Hammer, drove the Moslem invaders south through Gaul after the battle of Poitiers and gathered resources by confiscating the properties of churches; his son, Pepin the Short, tried to hold fast to southern Gaul while shaping his Franks into a catalyst people, to rule the others.

But only Charles, grandson of the Hammer and the son of Pepin the Short, received the name of Great. His rule became that of the Carolingian empire, which means simply the empire of Charles. It was different from others.

Then happened something quite unique in the west. The memory of this lost empire endured; it became a force that helped to shape a new world of the west. Charles himself became a legend, that of *Charlemagne*. The legend grew and spread through all the Christian lands. It was not merely the memory of an imagined golden age, or an extraordinary monarch. It was something belonging to all humankind, of a ruler who led them for a brief span of years toward unimagined things now lost to them. It passed, as it were, from the palaces and churches to abide within the homesteads and along the roads. It crept into songs. And it influenced events for four centuries.

This is the story of that man, as it can be reconstructed, and of the beginning of his legend.

CONTENTS

CHARLEMAGNE

Chapter I

THE FOREST LAND

After the vigils of Thomas, the apostle, he was sent forth for the first time on a venture of his own. Snow and mud made the tracks heavy that winter of the year 753.

Until then he had been given no armed band to lead, nor had he any land, either tilled or forest, to his name. He was then eleven years of age, over-tall and gangling, yet with a spread to his shoulders and wide bones in his hands that marked him for strength. They had cropped his dark hair close and his voice came shrill from his clumsy body.

Usually they called him that son of Pepin the Short. Those who hated him for one reason or another mouthed out his name as the Churl. It fitted him well enough, but his rightful name was Charles.

He said at once that he would go forth speedily, snow or no snow, on this venture alone to meet the visitors coming over the pass of the Alps to Frankland. After pulling a sheepskin cloak over his leather tunic, he rode from the court of Pepin, from the ancient Villa of Theodo. He forgot to take any presents for the strange visitors, although he remembered to take good led horses, one for each rider. As to those riders, Charles picked only Kerold, the swordsman, and the foresters who had hunted stags with him the day before. Having neither liegemen nor lords as sworn followers, the headstrong boy consorted with groomsmen and huntsmen, to gab with,

13

to drink with, and to swim when summer warmed the rivers.

When he vanished up the muddy trace into the drifting snow with his cavalcade, some of those who watched him off laughed and said lightly that the Churl set out to meet and to welcome the apostolic lord, the Pope himself, of St. Peter as if riding after a stag. Pepin himself said no word of blame or praise. It was the way of the dour Pepin, king of the Franks, to keep his first-born son at his side, to watch him rather than to school or counsel him. Whether good or ill came of that hard way of Pepin, no one could rightly say.

Riding hard and changing the saddles to the led beasts when the knee-deep mud tired the horses, Charles the prince and his forest lads followed the low sun south and came apace to the hostel at thirty leagues. Gladly he rode, being alone, without Fulrad the Abbot or the Constable to bid him be ware. This was the first mission to be given him by his father.

Gladly they sang as they rode, the steam of the laboring horses rising into the mist. The six who followed him felt lucky because the boy was gay.

Luck rode with the Arnulfings, he said. For Arnulf, the first of his family, had asked for a sign. Arnulf had thrown his seal ring into the river Seine, saying that if the ring came back to him it would be a sign he would rule over his fellow men. Well, the ring vanished into the water. Yet after years a fish was cut open on Arnulf's table and his ring fell out. Surely God had meant that to be a sign.

"There was the other river without a ford." Kerold, the man-at-arms, said his say. "And darkness coming on the earth and sky. When Charles rode up, a white hart sprang before him into the water, with antlers shining like gold i' the sun. Where this white hart drove into the water Charles followed. I' truth, there was a ford. Few who crossed it wet their leggings."

In many ways, as in such gabbing tales, Charles' memories were bound up with rivers, if not with hunting. He liked to

14

hear his comrades gab about his luck, because he had no trust in his own skill, or wisdom.

When they came late in the day to the hostel at thirty leagues, he thought that luck had served him well. Many horses clustered by the haystacks and stable hut, so it seemed as if the reverend visitors from Rome had arrived there.

At the hostel door, however, stood the lord Aucher. He was a battle leader who had fared to Rome, at command of Pepin the king. "How close does your father follow?" he demanded when he recognized the gangling Charles. A deft, hard-spoken seigneur, he gave no title of rank to Pepin in his words.

"He does not follow. He sent me on this road to greet Stephen, apostolic lord of Rome. Where is he?"

At this Aucher was not pleased. He looked long at the boy and explained that Stephen and his following of St. Peter's had had a hard passage over the mountains and were coming on slowly from the monastery of St. Maurice, where one had died.

Aucher and his men occupied the sleeping loft of the hostel and made no move to give their place to Charles and his foresters. Plainly he said it was neither courteous nor fitting for the king of the Franks to send only his youngling with forest fellows without gifts to meet and greet the Pope.

To this the boy made hasty and angry answer. He would not quarter himself at the hostel where Aucher abode in such comfort. He had been bidden to meet the great visitors, and he would ride on to carry out the bidding.

Aucher went back to the fire, with one word. "Churl."

Snow darkened the sky and cold settled in their fingers and feet when they rode on. The tired horses trod heavily away from the stable and stacks. Kerold and the forest fellows said nothing for they were Charles' men, faith-bound to obey him.

After dark the forest mesh closed about them, and they reined in to rest. Charles could not think where to look for shelter, but he would not turn back to sleep by a fire on stones where Aucher slept on the hay above him. He had a stubborn will.

Then suddenly he laughed, saying, "Now surely, dear friends, it is a time for that white hart to appear and show us a way to go."

They went on more readily after that, by reason of Charles' good cheer. It was like venturing through the darkness that befell Egypt, until one of the foresters pointed out a glimmer of flame ahead and they thought surely it would be the fire of a homestead.

But other lights flared along the track. These turned out to be the torches of a moving cavalcade. Charles and his band reined in because they had no force to stand against such a large company—likely to be marauders on the move at night.

Then Kerold swore, "Hart or no hart—strike me blind now if it is not the reverend henchman of St. Peter!"

So it turned out to be. The Pope's escort, benighted, was feeling its way along the road toward shelter. Charles forgot his weariness in his great excitement. This was the rarest luck!

When the outriders learned that he brought them the welcome of the Franks they led him to a muffled figure on a white horse. He heard a tired voice ask, where was the king?

Dismounting, stumbling in his excitement, Charles tried to explain that Pepin, son of Charles the Hammer, waited at Theodo's Villa in a warm high hall for the coming of the apostolic lord of Rome. Not knowing what else should be said, he waited anxiously. Another voice echoed his impulsive words in the clear Latin of the books.

Evidently the robed Romans felt misgivings because Pepin had not come forward on the road himself. Straining to understand their strange talk, he realized that it was a boorish welcome to send him and his fellows to greet this Stephen. For Stephen's voice whispered; it shook with the winds and the chill of the mountain passes.

Then he remembered that he had come without a present in his hands. The hot blood of shame pounded in his veins.

"Lord Pope," his shrill voice cried, "I would have brought gifts of fine woven stuffs and costly gold, but I have nothing except the weapons of hunting, and books—and few of those."

A face framed in the fur hood, white and weary under the torchlight, bent to examine him. "Valiant boy," the wayfarer made answer, "why do you speak of gifts? It is enough, Charles, that you have come through this forest wilderness— yes, at the hour of midnight, to lead us to shelter. Can you do that?"

It comforted Charles in his shame that this great apostolic lord pronounced his name clearly, so that it did not sound like a muffled Churl but like the ringing of a bell, *Carolus*.

He would not forget that sound of benison. When he rode back past the lance bearers, he was thinking about it. He had been lifted out of his shame.

And then he began to laugh, choking to keep from bursting into a loud guffaw. From the band of his companions, Kerold pressed to his side, whispering, "What has come upon you?"

"It has come over me," Charles gasped, "how we will turn the lord Aucher out of his snug nest in the coldest hour of the night to make sleeping space for all these bishops, presbyters, and clerks."

His laugh rang loud along the silent, snowbound road.

This first mission of Charles ended after the Christmas feast that marked the first day of the year 754 of salvation. When he sighted smoke rising from the wet roofs of Theodo's town, there was Fulrad, the archchaplain, waiting in his robes by the road, with the Constable armored and armed.

When he sighted the broken-down arch of the old Roman gate, there was his father waiting, wearing a new sky-blue mantle and the sword with the gold cross on the pommel. To Charles' surprise Pepin swung his broad body down from the

17

saddle and walked out in the mud to take the rein of the lord Pope's mount, to lead it through the gate. He did that like a groom.

"For all that Pepin does," muttered Aucher, "somebody will pay."

Charles cracked his thumbs loud in derision of such belittling words.

Yet when they all paced through the gathering of the seigneurs, both lay and church, in the warm high hall, and entered the oratory to make a prayer for Stephen's safe arrival after the long winter journey, an odd thing happened.

The weary wayfarer, the Pope himself, went down on his knees at the altar step before Pepin. "King of Frankland," the old man cried, "you see me a suppliant. I will not take your hand, to rise, until you have pledged me aid against my enemies."

Perhaps he was overtired, perhaps he was merely elderly and distressed; for tears ran from his eyes down his thin cheeks. Charles wanted to see his father lift Stephen with heartfelt swiftness.

Pepin, however, stood unmoving, with square chin outthrust. There was strength in his body and wariness in his mind. For a moment the weeping vicar and the meditating man of force made a picture like the mosaic figures behind the altar. That picture remained fixed in the mind of Charles.

Then without a word Pepin stretched down his arms and lifted the old Stephen.

With his mission ended, Charles returned to his duty at the palace, where as yet he held no office other than to go through the days as Pepin's bastard son.

Pepin the Short had not been born to rule in royalty. Like the Arnulfings before him, the dark, closemouthed nobleman had been Master—or as some said Mayor—of the Palace; he had been first among his peers of Frankland, who had still sworn faith to the rightful king, last of the Meroving line.

True, Pepin had carried on the actual task of ruling, with a hard quick hand. While the last of the Merovings had merely come forth from his homestead riding in the ritual cart drawn by plodding oxen, driven by a long-haired peasant, to the assembly each year. There the fat drone, the redhead Meroving, had faced the gathering of his folk and had given his consent to the things they had done or wished to do.

Two years before, the other lords of Frankland might have agreed and sworn together to elect a Master of the Palace other than Pepin. Yet Pepin, foremost among them, had firm guardsmen at his back; the armed host of the Franks had followed him out to the road of war each year. He held fast to this power because he had the ability to use it. So he had sent Fulrad as messenger to Rome to ask a question of the Pope: *Should not he who holds the power in a kingdom have the title as well?* The answer had been yes.

That was why the last Meroving, the almost forgotten Childerich III, had been led out not to the year's assembly but to a monastery in the forest. He had been driven away in his cart from his comfortable farm and cooks and women, to have his fine red hair shaved off. The assembly had hailed Pepin as king, the saintly Boniface had set the crown of beaten gold on his round dark head, and for two years he had ruled in royalty.

Yet the great lords such as Aucher had never bidden Pepin to the throne. They remembered him now as one of themselves. Perforce but not willingly they obeyed, so long as Pepin, son of the warrior Charles the Hammer, managed well for the folk whose throne he had usurped.

In these thankless days when the Christian world seemed to be sinking in darkness toward its end, all the Frankish folk held to a memory of long ago, of a golden age when the first Merovings had led them from the sea border, when gold had been plentiful and trade had been active along the routes from which the vestige of the Roman Empire had not vanished. The old days of prosperity and even peace——

No one taught the Churl this. It came to him in snatches of tales heard in the saddle, or in whispers where the eleven-year boy stood for interminable hours behind his father's back. From the hour of prime until the midday meal, Pepin kept him there listening to appeals and complaints brought to the king's mercy by his people. It was Pepin's hard way of schooling him.

His mother insisted on the study of the sacred books. Only in the drowsy hour after eating and before sleeping could Charles turn to these books and the deacons who taught the boys in the Palace School. Since the deacons were apt to be heavy with meat and wine, they skipped through the science of numbers—*If you gathered thirty chestnuts and ate five each day, how many days of the week would the chestnuts last? Until the Lord's day of rest*—and the science of physical things—*What is light? The torch that reveals everything*.

All the boys needed to learn were the answers to the questions. In rhetoric, they read aloud from the sacred books—*Weep over Saul who clothed you in scarlet . . . who put ornaments of gold upon your apparel*. They read how Saul died and how Sodom found its doom.

But these answers of the lessons, and the miraculous happenings of the books had nothing to do, in the mind of the boy, with the stress of human beings around his father.

Each day, as well, he was trained to use his weapons. They had been given him by Bernard, his uncle. After Fulrad blessed them at the altar, he had knelt to take in his hands the iron, pointed shield, the long sword with its girdle, and the light lance of ash wood. Now in the summer evenings an old swordsman, serving the Constable, exercised him with sword and shield and scramasax—the heavy curved knife used to parry a blow or get in a quick stab. Being long of limb, the boy could keep his shield out of the way of his horse well enough; he could grip the horse fast with his legs; but he was too clumsy to hurl the six-foot lance fairly, at a gallop, into the target.

"Let a boar run," he cried at his trainer, "and you will see me bring it down with a javelin."

His hunting weapons, the throwing javelins and small bow with long and short arrows, were familiar to his strong hands and he felt sure of them. The heavy iron point of the battle lance could not be brought down on a charging boar.

"Ay," grunted the war veteran, "but Your Honor's boar will not be carrying a shield."

It angered Charles, who knew he could keep up with the fastest riders. After watching him practice thus with his weapons, Bernard, commander of the East Frank levies, shook his head, as silent as Pepin. He rubbed his chin, and said, "Young comrade, you have skill but not the knack."

"If Your Excellency will set me a task, I will do it."

Bernard's gray eyes reproved the boy for his temper. "It is more than a task! A Northman does not make it a task to handle a boat. A Hun, now, is born to the saddle."

"And is not a Frank——"

"A Frank is born to the forest."

When Charles left the last pastures behind, with the fruit and nut trees, and entered the half-light of the forest, he felt alert and rested as well. He could follow the thread of a deer track through the thickest oak groves. From the corners of his eyes he glimpsed squirrels circling to the far side of the trunks, and the swift change in shadows that marked a panther stealing away. The hounds that coursed the hillsides spoke to him with warning and excitement.

On such a forest path he was master. Faint signs drew him on toward antlered stag or feeding bear. He kept direction by instinct, certain of finding his way out. If he chose to sleep through a night he could find a stream, and make a fire.

The forests had grown huge, marching down from the dark firs of the heights, encroaching into the tilled valley lands, since they had not been opposed in their march for centuries. Often he stumbled on the masonry of abandoned villages in their thickets.

His huntsmen believed that the Black Horseman still rode this *Wald,* and on the heights in the dark of the moon could be seen the fires of the Witches' Sabbath. There would be elf maids watching from the springs where laurel mingled with spreading oaks. Especially when the harvest moon hung like a beacon in the sky——

Before harvest that summer Charles discovered what Pepin had held back in his mind when he gave his hand and pledge to aid the beseeching Stephen. After the May Field assembly the court rode over to Paris. Thither Charles went gladly, because the river Seine was full of mullet and other gamesome fish.

The high lords could go easily because they had finished with the tilling and sowing of their lands. Pepin took his family to stay at the fallen-down palace of Julian on the hill near the island of Paris. The discarded Merovingian monarchs had thought to make a great town of Paris, especially Dagobert, who was buried there. But the ruder Arnulfings, perhaps because they wished to avoid treading in the steps of those other kings, had neglected the island, now overgrown with brambles and known better by its Roman name of "the Muddy."

For the first time Charles had a chamber to himself in this palace of Julian the Roman. Fulrad the Abbot, energetic as always at the coming of the king's family, told Charles that long ago the Roman troops had hailed Julian as their emperor in this very place. More than his father, Fulrad tried to explain ancient happenings to the boy; Pepin, busy when he was not brooding, became impatient when Charles did not understand such things.

It mattered more to the boy that the mosaic floor of his new room felt uncomfortable through his sleeping cloak, but he could climb out at night by a break in the wall and stretch out in sweet grass, where he could hear the chuckling of the river and visit the night lines he had set with the other lads, before sun drove the mist from the water.

Besides the lonely grandeur of his room and the bustling of Fulrad, his mother's dress gave him warning of the coming ceremony. It was no new garment for hall or horse but a robe shining with silk and gold thread, binding her tight on throat and arms while sweeping around her feet in a great circle. Although she could not walk in it very well, she flushed with joy and stepped out proudly when she tried it on, and her maidens clapped their hands. Although she did not have noble blood in her, he thought his mother, Bertrada, to be a noble sight in the new encircling dress.

When he shouted his approval Bertha—as he called her—bent her knee and bowed her head as if to pleasure a mighty person. She understood how he felt.

At first Charles had taken no thought to his birth. For Bertha had been the favored mistress of his silent father, who had singled her out by wedding her some years after the boy's birth. The folk made a jest of Charles' walking to the wedding altar.

But in the last two years he noticed—he was ever quick to notice such things—how men no longer jested about it. Kerold said if Pepin were truly king, there was bound to be a difference between a leman's brat and a queen wife's child. Charles did not think this to be important.

Perhaps, however, it made firm the bond between him and his vital, demanding mother. Bertha was ever swift to take his part in a quarrel—as if she felt there was a hidden balance to be adjusted on his side. While his father would never so favor Charles.

If anything, Pepin doted on the child born after the wedlock. Carloman was only three, delighting them all with his bright ways.

The day before the ceremony they all rode out to the gray stone basilica of St. Denis the Martyr—the Dionysius who had become a martyr by having his head cut off, and revered since then as the apostle of Paris. Stephen had gone there, to the monastery in the barley fields, to recuperate after his hard journey.

After vesper song Bertha asked Charles to stay with her to pray at the step. Charles wanted to explore the woods, which he had not seen for years.

"No, stay with me," she begged, and added swiftly, "Sweet son, a time is at hand when you may not follow your stubborn will as you have done before now."

Although this sounded like a hardship, the thought seemed to make her joyous. To be sure of his staying, she took his awkward hand in her warm fingers. She smelled of clean, washed hair and fresh linen. Willingly he stayed with her because the candles revealed a fascinating picture in the apse. There the headless St. Denis, or Dionysius, stooped to pick up his head from the ground at the feet of a stalwart swordsman.

Many of those who lingered for the candlelighting admired the sprightly woman and tall boy kneeling in prayer. Close to Charles came a slim girl with freckles under her eyes and tousled, unbound hair. But her gray eyes were fixed on him with mute respect. Ignoring the peering girl, he bent his head with stately dignity, well pleased that he had obeyed his mother.

Then the girl was pulled away. He contemplated St. Denis, near whose tomb rested his redoubtable grandsire Charles, who had been a muscle-bound peasant. No doubt such martyred churchmen, being seated now near the Lord God's throne in the heaven above the clouds, held vast power over all that happened. So his mother believed entirely. Yet he remembered Stephen kneeling to his father to invoke the strength of iron arms.

Which strength, then, would prevail over the other?

The day of the ceremony dawned fair and hot. A dry sweet smell came from the hayfields that encroached on the road.

Charles always thought of this month of July as the Hay Month.

No one labored in the fields because all had gathered at St. Denis' church, trampling around outside because the stone building was too small to hold more than the counts and the great seigneurs. But the crowd in the fields could listen to the trumpet-like peals of the new organum that had been fetched to add glory to the day. Although this strange instrument of music grated and hissed, from far off on the road it sounded, to Charles at least, like the horns of the archangels.

Ah, never had he beheld or heard such glory: his stately mother riding to the step of the entrance to avoid getting thorns in her skirt—the palace guards lined up with crimson plumes in their polished helmets, beating back with their spear butts those who were too reeling drunk to enter, fittingly, the house of God.

It seemed to the gangling Charles that the whole countryside had come to behold honor bestowed on his family. The organum itself had made the long journey hither from distant Constantinople, the soft high red slippers on his feet had been gleaned from a Moorish pack-trader.

Behind his father and mother he stood for long, while Stephen the lord Pope, in pure white robe and gleaming gold cloth about his thin neck, gave a blessing to the new altar of smooth marble. Although Charles could not understand many of the chanted words, he realized that the old Stephen was calling upon the mustered host of heaven to give power to the altar—upon the apostles, archangels, saints, martyrs, and other liegemen of the Lord.

After that Stephen performed the ceremony of the day by summoning Pepin to the altar, proclaiming him to be an illustrious man, king of the Franks and Patrician of the Romans. As he did so, Stephen let sweet-smelling oil drip on Pepin's bullethead from a tiny silver horn. He was anointing

Pepin as that other king, David, had been anointed sometime before in golden Jerusalem.

Then Stephen did something surprising. He summoned forth Bertha and let the oil fall upon her lovely head. She was no longer a woman of common blood, but queen of the Franks. How great was her pride when she turned to face the staring silent throng of dukes, counts, paladins, and bishops.

When Charles' turn came to kneel before Stephen, he heard the words plainly. "*Vir nobilis, filius regnatoris, patricius Romanoram.*"

So he was proclaimed the noble king's son, and Patrician of the Romans. What Patrician might mean, he did not know. At the moment he was aware of the cold drops of oil in the stubble of his hair and a thrill of delight that he had been named the noble son of Pepin.

Then as he returned to his place by Fulrad and the first of the paladins something took place for which he was not at all prepared. An old tiring woman gave the baby, his brother, to Bertha. While Bertha held the child Carloman, the frail Stephen went through the same business of naming Carloman a noble son and Patrician.

Just for an instant, Charles wanted to laugh loud. It was really funny to think of the baby as a prince Patrician. Then he saw that Bertha was flushed with exultation.

Swift as a knife thrust he felt a quick pain of jealousy. What had been given him, in honor, should not have been given a child in arms. He felt a deep sense of injury, and at once made up his mind that he would not speak of it.

Brooding over the honor divided between himself and Carloman, he paid little attention to what Stephen said next to all the assemblage. For one thing, he could not easily follow the intoned Latin of the books, for another the listening Frankish heroes did not appear to know how to make proper responses. While some clerics chanted "For the ages

—amen!" other nobles, who had been celebrating the occasion, shouted "Vivat!"

But a few words reached him clearly. "Henceforth your faith shall be given unto your king and those who are sprung from his loins, and to no others."

At the time the boy took some comfort from this joining of himself to his father. Only afterward he reflected that the Pope by these words had set Pepin's *family* apart as rulers. His sons and their sons were to reign over Frankland, regardless of any issue of the red Merovings, or the great vassal dukes. Pepin had secured the throne for his family—as kings by birth.

Only long afterward did Charles reflect that Pepin must have come to an understanding with Stephen. At the Field of May, Pepin had persuaded his doubting nobles to ride across the Alps to the aid of St. Peter; here in the church Stephen had announced that Pepin would be king by right as well as in name. No one in church could voice a protest. At least, no one did so.

While the men went to feast at the monastery's hall, Charles led out his shaggy horse to gallop headlong across the pastures to the river. He had not felt the sting of jealousy before. It was his way when humiliated or troubled to climb to a saddle and ride until the pulsing blood of his body eased the tightness in his head.

Along the river he rode fast, skirting huts and byres. When he sighted a gathering of youths from the palace stripped and swimming, he pulled up and flung himself down on the hot bank, tearing off his clean linen shirt wet with sweat. But he kept on the fine Córdoban slippers to stride down to the water. The boys, who knew him well, hailed him as the new Patrician of Rome.

"We Rhine heroes," shouted one, "deal in no such Patrician-abracadabra mummery! We are well enough able to kiss the girls and strike down our enemies with a single sword stroke—*pfwang!*"

"And cut their purses and throats with your knives," responded Charles dutifully—"*zhutt!*"

He was not quick to think up a taunt, yet he managed to make a suitable response. When he plunged into the river he outdistanced the other swimmers to the far bank. Already he could defeat many grown men at swimming, riding, or questing after game.

When Kerold and the serving lads brought cool beer to the noble swimmers, Charles emptied his bowl before the others. As the beer stirred his body, he thought of another response to make. "Of all the Frankish heroes my namesake and grandsire Charles could strike the hardest blow. For he had no need of the iron of sword or mace. With his bare fist he could break the skull of a charging bear."

"Then his bare fist had knuckles of wrought iron sprinkled with broken flints!"

"With a sword," continued Charles, paying no heed to that retort, "who had the strength of Pepin my sire?"

"The lion and the bull!" the wet swimmers responded in chorus. "Give us the recital of the sword and the lion and the bull—how Pepin dealt with them."

So bidden, Charles filled his bowl and drank, and tried to keep his shrill voice deep. "It was the time Pepin sat on his field stool before all his noble lords. First there came into the field a raging bull. Then there came a blood-hungered lion. That lion leaped upon the bull's back, to bite through its neck behind the hard bone. And Pepin cried to his liegemen, 'Noble sirs, take that beast from the bull or kill it, if you will.' Then the nobles trembled in dread—not a one of them moved to pull off the lion."

The beer boys and swimmers breathed slow to listen better, for this tale they had heard so often they loved it well.

"When Pepin saw how they moved not," Charles continued, "he sprang out from his field stool, whipping out his sword of the finest iron. With that sword he struck once. The blade struck through the lion's neck. It struck through the bull's neck, and deep into the ground. It was such a stroke as human eyes seldom see. When they beheld it, the Frankish heroes trembled and their voices failed with fear at such strength. Then after dealing in this fashion with the lion and bull, Pepin sheathed his sword and went back to his seat."

They were all merry there, at hearing the tale, while drinking on the sun-warmed grass. Stretching out, Charles waited for the water to dry on his skin, and felt comforted by the good fellowship and plunge through the water when he had been first of the swimmers.

He hid from his companions the pain that lingered around the memory of Carloman's anointing that morning. It was something personal to himself. He did not want to speak of it.

During the next years he learned to keep to himself many such hurts.

After thirteen years Charles stood six feet and more. Fullthroated, stout-limbed, his massive body could hurtle through the forests without tiring; he could swim his favorite rivers, the Meuse and the Rhine. His broad, restless head with its long nose and narrow dark mustache marked him as a true Arnulfing, descendant of the first Eagle-Wolf. His wide gray eyes had the penetrating vision of one who quests habitually through tangled outdoor growth. But the awkwardness of his body had not matured to ease; his shouting voice remained shrill as a boy's. When he roared with laughter, he worked his ears back and forth as if his body mimicked the mirth of his mind.

So he was young for his years, and he was fated to remain that way. This young self in Charles joyed to gallop ahead of his fellows, to loose arrow or pitch lance from the saddle, to share venison steak and boar's haunch with his hungry followers, to give away his gains with open hands, to hear praise of his strength, and gleeful voices rejoicing. He disliked to have his companions leave him, or to abide alone with his thoughts.

Like the falconers and foresters who followed his impetuous riding, he clad himself in itchy Frisian wool and leather against cold and wet. Being at ease with his henchmen, and the vital young girls of the countryside, he could hold them intent with tale or song. This Churl had an irresistible way with him. Women yielded quickly to the vitality of his body, and his urgent will.

The other Charles, the lonely self, kept silence, uneasily aware of its ignorance and shiftiness as it blundered into failures. His father was assured, moving with Mephistophelean ease through dangers, goaded on by his ambitious mother. His young sister Gisela had a grave way with her, reliant and yet withdrawn from the others.

Each year his smaller brother Carloman gained favor with the others. The monks of St. Denis, who had counseled Pepin's younger years, became the tutors of Carloman. Fulrad devoted his attention to the boy who mastered the art of reading Latin letters so easily. Quite evidently Carloman had the perception and judgment of his father.

For thirteen years the annals of the Franks hardly mention the name of Charles. He did not go with his father on those two successful journeys through the Alps to Italy. It is not altogether surprising, this silence of the records, which were kept, if at all, by some conscientious scribes in monasteries at the crossroads where travelers brought tidings of happenings elsewhere. These monkish chroniclers crowded their words in half-remembered Latin on small sheets of scraped parchment—because the papyri-paper of Roman times no longer came from the east.

They kept their record in this way of the important happenings each year since the creation of the world—5960 years had passed, by their reckoning, since the Lord made heaven and earth.

They noted the appearance of plagues, of comets in the sky, miracles, and rare events like "the coming of the organ to Frankland." One such scribe mentioned Charles in 761:

"Again the king Pepin arrived in Aquitaine with his armed host and his first-born son, Charles by name, and captured many castles." Another chronicler, Ado, in Vienne added that "In capturing Clermont they burned it all." From their silence it is only clear that the bastard Churl served his father without distinction and without rebellion.

News of the day, otherwise, passed by letter from king's hall to noble's *Hof*. Not that either Pepin or his Frankish lords could put pen to parchment; they made their mark under a scribe's writing.

One letter from the Pope at Rome urged Pepin not to divorce Bertrada, his wife.

It failed to explain why Pepin wanted to be rid of Charles' mother. Yet their youngest child had died after birth, just then. Bertha herself survived to a strong middle age, at more than forty years. The dominant queen of the Franks had a personality quite different from the comely mistress who had given birth to Charles.

And Pepin, like the peasant-born Arnulfings before him, had a way of summoning younger lasses to his bed. Whereupon Bertha, unmistakably, tried to enter politics.

In doing so, she opposed Pepin, and thereby made a mistake. So the letter of the Pope reached them, warning the king not to divorce his wife. In their conflict Charles must have drawn closer to the mother who held him in such love.

Charles had married a woman named Himiltrud. Only her name is revealed, and the fact that she came from no great Frankish family and caused no stir at court. Himiltrud bore him one son, christened Pepin—thereby carrying out the Arnulfing tradition of names, alternating between Charles and Pepin.

Yet all too soon it was apparent that the hand of the Lord had touched the child Pepin. So bright he was of face, so fragile of body, with a crook coming into his spine that made him peer sidewise up at his father. Pepin of the angelic face and hunch back.

It was an irony of fate that gave the lusty Charles a child so unlike Pepin the king who never forgave weakness. The feeble hunchback boy belonged to Charles' other, lonely self, claiming his love and protection. When Carloman had two sons they were sturdy enough.

As Charles had taken his family and wandering way of life for granted in that early year of his meeting with Stephen, he now seemed to take the homeland of the Franks under his father's rule for granted. Holding no title to any region, however, he made certain lands his own in an odd fashion. No one rode further afield than he, on mission or hunt. He coursed through the wilderness of forest where towns had ceased to exist, and he made some of these his own preserves by posting his foresters to guard the entrance trails and protect the deer, boar, and wild ox from any hunting but his own. In this way the dark ravines of the Ardennes (the *Arduenna Silva*— the Bitter Woods), the pine waste of the charcoal makers and the deserted heights of the Vosges became the small dominions of Charles.

For even in the silence of those early years it is clear that what Charles grasped for himself he held to firmly. He was stubborn in that respect.

Near the winding Meuse he liked to rest in an obscure valley. It lay not far from Cologne ("the Colony" of Roman days) along the sweet water of the Würm stream—a green valley of marshlands where wildfowl came, close to a miniature hunting forest. It was off the great river routes, and the stone-paved Roman military roads that the Franks used for highways. It had warm sulphur springs spreading to pools where wayfarers could bathe. The hamlet by the springs bore the old name of Aquis Granum, which might have meant Fertile Water to its long-departed inhabitants.

This valley Charles craved for his own.

Like isolated Aquis Granum, the homeland of the barbaric Franks lay apart from the outer active world. It lay, roughly, between the tributaries of the great river Rhine and the Loire. Because the wilderness was intruding steadily on the tilled lands of ancient times, these rivers served as frontier barriers and travel ways as well. Lacking roads, the folk often journeyed by small craft along the water; Charles could enter a coracle with a leather sail, up on the shoulders of the Alps, and make his way by the swift streams, down to the Rhine current and the stone hostels that had been barracks of the Roman legions at the Colony.

Those Roman legions had been gone for nearly three centuries, and with them had vanished the great Empire's mechanism of rule by standing army and colonists, by coded law and by the pulsing arteries of trade that extended outward through the known world.

Ancient skills were dying in the west. Unlike many other barbaric peoples, the Franks had never known the mechanism of the Empire. In their wanderings the Visigoths had pierced the frontiers to reach their abiding place in Spain, the Ostrogoths had settled within Italy itself, whither the agressive Lombards followed them. Even the erratic Vandals had been pushed by more warlike migrants across to the comfortable cities of Roman Africa.

In the adjacent island of Britain the seafarers, Angles, Saxons, and Jutes, had entered into the dying urban life of Romans. The Franks had no such memories of the marvels of a civilization that bred taxgatherers and chariot races.

Their name might have meant the Free, or the Fierce. Their folk memories were of hard living in the mists of the Baltic's shore. Their legendary king Meroveus—Son of the Sea —had been a tribal chieftain, ruling by personal whim and the consent of his clans after being raised on the warriors' shields. Forest-bred, hewing their way with axes in battle or cultivation from the Baltic wastes to milder, fertile lands, they had forged slowly to the Rhinelands, where the Austrasian Franks settled and outward to the Seine, where the Neustrian Franks had worked the land. Then, joined together by a king, Chlodovech or Clovis, they had thrust back the domesticated Visigoths deeper into southern Gaul.

Isolated within their forests, thrown on their own resources, they got food from the soil to ward off famine, they discarded their hewing axes for more efficient swords—a skilled smith had seemed to be something of a magician—they made their plow horses into battle steeds, their saga chanters into singing poets, and their ancestral kings into short-lived, anxious rulers. Beyond the will of their kings lay deep-rooted tribal tradition of personal freedom and the council of the warriors. A city meant to them a gathering of people who built huts. Civilization had no tangible meaning for them, unless in the ritual of their churches, or the rare Scripture books telling of a fabulous Garden of Eden somewhere to the eastward and the torments of the damned. The objects of civilization trickled in to them from the packs of traders wandering at hazard from the Middle Sea with its Arabian ships or from remote and dreamlike Constantinople, where an emperor survived within a palace of marble by a tree of gold where jeweled birds sang and organs played.

Perhaps their ancestors had ventured along the Baltic shore in fishing craft if not in dragon ships. That was the vaguest of memories, bound up with the Merovingian golden age, when the structure of Roman power had not dwindled away to skeletons of aqueducts, baths, and theaters that were no longer repaired and had no meaning. Nothing had been found to replace the power of the vanished Caesars. The wharves of ports like Boulogne had become deserted and overgrown with weeds.

The Franks had forged outward under such dynamic battlers as Clovis and Dagobert. Charles the Hammer had given them a taste of victories. Pepin, the schemer, moved more warily, avoiding headlong battle, making fast the tie to the shrine of St. Peter. He sought to make the Frankish hinterland a focus of authority between the pagan borderlands and the centers of faint culture in Aquitaine and Lombardy. He announced that those who entered Frankland from across the borders might keep their own law and not be subject to Frankish law.

Beyond his borders, however, a saying ran, "Have a Frank for a friend, but not for a neighbor."

In those years the deepest darkness of the ages covered western—and Christian—Europe. The human masses, speaking different dialects, moved in flux. There was no rule; there was no power to shape the flux. The glory of the past was fading from memory, and no hope for the future took its place.

In the minds of men lingered only the terrible and mystical hope of the ending of world life with the second coming of Christ.

Yet there was a freshening of vitality, the birth agony of something unknown. There were two human figures striving toward authority, the leader of the onward pressing Franks, the leader of the Church of St. Peter. Pepin, after taking thought, had given his hand to Stephen.

But the power of the iron sword prevailed over the authority of the priest of the apostle.

Oddly enough the resistance to Pepin came from the most enlightened region, the east border and the deep south. On the east the clannish Bavarians had contact with the trade artery of the broad Danube, and with the wealthy Lombards of Italy. Their duke, Tassilo, as young as Charles, clad himself in the fine scarlet velvet and gold arm rings of a king. He was Pepin's nephew, but he claimed as bride a Lombard princess and carried a barber and a poet around with him. Tassilo boasted that he deserved a Virgil. Charles did not understand what a Virgil might be.

One summer, long after the Field of May, Pepin the king had to wait at the sandy, swift-running Loire for Tassilo and the Bavarians to join him in answer to his ban of arms. Pepin was marching between sowing time and harvesting time into

the deep south of Aquitaine, where the duke as usual defied
him during the peacetime of winter. With the Bavarians he
planned to march through to the Pyrenees and end the resistance.

When Tassilo arrived at last with his mounted spearmen,
he walked with his scarlet mantle swinging between the lines
of Pepin's guards, whose dull brick-red mantles had been
soaked by rain until they resembled shabby fruit sacks.
Charles, waiting at Pepin's back, had never before noticed
how clownish the guards looked in their Roman type of uniform. But Tassilo's keen eyes had taken note of that, and of
the makeshift huts of the Frankish host. He also had a plan,
very different from Pepin's.

When he had greeted his uncle the king, he excused himself from the welcoming feast, saying bluntly that he had
come in duty-bound, being too ill to march with the punitive
expedition of the Franks. Handsome and eloquent, Tassilo
did not appear to have any sickness. "My heartfelt good will,
uncle," he observed, "will accompany Your Clemency on the
road, whether to peace or war."

As his habit was, Pepin took thought before answering.

"You swore an oath," he said then, "at the shrine of the
saintly Hilary to come without fail at my ban to arms."

Tassilo answered, with less force, that he would keep his
oath, made on the sacraments, if his strength permitted.
Being ill, he could not do so.

The headstrong Charles would have challenged his cousin,
charging him with *herisliz*—desertion in the face of the
enemy. Yet he could not take the word from Pepin. Moreover Tassilo cleverly made it seem as if this were not war but
merely marching around.

Long did Pepin think the matter over. If it came to a test
of weapons with the well-armed Bavarians, his Franks might
lose strength to go against the openly rebelling Aquitanians.
In the end he let Tassilo depart unchallenged.

"Do not have more than one enemy at a time," he said to

his bastard son. Charles did not understand that Pepin was
aware of a reason why the battle strength of the Franks
should not be tested.

It seemed to him for the first time that Pepin showed weakness. His father, in fact, appeared sluggish of late, often sitting drowsing on his carved high seat. His limbs became
swollen and the flesh bagged under his eyes.

"His folly of mind," Bertha stormed with strident words,
"led him to seek his aid beyond our sight, and where? At the
shrine above the bones of St. Peter! Has this Pope one lance
bearer or even a rascally bowman to send to war? No, not
one."

Her woman's mockery was inspired by the respect she had
had, aforetime, for Pepin the war wager who now sought
parleys and peace. She also had noticed the royal splendor
of Tassilo and his retinue. That scarlet mantle became in her
mind like the cloak of an archangel. Moreover she had
expected Pepin to keep the lordlings of Salzburg and Toulouse obedient as vassals to his will. That would have increased her pride because it increased her dignity in the eyes
of other women. Especially in the eyes of those mincing
females of luxurious Toulouse, those haughty southerners of
the Province and the gardens of Auvergne, so much fairer
than her own thatched villas of Soissons and Worms. For
these women of the deep south clung to the myth of their
ancestral, Roman nobility.

In Bertha's opinion, Pepin was losing his grip.

After the Bavarians had departed unharmed, Pepin led his
Franks across the Loire.

It seemed to Charles ironical that Tassilo, a well man,
should desert while his father, a sick man, went on with the
war.

Again, again, and a third time Pepin took the Frankish host
south. The third time, in the year of salvation 768 he had his
swollen body carried in a horse litter. The chronicle of that
year relates "when he marched on after the Paschal Feast, he

left behind him the lady Bertrada, the queen, with her family."

He marched on with his host to the land of the Rocky Heights, to the last land of his enemy. There the Aquitanian duke was slain by his own people, weary of conflict, and no rebel force remained in the field against Pepin. But Pepin did not survive to punish Tassilo for oath-breaking and desertion.

Swiftly his litter was carried back to where Bertha waited. Past Poitiers of the yellow harvest fields where Charles the Hammer had beaten back the Moslem horsemen, over the golden Loire, his litter was borne swiftly to St. Martin's at Tours. At this shrine of the soldier saint, Pepin gave a treasure in alms, in the hope that St. Martin would heal his sickness.

"Whence he journeyed," the chronicle states, "to St. Denis, dying there the eighth of the kalends of October." He was buried under the floor of the basilica by the tomb of Charles the Hammer.

Chapter II

THE RIDE TO CORBENY

Not long afterward Alcuin, a friend of Charles would describe their time as "these loveless days of the world's last age."

As the comfort of Charles' family life had broken down long since, the security of his kingdom ceased to exist the moment Pepin died. Perhaps the stocky Pepin had exhausted his strength in those last campaigns in the southland. The fragile hegemony that he had enforced over a half dozen barbaric peoples depended on his own personality. There was no rule established to function after him.

The silent Pepin had made no early decision as to his successor. He had turned over no country to Charles, or to Carloman, to manage. Only the day before his death, Pepin bequeathed half the kingdom to Charles and half to his younger brother. By this will of the dead man Charles would reign over the seacoasts and the Rhine frontier as far east as the Bavarian Alps. Carloman would hold the center of the kingdom, around the Burgundian land, with bright Toulouse and the fertile Provence.

In this way Pepin had given the massive and impetuous Churl the task of guarding the borders, while the more talented Carloman kept order in the heart of the dominion. Obediently the great seigneurs of Frankland escorted the brothers north, elevating Carloman on the shields and crowning him at Soissons and Charles at Noyon, just across the borderline between them.

For the two brothers never met again in friendship. The animosity between them needed only a spark to burst into conflict. With Carloman departed the wisest counselors—Fulrad the archchaplain, Duke Aucher, the Chancellor, and young Adalhard. No lord is named who stayed with Charles. He had the title of king at the age of twenty-six without evident purpose of his own.

It may be that, in his perplexity, he relied upon his forthright mother. To Bertha the death of Pepin had been a release, bringing power to her hands and the chance to do the opposite of Pepin's lifelong endeavor. Instead of a Frankland ruled by one man's will, she longed for security and dignity for her two sons. Why should they not be bound in alliance, if not in marriage, with the neighboring, more enlightened rulers—with the brilliant Tassilo and the distant king of the Lombards? It was such a simple and happy solution, to have four kings of western Christendom united in kinship and loyalty, inspired by the solitary queen mother Bertrada.

To this Charles made no objection. He was riding the circuit of his new lands with his gnome-like boy. He longed, in the vaguest way, to give this little Pepin honor and position that he himself had never known. Bertha knew more than he about the ways of courts. So he might have kept on, pottering around the borders aimlessly—in his first decree he signed himself only "devoted defender of the Church"—if a rebel had not appeared swiftly in the south. A certain Hunald came forth like a ghost from a monastery, to rouse Aquitaine against the Arnulfing novice kings.

This was something tangible to be dealt with. Excitedly, Charles sent to summon his brother to come with armed force after the spring tilling, and march with him. Swiftly, Charles rallied the Rhineland and coastal contingents, and rode hastily to meet Carloman.

But the more cautious brother would not venture out to

battle; he seemed to fancy that Charles had the duty of keeping the borders. The headstrong Charles left his brother to go on alone, as Pepin had done. Obviously he had no plan prepared, but luck served him well. Impatiently he pushed ahead with the best mounted spear bearers, and Hunald retired cautiously to the hills of Gascony.

Following fast, Charles paused beyond the Garonne, remembering that he might be attacked. While he built a rough stone fort, he sent messengers ahead to the duke of Gascony, warning the southerner to give up the traitor Hunald—"For I have come to Gascony and I shall not leave without him."

It was a boast, loosed on impulse. Yet Charles' headlong race had alarmed the countryside, where no one knew his actual strength. Very soon the rebellious Hunald was delivered up, bound. Charles laughed at his own luck, feasted the men who had followed him faithfully, and sent his enemy back to the monastery.

It was all rather like a hunt in a strange forest. As the small band of Franks circled back from the hills they beheld far to the south the gray rock summits of the Pyrenees, and the small cleft marking the pass of Roncesvalles.

The bastard son of Pepin might have rested content with his easy victory—gained more by the speed of his horses than the might of his swords—if it had not been for the intervention of his mother.

The annals of the Franks, and of the Germans and French who followed them for that matter, are filled with the calamities caused by energetic and beautiful women. More songs than the *Nibelungenlied* relate the slaying of the greatest warriors owing to the quarrels of their Brunhildas. The Arnulfings had always been susceptible to the allure of strange women, and the lusty Charles showed every indication of resembling his ancestors in this respect. No one was better aware of this than Bertha, who hoped to guide him through his kingship.

41

Charlemagne

The queen mother had left Frankland on a long journey without explaining her purpose in doing so. Now she returned triumphant. With her she brought Charles an offer of marriage to a young and royal woman, a princess of the Lombards. And she brought him an entirely new policy, already set in motion, which undid what Pepin had labored to do.

Bertha's motives are clear enough. Above all she longed to prevent the conflict brewing between her sons. The stubborn Charles would not forgive Carloman's defection in Aquitaine —or Carloman's claiming half his forest preserve of Ardennes. Instinctively Bertha felt that in war the hulking, shrill-voiced Churl would overcome the gentler ruler of the Seine. At the same time a cultured wife would add dignity to the uncouth Charles.

Her success, on the journey, was quite remarkable. But Bertha was a remarkable woman. Probably she had enlisted the aid of the powerful lords, counselors of Carloman, in persuading her younger son to ally himself with his cousin Tassilo, the Bavarian, and Desiderius, the Lombard king. By uniting Charles to a girl of the Lombard palace, she would draw her unruly son into this quadruple entente.

In doing so, Bertha ignored Pepin's single alliance, to the vicar of St. Peter. Pepin, in his Italian journeys, had soundly threshed the Lombards, who sought to make themselves overlords of Italy—and Rome. Pepin had pledged himself to safeguard the awkward church outside the walls of Rome. Yet Bertha had made a good impression even there, by appearing as a pilgrim at the shrine, while hinting that she was on a mission of peace.

"Blessed are the peacemakers," she reminded Charles, when she explained her triumph to him. She did not explain the dire consequences that might befall the church of St. Peter, the great apostle. Almost certainly Desiderius the Lombard had praised her plan and given her assurances of peace and well-being, because it would be a godsend to him to be rid of the hostility of the dangerous Franks—to have

Charles, the elder king, as a son-in-law occupied with quieting far-off Aquitaine.

"The southland is still smoldering, dear heart," she assured her son. "Princess Desirée is so fragile and tender. You must be gentle with her."

Soon Desiderata, or Desirée, arrived in the Rhineland as his bride to be, with a bevy of Latin-speaking courtiers. She was frail enough, being sickly, and she had a pride that Bertha had neglected to mention. Bertha also ignored the circumstance that Charles already had a wife.

To Charles' devotion to his mother was now joined the obvious necessity of wedding this distinguished girl. She attracted him.

Straightway he dismissed the wife of his youth, Himiltrud. She seems to have been a simple person, certainly no figure at the rude court of Frankland. But he kept with him the small Pepin Hunchback, when he wed his princess.

To Frankland the Lombard bride brought a sense of refinement, and surprising demands. She had a serf woman to dress her hair, and pages to carry forth silver platters of food, and even some cherished glass goblets for drink. She had silk for chamber robes and a bright way of pattering Latin.

Her royal husband knotted his own leg wrappings when he swung his big body out of bed at dawn; he pulled stained leather over his undertunic; he walked afoot through swine pens and stables, gorged himself with cheese and roast venison, and tramped from the bedchamber to pray at the laud's hour with a sheepskin pulled over his shoulders. To his anteroom flocked herdsmen, with keepers of dogs and falcons, because he would not order them out. Desirée's home had been the terraced palace of Pavia, where the women's apartments had masseuses waiting in marble-lined Roman baths. There was no palace of any sort in Frankland, no proper city, and very little hot water except in the warm mineral springs where Charles plunged naked with his gang of fellows.

He said his *sala regalis* awaited her at Ingelheim. This

royal abode proved to be separated from the market place by a wooden wall, banked with dung heaps where the swine rooted. The hall itself retained some reddish Roman paintings of fauns chasing nymphs, and it smelled of the cowsheds next door. Charles had planted an orchard around it, where a water wheel groaned, turning the stones of a grain mill. The palace brook flowed into the duck pond, where the royal Seneschal also raised chickens and fine pheasants.

Pigeons swarmed through the fruit trees, and were served at the festal table on wooden platters. Charles liked to have the venison carried smoking from the spits dripping in the fireplace. He said his *city* of Ingelheim enjoyed the king's peace, as well as the sanctity of the grave of a saint named Remi.

The roof over Desirée's head was planted with jubarb herbs which served to garnish meats and ward of lightning. Nameless Roman emperors in marble effigy adorned the garden, made gay by strutting peacocks that screamed before sunrise, when Charles awoke.

To Desirée it seemed that the *sala regalis* at Ingelheim was really a farm. The king, her husband, promised that he would take her to a finer garden, down the river.

He wanted to take her in his arms and leap into the odorous pool of a swampy valley called Aquis Granum, which he seemed to deem a garden spot! There he counted over the head of beasts in his herds, the wildfowl passing overhead, and it seemed to her as if he counted the very trees of the tangled grove so carefully reserved for his hunting. Wherever he went, his grotesque hunchback boy followed like a shadow.

On this impetuous bridal journey a surprising letter from the Papal chancellery was read to Charles by his notary. It had been written by the hand of the Pope and it vibrated with quite human rage, and it was addressed to the royal brothers, Charles and Carloman.

"Now a thing has come to our ears that we cannot speak

of without pain in our heart, namely, that Desiderius, king of the Lombards, seeks to persuade Your Excellencies that one of you should be joined in marriage to his daughter. If it be true, it is a veritable suggestion of the Devil. . . . What unmentionable folly is this—that one of you most excellent sons and illustrious Franks should be polluted by union with the treacherous and foully stinking race of Lombards, which is not numbered among the nations, except that the tribe of lepers has sprung from it."

This sounded like the cry of a man out of his mind. And in fact the guardians of St. Peter's had discovered the full consequence of Bertha's diplomacy, because their enemies the Lombards were grasping at the remaining Papal lands and towns with a clear conscience and a free hand, now that the dangerous Franks were allied to them.

To Charles, who had never been out of Frankland, who had scant information about the conflicts within Italy, this must have brought utter bewilderment. The end of the letter, however, rankled like a barb.

"You have promised firm friendship with St. Peter's successors. Their enemies were to be your enemies; their friends your friends——"

Yes, that had been Pepin's pledge. And the letter told how Stephen II had journeyed across the Alps to obtain it:

"—a journey which he might better never have made, if the Frank is going to join the Lombard against us. Where is your promise now? . . . So we urge you, unhappily, that neither of you two brothers take in marriage the daughter of the said Desiderius, nor shall your sister, the noble lady Gisela dear to God, be given to Desiderius' son; nor shall you dare to put away your wives."

With most men this violent protest would have weighed little against the actuality, that Charles had already married Desirée and so had leagued himself with the distant Lombards. But the headstrong Churl had his peculiar sensitivities. The vivid memory of Stephen shivering in the snow . . .

of Pepin's pledge . . . the crippled child with Pepin's name . . .

He, not Carloman, had put away his wife. The letter from Rome seemed to be directed at him alone. Carloman had envoys at Rome and must be aware of what was happening there.

Against Charles' anger at what he felt to be trickery, there was his devotion to Bertha and another thing. He had demanded that his people over the age of twelve take oath to him as king:

"I swear to my lord, Charles the king"—how well he knew the words—"and to his sons to keep faith with them all the rest of my life without deceit or ill will."

So also had the great seigneurs pledged loyalty, at his bidding, to his new queen Desirée.

Brooding, Charles continued on his Rhine journey with his bride as the spring plowing came to his homestead villas with Eastertide of the year 771. At the monasteries, pilgrims spoke feelingly of riots and blinding that terrorized the streets of Rome under the machinations of the Lombards.

Then arrived other strange letters addressed separately to Bertha, Charles, and Carloman, yet all much alike. The Pope was relieved, in his grievous distress by the aid—of all people —of the Lombard king. "Let Your Most Christian Excellency [Charles] recognize how . . . the most excellent and God-preserved king Desiderius has met us with all good will. And we have received from him full and entire satisfaction of all the claims of the blessed Peter."

This Charles did not believe. He had an instinct for scenting a false phrase. It seemed more likely that the harrassed and weak Pope Stephen III had yielded to the Lombards.

There was, seemingly, nothing to be done about it. This last letter surely absolved the new king of the Franks from any blame. And the whole matter lay outside his authority. But he could not dismiss it from his memory. Gisela refused to marry a Lombard.

The Ride to Corbeny

The Pope even congratulated Carloman on the birth of a son. Carloman's lands ran with the Lombard's, and with Tassilo's, who now claimed to be a king. Why, they were all delighted with success, and Charles alone could hardly oppose himself to the other three—and Desirée as well——

What he did in his bewildered frustration was impulsive, and utterly unreasonable. He told Desirée that he divorced her. She was no longer his queen or his wife.

The proud Lombard woman did not linger in his homestead. To be sent off like a tribal slut by this hulk of a man with the squeaking voice was a shame undreamed of. She stayed only to ask by what reason he divorced her.

He had no reason. It was his will to do it.

Desirée went, with her serving women and courtiers, not waiting to pack the silver she had brought as bride. She passed like the breath of a storm up the river toward the Alps.

His mother hastened to him, tight-lipped with anger, weeping when she could not move his mind. From that moment Charles no longer sought her counsel. Nor did Bertha journey forth again to experiment with diplomacy. The chronicles say she devoted herself to good works at the religious house of Prüm.

To him hurried his young cousin Adalhard, white with fury. Heedlessly the boy cried out what was in his mind. "Animal that you are! A donkey with twitching ears has more sense. You have made yourself an adulterer. You have made me a perjurer, with all the Franks who swore loyalty to your queen."

Charles did not lift hand against the boy. Nor did he send to summon Desirée back. Adalhard departed from the villa and did not enter his king's presence again for many years.

There was a dark-haired girl thirteen years old, Hildegard by name, who had come early to the harvesting fair that year with her noble Swabian family. Charles noticed her among the throng around the fiddle folk who struck up music at his coming. He went out of his way to greet her and found her voice to be shy and pleasing. Her hand, when he took it in his heavy fingers, was firm and warm. Her eyes followed him away.

Charles thought about Hildegard, and flung back his great head, laughing. "I am the Lord's fool!" he shouted to the sky.

Like the letter from Rome, the tidings from Corbeny came with an echo of thunder. His brother Carloman was wasting swiftly in illness.

While he had puzzled hopelessly over the letter, the massive Frank reacted differently and swiftly to this message. Summoning falconers and huntsmen, he rode south through the forest as if searching for deer. Yet he took a strong escort of the swordsmen who had raced with him through Gascony.

Then he waited at a cabin close to the boundary of the twin domains. No sooner had a forester brought him word of Carloman's death than he was off with his followers.

At Corbeny the dead king's counselors had gathered, and all of them had great names—the archbishop, with Fulrad, the count Warin, duke Aucher, and the two uncles who led the armed host, Bernard and Thierry.

Without announcing his coming, Charles walked into their gathering at night. Outside the hall his armed men waited by their horses.

When they had greeted him, Charles stood to face them, and said simply, "Our father Pepin gave the rule to his two sons. Now Carloman also has left us in death, and so the rule shall be mine."

Some of them spoke of Carloman's two boys. The father's share descended to the sons. There should be a guardian of the children, to hold this right of theirs, until they came of age.

"For how many years?" Charles asked, and shook his head. "No."

Aucher, who held lands within Carloman's domain, dared retort, "They have a mother, rightly wed, of good family."

He might as well have reminded all the listeners how

Charles had dismissed the daughter of the Lombard. Into the gathering came the sharp feeling of strife. For a moment Charles made no answer, staring into the fire that rose from the middle of the room, the smoke swirling around the ceiling vent. Then he seemed to the watchers to relax.

Going to the silent Fulrad, he took the abbot's hand, saying quietly. "Good friend you have been to Pepin's son. I say, let your word decide now for Pepin's kingdom and the grandchildren."

With that he went out, to wait in the cold of the courtyard. He left them all surprised, with a feeling of new responsibility. They had expected harder words.

Fulrad gave his word that the kingdom in this troubled time must be held by a man's strength, and so by Charles. The two uncles thought of Aquitaine, and added their words to his. That proved to be the will of the council. But Lord Aucher, who had no amity for Charles, went out to seek the widow, Gerberga.

After the counselors made known their will, Carloman's queen fled with Aucher and the young children on the road toward Pavia.

"Does it matter?" Charles asked. He seemed indifferent to their flight. Nor would he send to stay them.

"It matters much," Fulrad responded gravely.

The two boys, born in wedlock, were true heirs of Carloman, and in the hands of the Lombard king might be made to trouble the later years of Frankland.

Still Charles would not change his mind. To one part of his mind it seemed amusing that the true-born descendants of the Arnulfings should be fugitives from the country, leaving behind only himself, a bastard, and his crippled child. So he laughed and shook his head. Someone must take the responsibility now, and by the providence of God, he alone was left to do that. No, the kingdom had come into his hands. The rest did not matter.

So he seemed to think. But how judiciously, if at all, did Pepin's first-born son think such problems out?

He had acted like a fool, apparently on impulse. He had driven off two wives without cause, and by sending Desirée packing he had sown the seeds of deadly enmity in the fertile antagonism of the proud Lombards. He had seized his brother's heritage, and by further folly had driven his brother's children into the hands of the very enemy who could best use them as hostages of power. Furthermore, his actions opened up a family feud with his cousin Tassilo, who had wed a sister of Desirée.

No, his cousin Adalhard had told him the plain truth—his animal-like conduct made him an adulterer and the lords of Frankland perjurers. (And chroniclers of the reign of Charles in later years would seek to gloss over his brutish behavior by calling Himiltrud his mistress, and explaining that he had divorced Desirée because she was sickly and unable to bear children. That was not so, because the fugitive queen died in childbed soon after reaching her father's palace. Charles' second child had such a sorry fate.)

Apparently Charles acted in fury when he realized his mistake in following his mother's advice. The younger brother, the careful Carloman, had been the wiser head. Certainly the oldest counselors had taken Carloman's side. Yet Charles, in all his folly, had managed to win the allegiance of the great seigneurs who were preparing to desert him at Corbeny. By the sudden force of his appearance he startled them. Then, by his surprising gentleness in leaving the archchaplain, Fulrad, to decide his case while he stepped out, he led them to decide for him. They said afterward that he charmed them. He had this gift of winning friends of every sort.

His stubbornness hardened into an inflexible will. By cajolery, by sleight of hand, by persistence, or by force this unusual man would get his way. He had made his own people take an oath of loyalty. Now Charles imposed the same oath on Carloman's folk, *on every male over twelve years of age*. Lads throwing staves to knock acorns down for pigs had to swear faith to Charles. Or at least they were asked to do so.

Now this was something unheard of before then, and indeed for long centuries afterward. Of course in that age a boy or girl of twelve was matured for labor, for arms, or child-bearing, and had in truth lived half the expected life span. But until then only the lords of the land had taken such an oath to the king. Charles had called on all his folk to become *fideles*, faithful to him alone. If they neglected to do so, as most often happened, they would then be unfaithful. The consequences of that were not immediately apparent to them.

Oddly enough—and Charles' folly was to bring about some fantastic happenings—those who took the new pledge most seriously were the southern rebels, the Aquitanians. Perhaps former enemies pondered this question of a loyalty oath more carefully than the home folk, the Franks, Burgundians, Swabians, and others; perhaps they discerned something attractive in the erratic Churl; more probably they remembered too well the ravaging of Pepin's eight campaigns. At any rate the volatile Gallo-Romans of yesterday—the Gascons and Provençals of tomorrow—took the *fideles* pledge and refrained from conspiring against Charles although many of his own folk and family were to do so.

Meanwhile, in the Grass Month of the next spring, of the year 772, having rid himself of his mother's guidance, and stirred up a hornets' nest of intrigue against him in Italy, Charles began his task of ruling all of Frankland by wedding the dark-eyed Hildegard, and going off to spoil the pagan Saxons across the Rhine border.

Hildegard had all a well-brought-up girl's readiness to labor, at the women's looms, at keeping the toll list of the king's possessions, at providing ample meat for the spits in winter or hunger time, in weaving neat garments for herself—not the flimsy silks of a foreign princess—and at quick pregnancy. Moreover, being so young and gentle, she was kind to the little Pepin. Charles became buoyant with such happiness at home, wherever he might choose to quarter himself. In consequence he expected her to keep him company in all his journeying, and she did so.

But Hildegard did not cross into Saxonland that first summer. Even Charles would not take his bride into that wilderness of forest, marshes, and ridged mountains where the hatred of the pagans awaited him. Being akin to the Germanic Franks, and even more barbaric, the Saxon tribes would keep to no peace with them—any more than would the Franks with the Saxons. Behind this perpetual feud lay the devotion of the Saxon folk to the old gods, which the baptized Franks now held to be devils.

Behind the stubborn enmity of the Saxons lay another motive unperceived as yet by Charles. "Saxonland" stretched from the dark summits of the Harz to the Baltic shore; it was the homeland of the folk, their last refuge. In defending it against the warlike Charles the Hammer, they fought for their own soil. In consequence the raiding Franks had burned villages, carried off some livestock and harvested grain and a few captives to become slaves, but had not won possession of so much as a river valley. Pepin, the organizer, had left the Saxons pretty much alone for the last fifteen years.

It is easy to say that Charles, the new king, led forth his restless nobles that first July in a simple, warming-up foray rather than risk an expedition elsewhere. Such raids for "vengeance and spoil"—as the annals liked to say—were popular enough. Perhaps he thought of that, but he was doing little planning as yet and more probably he wanted to retaliate for the burning of a border church by the pagans.

It was not by accident, however, that he achieved an odd and spectacular success. As the annals of Frankland all mentioned the year when "the organ came" they wrote down this summer as the one when Charles "overturned Irminsul."

The novice king led his mustered horsemen and their

archers on foot cautiously along the rivers beyond the Rhine, gathering up the grain and swine in the clearings, and watching for ambushes where the forest closed in. The Saxons had learned how to make and use Roman war engines. He drove them out of a hilltop guarded by log walls, and searched for the hidden place of Irminsul, which the fort defended.

The way led down a stream to a hidden valley where a mighty grove of trees rose like a colonnade. In that grove the Saxons had made their sanctuary, the place of blood sacrifice and soothsaying, deserted now. Curiously the Rhinelanders explored it. Old men-at-arms like Kerold looked for signs of an ambush. For in the silent heart of the grove rose Irminsul, tree god of the Saxons.

It was a little unearthly, this silent grove and the giant trunk carved into a head without eyes. Charles studied it while his liegemen searched the huts of the idol's priests for treasure, finding little. "Hew the thing down," he ordered them then.

Axes labored long before the great tree fell. It crashed into the huts of the shrine, rending them apart. And in the wreckage gleamed the gold and silver of coins and vessels that the forest folk had hidden away at the shrine. A goodly trove.

Laughing, Charles said that they had found their reward for overthrowing the Irminsul. The trove he divided at once among his followers, keeping a silver drinking bowl as a gift for Hildegard. The bowl had a rude column resembling Irminsul scratched on it, and he wanted to give a token of his success to his young wife. He had avenged the burning of the Frankish church. Drouth came with the summer's end, and the forest streams dwindled to mud channels. Charles ordered his small host to ride back to the Rhine. On the way, as men and horses suffered from thirst, heavy rains deluged them.

The priests among them said that this water in the wilderness came from the Lord's hand. To the wealth of Irminsul, they added the benevolence of a seeming miracle.

Charles thought at least the summer's march had been an odd one. With the first snow he disbanded his liegemen to seek their homes. He rejoined Hildegard in the hall of Theodo's Villa (Thionville). From Christmastide to the end of the spring thaw, at Easter's feast, the Franks hibernated in their farms because snow closed the tracks.

So Charles was abiding in content by his fireside and wife when the man named Peter arrived out of the storms. This Peter had made his way from Rome to Frankland by sea because he could not get through otherwise. Not the winter weather but the enmity of the Lombards had kept him from the passes of the Alps.

"For the king, Desiderius, now holds in his protection the wife, Gerberga, of Your Excellency's brother—yes, and her two young sons. The king of the Lombards has seized upon the towns of St. Peter outside of Rome. He threatens to invade Rome and make himself master of the city."

While Charles had been off in the Saxon forest, the Lombards had acted. The predicament of Rome and its Pope was indeed far afield from Charles' villa. Yet it held so many threads to his own life woof. The pledge of Pepin—the fugitive Gerberga—his own setting out into the storm twenty years before to meet the aged Stephen—he felt all these intangible bonds of the past. As Fulrad had warned him, they did matter much.

Still, there was a new apostolic lord in St. Peter's, Hadrian by name. Charles knew nothing about him, except that Peter said Hadrian the Pope had defied Desiderius by answering that he would not meet with the Lombard as an equal noi would he give up his city of Rome.

Peter did not tell Charles how Hadrian had sought first to reason with the Lombards, and then had appealed vainly to the far-off emperor in Constantinople before turning in desperation to the barbarous Frank.

Charles thought about it by his fireside. Then he sent

messengers out to the roads with the king's order to his seigneurs to come to the Field of May with arms and provender for a march to the Alps.

He was certain that few of them would be willing to do that.

Chapter III

JOURNEY BEYOND THE ALPS

THE GLORIOUS KING Charles led his armed host to Geneva. There he divided it and went himself with one part beyond the Alps."

So the annals said, later on. It sounds very simple. We think of a ghostly, glittering array of knights in armor following a majestic *Charlemagne* across the mountains. In reality, however, the inexperienced and inglorious Charles attempted a most difficult task.

He had no reliable army. At his summons perhaps three to four thousand horsemen joined him, the levies of East Franks, Alemanni, Burgundians. (They had a superstitious dislike of being numbered exactly.) These furnished their own light lances, haubergeons of iron plates or rings sewn upon leather tunics, iron half-helms, long slashing swords and short, curved ripping knives. They had the new, heavy pointed iron shields. These Frankish warriors were not, as Bernard had observed, natural riders; they had taken to horseback to meet the more able Goths and Arabs. Formed into troops—*turmae*—and squads—*scarae*—they obeyed the orders of their local leaders, who might or might not obey Charles. Trumpets gave them the signal to charge, which they did with headlong courage; they fled away just as quickly.

The foot fighters came from small farms, peasants bearing round wooden shields painted either blue or red, wearing iron caps, and carrying bows of yew wood imitated from the Byzantines. (Pepin had tried to make his horsemen use such bows, like the efficient Byzantine cataphracts, without success.) Waggoners, servants, and venturesome boys—with the contingent of Charles' personal guards—made up the rest of the highly undisciplined armed host of Frankland.

Except for the hero type of warrior, the levies that mustered after the Field of May expected to be back on their farms by harvest time. Except for the recent foray against the Saxons, the army had not been out of Frankland for seventeen years, and even the veterans had grown accustomed to taking "vengeance and spoil" along the borders rather than standing in battle. Pepin had realized, and Charles was beginning to discover, that the once redoubtable Frankish host could not be relied on in bloody battle. Dagobert's lusty warriors had become farming folk, all too mindful of their families and fields.

Such were the levies that Charles sought to lead, by persuasion and their traditional loyalty to a king, across a mountain barrier against more intelligent enemies based on large cities defended by massive Roman walls. He had the aid of Bernard's advice and of his own sagacity in judging what his armed host could not do. Already, before the mobilization, he had sent three trusted envoys over into the Lombard domain to make certain that Peter had told the truth about the situation and to bargain with the Lombard king for peace without war.

The last levies came in from the lower Rhine to the rendezvous by the lake of Geneva. There Charles set up the two standards, of the ancient image of a dragon and of the newer Christian cross, before the pavilion where he quartered Hildegard. The melting snows of summer made the high mountain pastures luxuriant, and the army could supply its three needs: water, wood, and forage.

There at Geneva his envoys returned to report, "Neither by

their prayers nor the gifts of Charles did they avail to change the savage heart of the Lombard king."

That reply gave Charles his *casus belli*. He called a council of his nobles—his own Constable ("Count of the Stables") and Seneschal ("Elder Servant," in charge of supplies) his paladins, or officers of the palace, and the dukes or leaders of military affairs, and the counts or governors of districts, and the all-important bishops, who interpreted the will of the Lord. Most of them disliked his policy, which had been Pepin's policy, of warring with the Lombards for the sake of the city of Rome. Charles felt a sense of responsibility for St. Peter's because it had been Pepin's responsibility. To his liege lords he explained that he had offered fair terms, with kingly gifts, to Desiderius and had been refused. Moreover he meant to enforce his will on the army.

Most of his peasant fighters believed vaguely that the blessed St. Peter was still alive, besieged in Rome.

So Charles got his way. Small as the army was, it needed to divide to get through the narrow passes of the Alps, where grazing lacked. Hildegard and the hunchback boy were left at Geneva. Bernard took the weaker half over the pass of the Mount of Jove (the Great St. Bernard). Charles led the best of the host around Mount Cenis, toward "summits rising to the sky, with bitter rocks." Oxen struggled up the pass with leather covered waggons of grain, pork, and wine kegs. Donkeys and mules plodded up under the parts of demountable boats which served to ferry over rivers, or, roped together, made a bridge. The army's meat climbed up alive, on the hoof.

Charles called for hymn singing on the road. Sweating up the waggons, the men sang: "Turn your heads . . . and look again . . . This road will bring us back . . . to the fatherland."

It seemed as if his luck held good because no sign of the enemy appeared at the summits. With loud songs the column started down into a narrow gorge—and found it blocked by a cemented stone wall with war engines atop it and plenty of enemies visible along the parapet. An attack failed to break through this fortification.

After the failure of his assault detachments, Charles showed bad leadership. He asked for truce, sent envoys to the Lombards offering fourteen thousand pieces of silver if hostages would be given and peace sworn. Truce and terms were refused.

It seemed that Desiderius, encamped with his court in the valley below the gorge, was a mountain man, peasant-born like Charles, and more cunning in negotiation. The parley dragged, and the lords of Frankland grumbled in their tents that food was giving out, while the road was closed. Instead of rousing them out, the big Arnulfing made the mistake of begging them not to desert him. Whereupon their spokesmen reminded him that the summer was passing, and time lacked to reach home for the harvesting.

Apparently the king of the Franks had no hope of going on with the war when a few experienced officers of the old count Thierry came to talk in his tent. If the gut of the gorge was closed, they explained, a way around it might be found over the heights. Charles allowed them to try, with their *scarae* of horsemen.

They succeeded beyond expectation. Kerold and his mates called it the Arnulfing luck. (Solemn military commentators, including Napoleon Bonaparte, paid tribute long afterward to the genius of *Charlemagne* in dividing his armies and forcing the passes of the Alps.) What actually happened remains obscure. But when the flanking party appeared on the heights, panic seized the Lombard garrison of the gorge. It ran away.

Panic is like a plague. The fleeing garrison struck fear into the Lombard royal camp. When the Franks got past the abandoned wall, they cascaded down the valley and reaped rich spoil in the deserted camp. Their lances and swinging swords harried the fleeing Lombards out of the hills.

"Thus the lord king Charles," the annals relate, "by the

59

intervention of God, found the roads into Italy open to himself and his *fideles*."

Debouching from his valley, Bernard and his array joined the pursuit, sweeping down the river Po, on to the walls of Pavia—"the Palace."

In that gorge under Mount Cenis, the big Arnulfing learned a lesson he never forgot. The action of a few *fideles*, a few faithful to him, might bring him victory in spite of armies or calamities.

Very quickly he put the lesson into practice. By September 773 he had his Franks encamped outside the walls of Pavia, while his enemy Desiderius waited inside with his family and court. The Franks had no siege engines to break through the high, towered walls swept by the deep river on one side. It being harvest time, however, they could gather in the fruit and crops of the rich valley of the Po.

Since he could do nothing more there, Charles decided to take himself and a few troops of *fideles*—the spearhead of horsemen on whom he could rely—elsewhere, to get something done.

Intentionally or not, he abandoned military strategy to begin a conflict of personality between the barbarian Frank and more cultured Lombard.

Once these Lombards—the Longbeards or Langobards— had been the proudest if not the most formidable of the German migrants who had settled forcibly within the Roman Empire. They had been pushed into Italy by the pressure of the more savage Avars. Then for some two centuries they had kept to their tribal ways and tradition and speech. After that they moved into the cities.

Only in the last two generations had the former Longbeards abandoned their clan grouping and traditions while beginning to speak the lingua Romana of the country. Desirée, in coming to Frankland, had been like a city dweller entering a tribal wilderness. Oddly, while taking at last to urban life, and intermarrying with the natives, the Lombard overlords insisted upon the local people adopting their costume of trousers and mantles, with beards and forehead hair grown long, and the backs of the heads shaved. Their pride turned into conceit, their ferocity into cunning.

Nevertheless the strongest of their kings, like Liutprand, had sought to unite the Italian peninsula from the Venetian isles to sunny Benevento under their single rule. Even the crafty Desiderius when he pounded at the gates of Rome the year before, seemed on his way to possess Italy entire, as Theodoric the great Goth had once possessed it.

In that endeavor he had been opposed only by Hadrian, who locked the doors of St. Peter's and sealed up the city gates, to defy him. Hadrian the Pope held to the memory of the vanished Roman world empire, to the glory of his half-ruined city, and to the firm conviction that the vicar of St. Peter could never be made the subject of an earthly monarch. Hadrian's gesture had been one of spirit rather than force because he had only the unruly city guards to defend him. (Then Charles had mustered his expedition at Geneva, and Desiderius had fared north with his son to the mountain passes.)

Formidable as the mighty cities of Lombardy seemed to the Franks—who thought of Italy as "Lombardy"—there was weakness in the rule of Desiderius. The richest cities such as Benevento, Spoleto, or Friuli (Forum Julii) were occupied by self-seeking *Gastalds* busied in building up their own domains, and strongly resistant to any central authority. So much Charles soon discovered.

While he must have doubted, after Mount Cenis, the ability of his army to hew its way through a battle, he was not at all disposed to allow his *fideles* to feast slothfully in their tents. Moreover, the sun-warmed grandeur of the Po valley, with vineyards and fruit orchards clustered beneath gray castles and basilicas, excited this restless rover of untilled woodlands. Why, here the paved roads crossed streams on stone bridges, and beggars picked out their lice on mosaic floors of Roman baths! Never before had he beheld the wonders of urban life.

Unwilling to wait to besiege Pavia's walls as tactics demanded, he left Bernard and other paladins there, while he started off headlong with the pick of his horsemen along the Po. He had scored success with such mounted spearheads down in Gascony and at the pass of Mount Cenis.

His gallop this time took him far, to Verona, where forty-eight towers crowned the wall encircling its hilltop. By some means unknown his riders got into this fortress, into its ancient forum flanked by temples to forgotten Roman gods. From Verona fled the son of Desiderius. But there Charles captured the fugitive Gerberga with her children and the exiled lord Aucher. He had regained the hostages, his brother's heirs.

"You went far," he told the defiant Aucher, "to find a hiding place."

That night he fetched the trembling Gerberga to his own table at the palace. Wine he poured for her with his own hand. She was afraid to let the children out of her sight. So, to ease her mind, Charles ordered a mantle to be spread on straw where she could watch the sleeping infants. He seemed to think of them now as part of his family.

Word went out along the roads that the victorious Frank feasted his captives merrily instead of slaying them. The dukes of Lombard cities elsewhere remembered that he had offered gifts and a fair peace to the Lombard king before arriving with swords drawn. They decided to remain quietly behind their walls to learn what would happen next. What happened was that Charles galloped back across Lombardy, taking in more cities.

But the force of his coming lingered in memory. Three generations afterwards a monk of St. Gall wrote down this tall tale of his coming that he heard from the old soldier, Adalbert, who had served with the sons of Kerold.

"Now it happened that one of the first nobles called Otker [Aucher] had fled for refuge to Desiderius. When these two knew that the dreaded Charles approached, they went up into a high tower to behold at a vast distance anyone who approached. When the baggage waggons appeared, swifter than the chariots of Darius, then Desiderius asked of Otker, 'Is not Charles in that vast array?' And Otker answered, 'Not yet.' When they beheld the vast force of nations gathering near, he cried at Otker, 'Surely Charles is in that force!' But Otker told him, 'Not yet, not yet.'

"Then they beheld the bishops and the abbots, and Otker, trembling, responded, 'When you see these fields bristling with an iron harvest, and the waters of this river beat against our walls with the darkness of gleaming iron, then you will know that Charles is nigh.'

"Hardly had he spoken when a black cloud dimmed the brightness of day. Weapons gleamed like flame in the night. Then came on that man of iron, Charles, helmeted with iron, his hands clad in iron, an iron spear raised high in his left hand. All who went beside him, and followed him, filled the fields with their power, until the water of the river gleamed with their iron. The walls shook. The citizens cried in fear, 'Oh, the iron! Alack!'

"Now when the truth-speaking Otker saw all this in one swift glance, he said to Desiderius, 'There is the Charles you desired so much to see.'"

So did the legend make much of his force. The living Charles, however, could not break into the walls of Pavia. Winter passed. Fretting, he sent for Hildegard and the two boys to solace him. With the melting of the snows they appeared from Mount Cenis, and he rejoiced in his family and his victory. For no enemy remained to confront him outside a city.

Then Charles started off again, with his family and high dukes and bishops, telling them all to bring their robes of honor. They would pass that happy Eastertide as pilgrims, at Rome itself.

In setting out so impulsively for the Holy City, he failed to notify Hadrian, the Pope, of his coming. But he did not fail to take along his serviceable spearhead of chosen horsemen.

Merrily his cavalcade threaded through the hills of Tuscany, down to the Roman plain where stone aqueducts strode like inanimate giants across the marshes. At the last night's camp Charles saw to it that his nobles donned their blue and crimson mantles, while he girded on a sword with a hilt of gold. His middle had swelled with the good Italian food. He remembered that he was, by title, a Patrician of Rome. "Dear and valiant brothers," he cautioned his nobles, "I will hold faithless and fit for the swine any one of you who falls drunk at this Easter feast."

"I give my word in faith," swore Warin the Count, "to Your Excellence that all the comrades of Frankland will fare on with high and reverent hearts as true pilgrims, and none of them will fall down because of wine swilling."

Like a play master the Arnulfing arranged his lay and clerical lords, his trumpeters, and bearers of the standard of the dragon and standard of the cross behind him. Being doubtful of his own appearance, he craved both splendor and power to hedge him in.

Then on the Via Clodia, at a village by a lake, throngs lined the road to hail him. Roman militiamen clashed their spears, acolytes waved palm branches, and a boys' choir sang out *"Vexilla regis prodeunt . . ."*

Beside him paced the standard-bearers of the churches. At such splendor and harmony, Charles' heart expanded. Dismounting, he went forward on foot. Never before had a king of Frankland set eyes on this Holy City, behind its massive brown wall.

Nearing it, watching to see that his following did not straggle, Charles was led aside by his palm-bearing guides.

"This is the way of triumph. Will the Great Clemency of the Franks proceed upon this path of the ancient victorious Caesars?"

In this manner they led him away from the city gate toward the church of St. Peter. Happily, Charles walked on, listening to the hymn singing so much more tuneful than the hoarse chanting of his Frankish clerics.

Hadrian had resolved not to let him march into the city.

According to the author of his life, Hadrian had fallen at the news of Charles' immediate arrival "into an ecstasy of amazement."

The truth is, the Pope was stunned.

Hadrian came of a distinguished Roman family. A man of poise, determination—rather than clerical learning—and wide political experience, he had squelched and punished black conspiracy within the cliques of Rome, had fought a one-man battle against the wiles of Desiderius, while he dreamed of rebuilding the shattered monuments of his city. He was that rare combination, a diplomat of great force of character.

The problem he faced seemed almost insoluble. Cut off from the eastern patriarch in Constantinople, this bishop, traditional successor to St. Peter, had become by circumstances sole master of riotous and impoverished Rome, city of his distinguished ancestors, supplying itself precariously with food and a little money by the lands of the Roman duchy. He was, himself, the last vestige of the *Respublica Romana*. As such, he existed by sufferance of the Lombards, who were, at the worst, more refined and outwardly devout than other barbarian kings. To sustain his enfeebled city, Hadrian must have more territory in Italy—which he claimed as the patrimony of St. Peter—territory that neither the covetous Desiderius, nor the independent dukes, nor the distant emperor in Constantinople would think of yielding up. So Hadrian prepared to defend his walls of Rome desperately with priests, militia, and pilgrims, when the advent of the Franks across the Alps relieved the Lombard pressure.

Not only that. Charles' seizure of Verona decided the southern Lombard dukes to make their peace with the least menacing power of the three contending for Italy, with Hadrian himself. From Benevento, Spoleto, and other cities they hurried to St. Peter's to be shaven of their beards and long hair and to offer their fealty to this apostolic lord before the Frankish king or the Lombard, as the fate of Pavia might decide, could crush them. These dukes were present in Rome as devout and suddenly submissive pilgrims, and Hadrian was beholding the territory he needed thrust, as it were, into his hand when he heard that the barbarian Frank was riding, unannounced, into Rome.

Being a well-read man, although a poor Latinist, Hadrian may have reflected upon the fate of the frogs as related by that humorous Syrian slave, Aesop, when they tried to rid themselves of their King Log by summoning in King Stork. As at the coming of Desiderius, he determined to defend his city, but with discretion, because the forcible Frank was still an unknown quantity. Hence he sent for his guides and welcomers to lead Charles aside, to quarter the armed Franks safely beyond the walls in the Field of Nero, and to conduct Charles himself to the portal of St. Peter's.

There, since dawn Hadrian waited anxiously, at the head of his clergy with the massed Benedictines. Thither strode Charles, with a flicker of gold from the hilt of his sword and crown circlet. On his knees he climbed the steps, laboring up the weight of his great body. He kissed the hand that Hadrian held out to him with the greeting, "Blessed is he that comes in the name of the Lord."

For a moment the prelate studied the towering barbarian. Charles beamed with exultation when the thronged monks chanted a prayer. He felt as if he had come into a great and festive hall. Gripping Hadrian's hand, he was led through the atrium into the very door of the apostle's church, up the nave

66

between ninety-six columns, to the altar where a hundred lighted candles shone above the holy tomb. The light gleamed on plates of silver and gold, and the mosaic wall pictures. Never had Charles imagined such splendor.

Humbly he made his prayer at the confessional, and stole a glance over his shoulder at Hildegard and the watching Pepin. He heard Hadrian's voice, when they rose, saying that he had laid low the heads of proud enemies and had served St. Peter by his strength. What was he minded to do at Rome?

Charles murmured that he wished to visit the shrines during the four Easter days, and then depart.

Hadrian was not quite ready to believe that. He kept at Charles' side, a gracious host serving his uninvited guest.

Frankly he asked Charles to pledge faith and comradeship in peace with him. After doing so, Charles bade all his Frankish nobles and clerics take the same oath. Hadrian was satisfied, but he kept at the warrior's side.

"Yours is a joyous entry," he said at the gate. Charles did not seem to mind sleeping outside, in Nero's Field. All Easter Sunday the big Frank went around in a daze of wilderment, at the gathering of Roman magistrates and high lords to greet him, at the stately Mass within St. Maria Maiora, and the thronged feast in the hall of the Lateran. He was entering not only a holy city but a mighty metropolis of the world where pilgrims from Africa and the island of Britain elbowed their way to the shrines, carrying scripts listing the *mirabilia* to be visited, and buying tiny crosses and sometimes relics wherever they went. A longing gripped him to carry off a relic of Paul and even Peter, to the altars of St. Martin and St. Denis. When Hadrian showed him an entire chamber filled with books lying on shelves, he shouted in amazement and begged for some of the illuminated sacramentaries, so splendidly inscribed and painted, to take back to his homeland.

For three days Hadrian puzzled over this man with the eager mind of a boy, who might become either the master or

67

the protector of Rome. In Charles he sensed a stubborn will, and a disposition to accept responsibility. The Frank had a trick of picking up his crippled boy to show the child anything that pleased him. Thereafter Hadrian always asked if Charles would do a thing, never if he could do it; he pleaded for protection against enemies rather than for aid to himself.

The observant Hadrian came close to guessing the secret of Charles' personality. But that the powerful barbarian kept hidden, because it came from a suppressed and terrifying fear. Fear, to Charles, was a shameful thing and he fought against revealing it.

Hadrian did wonder, silently, at the way Charles haunted the spots of sacred tradition—the crypt of Peter's prisoning, the stones of the apostle's confessional, the golden reliquaries. No ordinary pilgrim wanted so to carry off a fragment of stone. Then, too, the Frank's joy seemed overmastering when he pushed his big frame into such a spot. He seemed to be hilarious with relief. Briefly Hadrian wondered if he were trying to escape, physically, from some fancied pursuit. But that did not seem possible.

After the third day's Mass at St. Paul's outside the walls, the Franks prepared to depart. But before they could do so on the fourth day, Hadrian requested them to meet—he realized now that Charles never liked to be separated from his family and liegemen—again at St. Peter's altar. There, quietly, he reminded Charles of the promise his father Pepin had given Stephen of blessed memory in Frankland—the promise of certain cities and lands to be handed over to St. Peter and his vicars. He then asked Charles if he and his nobles would confirm the promise so made.

Readily, Charles assented. Had he not crossed the Alps to redeem that very pledge?

Then Hadrian had a secretary read the written items of Pepin's donation. Charles could not follow the swift intoned Latin too well.

". . . from the isle of Corsica . . . thence to Mount Bardo, to

Parma . . . from thence to Mantua and Mount Silicis, together with the whole . . . of Ravenna, as it was in old time, and the provinces of Venetiae with Istria . . . and the whole of Spoletium and Beneventum."

Many of the names Charles did not know. Only the roads over which he had ridden in Italy were familiar to him. He had never laid eyes on a map. So he could not have realized that the recited boundaries took in two thirds of Italy.

Understanding that this was what Hadrian needed to have bestowed, he agreed readily. Some who watched the scene say that Charles had his chaplain copy the list, and that he himself placed the script of the copy beneath the Gospels that lay on the tomb under the altar.

The resolute Hadrian had been promised more than he ever hoped to possess.

On his part Charles took away a Roman priest to teach his Franks to chant correctly, together with a learned doctor, Peter of Pisa, to teach him grammar and writing. More than that, he bore away with him a craving for the libraries, the buildings of civilization, and the relief that had come to him so unexpectedly at the shrines of Rome.

After that his cup of happiness flowed over. Hildegard bore him a daughter, and early in June the defense of Pavia ended under the ordeal of hunger and fever. Desiderius walked out, empty-handed, with his family, to surrender. He proved to be only a plump, morose little man, fearful of offending Charles, who laughed heartily at such anxiety. Ansa, his wife, was a fine-looking female.

When his Franks swarmed into the gates, Charles rode in as victor, admiring the long colonnades and warm spring baths of this city of palaces. Desirée, who had been his wife, was dead, and Pavia was his. In high good humor he watched the treasures sorted out, ordering them given entire to his liegemen, who had besieged the walls so long. Delighted, they shouted approval of Charles' generosity and luck in

69

gaining a profitable victory with so little bloodshed. From that day he signed himself "Charles, king by the grace of God of the Franks and the Lombards, and Patrician of the Romans."

Desiderius and Ansa he sent away, guarded, to monastic retreat at Corbie. No burden of Frankish law or tribute did he lay upon the other Lombards, nor did he claim aught of their lands or cities for himself. He was merely king "of the Lombards," not of their country. They could manage as they had done before.

Then he was off, swiftly for his homeland. In passing the heights of the Rhone glacier, Hildegard's child died.

To the Lombard nobles, deserted by their conqueror, such heedless mercy seemed fantastic. One of them wrote, "The king of the Franks, who could have destroyed our possessions, showed himself merciful and indulgent."

That had never happened before in Italy.

Within a year Charles' peace policy raised up rebellion. Strong as the hatred of Saxons for their kinsmen the Franks was the antagonism of the humbled Lombards to their new masters. With the weak Desiderius removed, the northern dukes banded together to take over the country. In Rome, the anxious Hadrian heard that the son of Desiderius was leading back a fleet from Constantinople. With rebellion in the air, all semblance of rule broke down.

Hadrian, who had hoped for so much from Charles, found that the powerful Frank, engaged with the Saxons, paid no apparent heed to the plight of Italy. Eloquently the worried vicar wrote to his friend the "Great and Excellent King," saluting his wife and children—well did Hadrian recall Charles' devotion to his family—and warning him that chaos was setting in around St. Peter's. Armed bands held the roads. Ravenna claimed sovereignty in the north, while Rotgad, duke of Friuli, mustered an army.

In response Charles, occupied that summer of 775 on the

Saxon front, sent no visible token of his authority. Only a pair of bishops arrived from Frankland to trot their mules between Spoleto and Benevento, to sit in talk with the chieftains there. "Be wise and wait," warned these harmless bishops, "for Charles is coming."

They also sent back to Frankland by courier their opinion of the situation.

"What worth has this king of the Franks," Rotgad taunted the envoys of the Pope, "that the Romans put their trust in him?"

Hadrian sent on the taunt to the wandering Charles. No response in the clear script of Peter of Pisa came back to him. When winter set in and snow closed the mountain passes to an army, Hadrian lost hope.

Then after Christmas Charles came through the snow barrier. Leading only his column of picked horsemen, he was able to surmount the passes. This time he did not pause at Pavia but hurtled down the river, and up into the eastern hills, battering in bloody action through the defense of a river. The tale is told how Rotgad fought and fled, to be killed by his own men in the mountains, and how Treviso fell to the Franks in a siege.

With Desiderius the king of the Franks had shown gentleness; with the rebellion he dealt swiftly and harshly, hanging leaders, exiling dukes, confiscating lands, leaving his Frankish counts to rule with a garrison to back them in the north. He had named himself king of the Lombards and that was what he meant to be. Even in absence, he was their lawful king. The Spoletans and Beneventans who had talked with his bishops kept apart from the rebellion.

He made no pilgrimage to Rome. When he paused to celebrate Easter it was on the mountain road to Frankland. He got home in time for the hay mowing in July.

After that the future of Italy rested in balance between the unpredictable will of Charles and the determination of the Roman Hadrian.

Physically, the son of Pepin felt no fear. His rugged and now massive body could absorb punishment, and wounds left only scars. He had forced a thousand men to follow him over the snow heights that last winter, sleeping under no roof.

His foresters told how Charles met with an aurochs while hunting. This giant wild ox was, more than the lion, the king of beasts in Europe. Naturally in telling about it, the huntsmen made much of Charles as a hero.

"The gift-giving Charles, who would never endure idleness or sloth, went out to hunt the aurochs. When those attending him saw such an immense animal they fled. But the fearless Charles, riding a spirited war horse, drew close to the aurochs and tried to cut through its neck with his sword. Yet he missed his stroke and the monstrous beast ripped up the boot and leg thongs of the great king, slightly wounding his calf with the tip of its horn, making him limp. Then it fled to the shelter of trees and stones. Many of his servants wanted to take off their leg wrappings to give him, but he forbade them, saying, 'I mean to go like this to Hildegard.'

"Then Isambard the son of Warin ran to the beast and threw his lance, piercing it to the heart between shoulder bone and windpipe. They dragged the still warm beast to the great king.

"He seemed not to notice it, except to give the carcass to his companions, and afterwards he went home. There he showed his torn leg coverings to his queen, and asked, 'What does the man deserve who slew the beast that did this to me?' She made answer, 'He deserves the highest gift.' Then the great king had the horns of the beast brought forth, as witness of his truth, so that the queen sighed and beat her breast."

Because Hildegard felt such fear for his sake, the Arnulfing, who did not like Isambard, rewarded the young noble with a pound of silver for his act, and handfasted him in friendship.

Charles did not fear for his body, nor, after his ride to Verona, did he dread the machinations of an enemy. The dread that preyed on him, more and more, crept into his mind. As a boy he had not known it, in the loving kindness of his family; as the eldest son and shadow of the aging Pepin, he had not been aware of it.

But now that he was alone, except for the unthinking Hildegard, it rose to face him in the saddle or throne seat. It appeared everywhere in his homeland, like a dance of death, seen by no other eyes but his. It warned him every day of decay and death closing in upon his people, the Franks.

In the market of Ingelheim he came upon a sly seller of miracles, a fat man in cowl and goat-hair shirt offering amulets of twisted vines for a few pence, to heal dropsy, blindness, or black vomit. A man-witch.

Charles had a way of wandering alone, wearing his workaday Frisian wool, and it often happened that he was not recognized as the king. Once in doing so he found the folk of a hamlet gathered with their children about the wooden cross used for the ordeal of crucifixion; but they were all watching a free Swabian accused of thieving. The priests poured boiling water from a caldron into a keg as high as the Swabian's belt. Then they dropped a small stone into the keg, and rolled up the sleeve on the right arm of the accused man, who had offered to be judged by God's will through the ordeal of the boiling water.

When the throng pushed closer, to see if the Swabian could give proof of his innocence by pulling the stone from the steaming water, Charles buffeted his way in to the keg. If the Swabian failed to come up with the stone, his hand would be cut off with an ax, and most of the spectators wanted to behold that. Charles, who had a quick, keen eye, noticed that the Swabian was not sweating with anxiety. The man waited until a priest muttered some ragtag Latin, then plunged in his arm. He shouted as if in pain and jerked up his fist, which

73

a shorn cleric caught and held up a stone which seemed to come from his fingers. "*Ita—impenitus videtur!*" The priest cried the man's innocence.

The crowd exclaimed, while Charles bent over the keg, observing the stone lying untouched on the bottom. Angered by this mockery of a trial, he grasped both Swabian and cleric by the neck and thrust their heads into the simmering water. With howls of real agony, they tore away from him, while the throng stared at him in brutish wilderment.

Then, again, he found Frankish freemen laboring as serfs on the glebe, getting in a poor crop of barley. Although freemen, entitled to carry weapons, these Franks chose to grub for grain to fill their bodies and escape harder duties.

In such folk he sensed the ending of their ancient Teutonic pride; they were sinking into wine swilling, jostling to their death like the Gadarene herd——

At the vespers hour, he dismounted by a road chapel of St. Remi to say a Magnificat. His attendants waited outside to stretch themselves. The roof sagged over the dark altar, where two men whispered—a freeholder apparently confessing to a deacon, whose robe had been pulled on over hunting trousers. The floor was fouled by animal droppings. Such things the Arnulfing took for granted, but as he murmured his prayer he heard the methodical clink of silver coins, and a voice counting, ". . . four, for the item of the herder wench, five pays the item of the tallow weighed twice, six, that little trick on the mindless boy . . ." The voice confessing sank to a faint whisper, and ended sharply. "By the hallowed bones of Remi, I swear I have no more than seven pence."

It crossed Charles' mind that the word of a free Frank was no longer heeded, unless he swore by well-known relics. Then he understood that this penitent was paying his coins for the redemption of his sins, because some of the folk believed the words of the prophet Daniel, "*Redeem thy sins by almsgiving,*" meant to pay out the sum of them in money.

How could their dull minds understand the *meaning* of

such words? The clerics who should guide them often could not read.

After dwelling in the palace of Pavia and listening to wise Hadrian, Charles realized his own ignorance and the sottishness of his people, in their wattle and daub huts and log churches. For a moment, in the wonder of the vast Roman churches, he had been uplifted as with wine, believing himself close to a miraculous power. Yet in his homeland that exaltation vanished. He brought back relics. But were they, in this forest, any different from the fragments and wood of local shrines? Could they effect a miracle among the Franks?

Charles was brooding over that when he had his words with Sturm. Riding the road of the Rhine's right bank, among the frontier settlements, he found Sturm slashing branches in a fir wood, to build a night's barricade against stray beasts. Although disciple of Boniface and abbot of Fulda in the Saxon hills, old Sturm still traveled across country afoot, as in his missioner days. Even when he recognized Charles the king, the giant abbot went on swinging his scramasax, and weaving branches. Without thanks he sat at the fire the king's henchmen made, and shared the king's supper meat, bread, and honey. Without comment, he heard Charles' complaint of the sloth and gluttony and decay of minds among his Franks. And when Charles waited for his response, old Sturm roused from his meditation and said a strange thing. "My son, send away your huntsmen and groomsmen and guards. Abide here by the fire and make your prayer at complin hour."

"My prayer?"

"Yours."

Charles had hoped for wise advice from the weathered man who had walked the wilderness with Boniface, the apostle. Sturm had started building his monastery, Fulda, by felling logs on a hilltop, to make a place for the bones of Boniface.

Sturm's gray eyes peered up beneath the white tangle of his brows at the stars beyond the smoke. "It is near the hour now. My lord of Frankland, are not these tall trees like pillars of the nave of the Lord's temple? Do you have any fear here?"

Impatiently, Charles demanded, "Speak your mind, Father! Why do you call me to pray at this hour?"

The abbot's gnarled hands tightened the girdle at his waist. Then he rose up, and let out his strong, dry voice. "If your Frankish people sink into ignorance and fornication—the responsibility lies upon their priests. If the priests of Frankland are losing their minds and will—*hinc inde potestas terribilis*. That is because of one terrible power." He pointed his finger at Charles. "Yours. Your word is the law. All these human souls wait for your nod of consent, or frown of anger. Your power is a terrible power. You may not share it, or avoid it. Pray, therefore, that you use it aright. My lord, you bade me speak my mind."

After they knelt together in the barricade of branches, Charles pondered all that Sturm had said. It was not easy for him to understand such things. He thought of the last rightful king of the Franks, the Meroving, unwieldy with fat, rocking over the ruts in the ritual oxcart. He saw him again with a child's eyes. The last king, as some child of his might be, in turn. A mindless soul, trundled away from the cooking pots. That was what he feared.

Old Sturm leaned forward to drop dry branches on the fire. Something odd came into his gray eyes as he watched the giant Charles. "My son, do not think of changing human nature in a night. How often have I baptized my Saxon *kunkelds*—to find them sacrificing a goat, or even a bull, to propitiate their old forest gods the next morning. I am glad, then, that they do not let out the blood of a human slave."

Charles had not thought the priest of the frontier could be so tolerant. When Sturm prepared his cloak for sleeping, he nodded at the barrier of branches. "As for animals, they pay more attention to a barricade around a fire than to any prayer."

So old Sturm gave his advice to Charles.

Although he could not reason out his dread, the Arnulfing reacted against it with physical vitality. If his mind needed to be schooled, even at mature age, he would school it. From his new tutor, Peter of Pisa, he tried to learn how to put thoughtless words into clear sentences. The old Lombard doctor read him the grim song of Virgil, telling of the downfall of Troy, and Aeneas fleeing by the light of its burning, carrying his ancestral gods.

"What befell his folk?" Charles demanded.

"They were conquered. For conquered men there is only one safety, and that is to hope for none."

Charles became interested in this Aeneas who bred a new people beyond the sea.

Sometimes when dread of his own inability lay heavy on the Arnulfing, he strode off to the woods, following no path, to a grove like that of Irminsul but smaller. There in a hut dwelt some aged scops, and he gave them alms. Then the scops stroked a harp and chanted the ancient heroism of the Frankish folk when they rode the long ways of the sea.

Such ancestor tales had never been written down by a Virgil. Charles gleaned them from the memory of the old bards. Out of them came the glow of a golden age when power dwelt in the hands of heroes under the protection of the earth gods. Charles thought at length about the Irminsul he had hewn down.

At such a time he wondered how Pepin had meant to deal with the unsubmissive Saxon folk. For up to now—except in riding to Rome for Easter—Charles had followed out Pepin's ideas more than he chose to admit. The rudimentary Frankish state remained much as it had been, more like a personal estate of the king. The royal palace—differing greatly from Pavia—was merely the *aula* or hall where Charles happened to be. With himself, the eleven paladins or officers of the palace made up the council that decided matters. The Count

77

of the Palace took responsibility when Charles could not be present.

After dwelling at St. Peter's, Charles became conscious of the barbarity of his rule. His Chamberlain managed herds and lands more than any court; his Seneschal planned out the food and fodder along his line of march, and both of them had their heads together with Hildegard, who kept close track of the additions and subtractions of the treasury—gifts made to the king at feast days, and the corresponding gifts paid out; the tolls paid in from frontier posts and bridges, and the amends paid to the courts, as well as the king's share of booty from the enemy.

Hildegard never ceased hoarding their possessions, especially the crop and animal yield of their home farms. Charles had a secret conviction that this brought bad luck. It satisfied his careful Swabian wife if they had, at each hall, enough cheese, game, beer, linen, honey, grain, and tallow candles for their needs.

"Since your God-protected father died," she observed with satisfaction, "we have had no famine in the land."

Charles could not understand how Hildegard somehow joined God's protection with the yield of meat from the herds, but apparently it was perfectly simple to her, and she did not want anything changed for the worse.

For the first time, in these years, Charles departed from the policy of Pepin. He planned to subdue those nearest and most hated antagonists, the Saxons, and to change their deceitful pagan nature by converting them. "That nation, which has been given over to demons since the beginning of time, will enter into the sweet yoke of Christ." His council agreed with him.

Devout missionaries like Boniface had ventured among the pagans across the Rhine, and had usually been killed by them. Armed columns had invaded the wilderness to punish them. But missionaries had never marched with the armed hosts before.

Journey Beyond the Alps

It was a novel experiment, to attempt conversion by force, and it was destined to cause terror for thirty years.

Something had to be tried. No doubt about that. No sooner had the Frankish host gone off to Italy the first time than the border Saxons stormed and burned the abbey of Fritzlar, stabling their horses in the chapel, in revenge for the overthrow of Irminsul.

During that winter his council planned to end all such partisan strife by a single massive invasion—a full levy of arms of the Frankish *fideles*. They would build block houses along the wilderness roads and erect churches within them. (They had been absorbed in this all the summer of 775 while Hadrian besought Charles to return to Rome.)

Far into the pagan lands the embittered king's warriors forged, burning and slaying when they came up with the elusive forest folk, storming the twin hill forts of Sigiburg and Eresburg, pressing down the valley of Irminsul to the river Weser, scattering resistance at that barrier. The great clans, Westfalians and Eastfalians, felt the weight of the iron swords. The Frankish chivalry sighted the dark mass of the Süntal, after threading through the valley of the Ruhr. They appeared to have scattered all visible foemen.

Then back on the Weser one of Charles' divisions engaged in building a settlement was surprised and massacred. The forests still concealed the strength of the Saxon war bands. When word of the calamity reached him, he took the forces nearest him in pursuit, only to find resistance vanishing. Villagers appeared in his path to offer hostages and submission. (Then Charles had taken the best of his horsemen on that long winter ride to Italy.)

And there a courier had reached him with news that his forts of Sigiburg and Eresburg were besieged. He hastened back from the Rhone headwaters to the Rhine, appearing so unexpectedly with his wearied veterans that the forest folk took to their impassable heights. Charles was learning, at cost, the futility of invasion where no cities existed to be captured with their populations. True, no army had withstood him, yet he held securely no more than the two frontier forts and the valley roads leading from the great Hessian plateau.

He had roused against him the silent, inflexible resistance of all the Saxon peoples as far as the untouched northern plain and the Elbe and the Baltic shore.

Against such enmity his missioners prevailed little. With armed guards around them they preached a stammering message to sullen hostages and starving villagers. Charles held them to blame for their futility. Avidly he longed for a Boniface to carry his summons to conversion into Saxonland. Then he remembered the aged and forcible frontier preacher, the abbot Sturm, and sent for him.

"Tell me," Sturm demanded, "if you are fighting off wolves or leading forth sheep?"

When Charles could not answer this difficult question, the sun-darkened priest of the forest explained the riddle. The Saxons were a warrior race and like unto wolves. Attacked with weapons, they might be killed but they could not be changed into something different. No, to change the nature of wolves you had to sheath your weapons and dwell among them, sharing food with them, leaving them otherwise at liberty.

It angered the impatient Arnulfing to hear that. "How many times have I offered peace to those faithless ones?"

"Often enough. Yet you have done so after punishing them with iron weapons."

"They will not submit otherwise."

Old Sturm held out his gnarled hands. "Offer them a truce with open hands."

"How?"

"By God's will, you are the king. It is your task to arrange terms with these people lost to God."

Sturm's demand went beyond reason. Yet it echoed Charles' misgiving. Although brutish and pagan, the Saxons held to their old gods and ancient valor. More than the Lombards, and more even than his Franks, they had preserved the courage of their race.

In name Charles was king, *gratia Dei*. But what folk had the Lord willed him to rule? Lombard captives from Treviso and the far eastern mountains had taken oath to serve him, and so had become his men. Old Peter, his schoolmaster, hied from the city of Pisa. Although his rule stretched far, Charles possessed no city as a home. Instead he called on men of differing race and speech to take the oath of loyalty——

Out of Charles' brooding, and Sturm's insistence, came a new offer to the recalcitrant Saxon chieftains. The king of the Franks bade them assemble in freedom, to receive the baptism of the Church, and to take oath of loyalty to him. Within their lands he announced that he would build not a fort but a new town wherein chapels could be raised. Except that he would become their overlord, the Saxons would keep to their own laws and customs as before.

The site of the new town he selected himself beyond the contested borderline of Sigiburg and Eresburg, near the headwaters of the river Lippe. There stretched a watered plain, a junction of the wilderness roads, offering good bathing and hunting. It was like his favored valley of Aquis Granum which he had been unable to visit these last years. Because it straddled a fishing stream, the Padra, Charles christened this new friendship town Padrabrunnen, or Paderborn. The first building marked out with felled logs was a church.

In his chronicle for the year of the building, 776, Archbishop Ado wrote: "Where the Lippe arises, he received all the Saxon people, with their wives and children. Baptized, they joined themselves to him, in faith. At Padrabrunnen he held an assembly, as much of the Saxons as of the Franks."

This unusual gathering (in the summer of 777) the energetic Frank staged with his instinct for showmanship. As at the gates of Rome, robed bishops and counts in full regalia

81

surrounded him. Bearded Lombards paraded with swaggering Bavarians. Abbot Sturm, summoned to consecrate the log church, baptized incoming Saxon clans, Hessians, Westfalians, and Eastfalians in masses, standing waist deep in the streams. The dragon standard and the cross standard that had been carried to victory in Italy were paraded through the campfires, while Sturm's monks, coached by the Roman choirmaster, chanted *"Vexilla regis prodeunt."*

Meat, wine, beer, and honey loaded the tables by the fires; old Sturm preached the Word with a full heart. Bright-eyed, jesting, promising, Charles circulated through this camp meeting. He was a gifted spellbinder. His massive figure in leather hunting trousers and wolfskins pushed into the beer-joyous throngs of upstanding, long-haired Saxons. He drank, horn for horn, with their chieftains, and unexpectedly joined in their chants of heroes who sought Wotan in the heaven-hall of Valhalla.

His cup of joy overflowed when a strange cavalcade appeared—riders in silvered chain mail with spotless cloaks, sitting easily their high saddles on nervous horses. They were Arabs, nobles of Islam, from Spain beyond the Pyrenees, seeking a truce with the king of the Franks.

No master of a show could have welcomed a new attraction as eagerly as Charles greeted these distinguished guests. Not only were they a visible and unquestioned sign of his growing power, but they appeared like chieftains of another world to the forest-bound Saxons. Charles took pains that the newly converted Saxons should behold him in stately conference with the Arab lords.

In this way he found an answer to Sturm's challenge to offer a king's truce. Apparently he had won another victory without combat. Certainly he believed so, and his optimism was to cause him almost immediate grief.

With the advantage of afterknowledge, the good Ado ended his writing with the words: "Witukind and certain rebellious Saxons went over to the Northmen, asking their aid against the glorious Charles."

Witukind. His name had been heard along the forest roads during the last resistance. He absented himself from the church raising, the baptism, and the loyalty oath. Without clan or land of his own, Witukind was the one chieftain to whom all others listened, and he had warned them never to give the Frank a footing beyond the Rhine. Charles had no means of knowing that Witukind was the prime mover of the pagan resistance.

That summer of 777 yielded the best of omens. The date itself combined the beneficent figure 7—number of the days of Creation—with fortunate 3—number of the Trinity. Hildegard bore him another healthy son. Apparently he had made converts and friends of the stubborn Saxons.

By this revival meeting at Paderborn, however, Charles managed to convert no one more than himself. His ready enthusiasm overflowed. No longer did folk mouth his name as Churl, or snicker at the circumstance of his birth; he had made himself a king in deed as well as in name. Cultured Saracen lords sought him out in the wilderness. He had done more than Pepin, in binding Aquitaine fast and stretching his authority afar, to Hadrian in Rome.

A change was taking place in Frankland. The memory of the Merovingian kings, and of Neustrian and Austrasian Franks was fading out, to be replaced by the presence of the genial Arnulfing. Because he rode among them ceaselessly, the varied peoples of mountain hostels and lowland byres knew his ruddy face. He spoke their dialects and slept in their lofts. He left gifts with the roadside shrines. So, accordingly, from all frontiers free men journeyed to seek not the king's authority but Charles himself. A Frisian of the marshlands, when questioned by road guards, said, "I search for Charles the king." A Gascon explained, "I am Charles' man."

This in turn was having an effect on the eager Arnulfing.

Realizing the weakness of his Franks, he welcomed new allegiance. He felt—after Paderborn—that nations were ready to gather around his standard.

During his nightly musing he pondered the nature of this new following of peoples. One thing they all had in common; they were sheep of Christ's fold. Lombards, Bretons, or Saxons—they were Christians. Might he not become in time leader of one great Christian nation? That thought he kept to himself as yet.

But something tangible came out of it, in his mind. At the first he had claimed to be "defender of the Holy Church." And he had spent most of his nine years of ruling in defending churches on different frontiers. As far as those churches extended, people sought his aid. So they were opening up new frontiers to him.

Why to him? In Europe only two other monarchs had equal power. One, Tassilo, sought only to enlarge his Bavaria; the other, Abd al Rahman, emir of Córdoba, was a Moslem and hence a pagan.

Charles alone might claim to lead the *Christian people*.

When he roused from his meditation at dawn to go to the chapel for prayer and praise, the thought grew upon him. He could lead out the army of the Christian peoples. Then, indeed, he might rule them, by right.

The thought fitted well with his desire to conquer them.

Chapter IV

RONCESVALLES

During their winter hibernation between Christmas and Easter the council of the Franks planned the campaign of the coming summer. By now the elders, the counts Bernard and Thierry with the aged Fulrad, seldom shaped the decisions. They gave heed to Charles. It was not so much that he insisted on getting his own way, as that no one could argue against his enthusiasm.

That winter on the Rhine he spoke for an invasion of Spain. Although his advisers and paladins may have been surprised, they had to agree that his reasons were good.

Not for many years, Charles pointed out, had the Frankish host visited Aquitaine, abounding in food. With the Saxon peril laid to rest along the Rhine, there remained the greater menace of the Saracens beyond the Pyrenees. That frontier had been quiet for a decade only because of the civil war waged between factions there, where the Ommayid Moslems had gained mastery over the Abbasids. Out of this conflict emerged a strong leader Abd al Rahman, emir of Córdoba. Soon or late this warrior lord would strike against the Christians, as in the day of Charles the Hammer. It would be wiser to enter the field first against him.

Not only that. All along the Pyrenees Christian peoples had taken refuge from the Saracen invasion. These Wascons—Gascons and the Basques—and proud Visigoth refugees in the Asturias could be liberated by the Franks, and would unquestionably join with Charles in setting up a new and stronger frontier to the south, along the river Ebro.

So he argued with conviction. He did not explain that he meant to take, in this way, his first step upon his new mission of leading forth a truly Christian army against the pagan Moslems of Spain.

Most of the paladins of his council agreed with him. Count Thierry had a son, William, in the southland, old enough to win honor on the battlefield; Eggihard the Seneschal hoped to take richer spoils in Spain than in Saxonland; Count Roland (Hroudland), Warden of the Breton March, was eager to conquer a pagan land.

Charles' high enthusiasm carried them along with him. Orders went out to assemble the war bands far south on the river Garonne at the heights of Gascony, and early—at Easter instead of the usual Field of May. His eagerness sent the messengers galloping and the paladins to readying the weapons stored in the arsenals. Secretly he thought of the new host not as Franks, Burgundians, Lombards, and Aquitanians but as the army of Christendom.

In preparing for the journey, the impetuous Arnulfing contrived ingeniously to double his own working hours. Waking by candlelight, he carried his mantle and leg wrappings out to the antechamber, to groups waiting for him to judge their cases. Breakfasting on bread and wine, he listened to their appeals and usually granted them against the judgments of his counts and bishops, who had a habit of exacting fines— of which they kept a third. His dinner he limited to four platters, not counting the cherished roasts brought in by his huntsmen, and three bowls of wine. Yet while they all ate, merry with him, he had dry Peter of Pisa read aloud from Augustine's *The City of God*.

It seemed to Charles, in his preoccupation with Spain, that the learned Augustine, who foretold the end of the Roman rule of the world and the arising of the city of God on earth to take its place, had predicted what might happen in their own time. Moreover the book fairly echoed his own thoughts when it related ". . . the most savage animals—and man himself is said to have been once almost a wild beast—hedge in their own kind with a ring of protecting peace . . . they beget, suckle and raise their young . . . even the solitary vulture builds its nest and cares for the mother that guards the young."

So Charles devoted himself to his offspring, and to Hildegard, who was again with child.

"And so all men seek peace with their own circle, whom they desire to govern. Even those they war against, they wish to make their own, to impose on them the laws of their own peace."

Was that not, in so many words, almost Charles' thought? Did he not seek to make this gathering of people his own? Beyond doubt he was going to war against the Saracens to impose his own peace on them.

Finally, it seemed providential that these two Saracen lords should seek his aid against Abd al Rahman, with whom they had quarreled. They won Charles' respect. One of them named Sulaiman ibn Arabi, Solomon the Arab's son, had been a power in Saragossa, the stronghold on the Ebro. The other, called the Slave, had a haughty bearing; he brought gifts of incense that pleased Hildegard, and painted glass lamps, with strings of pearls and brocades with the design of a strange beast called the elephant. The Slave explained that he had seen an elephant almost as large as the chapel of Paderborn.

Sulaiman and the Slave had some peculiarities: they turned their heads away from the Frankish women, the fair ones as well as the ugly; they went apart with their slaves to pray, without books or priests to aid them, only washing themselves first and spreading a rug on the ground. Sulaiman pledged his faith that if the king of Frankland marched into Spain the gates of Saragossa would be opened to him, without battle.

That suited Charles, who had discovered the advantage of dividing an enemy before advancing against him. In the case of the Lombards, he had created a faction favoring him before crossing the Alps. Even in hurrying to put down Rotgad's rebellion, he had sent his innocent-seeming bishops ahead, to hold aloof the strong Beneventans.

Now his new Arab allies prepared the way for him in Spain. He needed only to march in, to victory.

They rode as if to a festival. Thousands of stark horsemen followed after the standard of the cross—for Charles left the dragon standard where Hildegard and her ladies waited his return on the shore of the swift Garonne that spring of 778. As he had done at the Alps, he sent part of the host aside to the pass of the Perch, toward Barcelona. With him he kept all the paladins and Rhineland heroes.

Fair weather sped Charles' array, through the Land of Rocks, into the Gascon heights. Morning mists veiled the mountains ahead. Never before had the Franks crossed in this fashion into Spain.

Earlier even than the exultant Charles, the young lord of Toulouse, William, was afoot at the horse lines, staring into the mist. This William, son of the warrior count Thierry, wore the short Gascon cape; he beheld no good omens at the dawning. The mountain way before them was empty of human beings.

"They keep to their manors," quoth Charles, who thought the quiet to be a sign of good.

"They have left their huts, lord king of Frankland," answered the closemouthed Aquitanian. "They have driven off their herds."

The inanimate mountains, Charles argued, could not harm such a great host. William of fair Toulouse felt misgiving because the mountain folk, the Basques and Gascons, were wild as horned sheep, giving allegiance to no prince.

Hearing him say this, the careful Charles sent forth huntsmen and bowmen with great warning horns, to climb to the heights and to sound their horns if they spied armed men ahead.

No warning was heard, no foemen were found. Over the narrow rock-bound pass the Frankish host wound its way, down through the forested slopes and the pine-grown plateau of Navarre, to the gates of the guarding town, Pampalona, by a peaceful waterfall. The gates stood open. The folk, short dark Basques, in silence offered grain and cheese to the army. Charles came upon a garden with a marble pool over which a fountain played as the wind blew. At this he marveled.

With Pampalona held secure by a rear guard of Franks, he fared on eagerly, down the stream to the wide river Ebro, where sails of boats moved between white villages that clung to the sides of hills. To the army camp came Berber and Jewish traders with luxury goods; they had Arab coins of heavy gold, and they made little of the silver pence of the Franks. Charles bade his liegemen bargain fairly with the merchants, because no other folk had shown them such good will in this strange land of white walls and fountains.

Fortune favored him. The Arab lord, Sulaiman, brought him a noble hostage, commander of an army of the emir of Córdoba. This lord, Ta'laba by name, had been defeated and captured by the garrison of Saragossa, who awaited Charles' coming. So said Sulaiman.

Even William of Toulouse, who rode more easily now that the mountains were left behind, held Sulaiman and the Slave to be worthy of belief. For one thing, Charles kept their sons as hostages; for another, they hated Abd al Rahman more than they disliked Charles.

"Why is a proud lord who has made pilgrimage and crossed the sea called the Slave?" the curious Arnulfing asked.

Rarely did the silent William smile, as he did then. "Because he is ruddy of face and light of eye as Your Excellence. Ay, he looks much like a Christian."

"In what way does that make him out to be a slave?"

"It is no slight or shame. They have conquered many Christian lands."

Down the Ebro fared the armed host, to be joined by the column from the eastern pass. Reunited, the Franks felt assured of their strength. They sighted the high walls of Saragossa on the right bank, and crossed over on their portable boats.

The gates of Saragossa were closed, and the city defended against them. In vain Sulaiman and the Slave sent messengers to urge the garrison to let in the Christians. The walls were of cemented stone as strong as Pavia's. And the Franks had no siege engines.

"Now it seems," quoth William bitterly, "they hate us more than they dislike the emir of Córdoba."

Wait, Sulaiman ibn Arabi advised Charles—wait aloof while food gives out within the city; then the rebels will come to terms.

By midsummer the Franks were still waiting in their tents, astride the river. At night fishing craft stole down the current carrying food and arms to the defenders of Saragossa. So the Moslems named this ancient Roman stronghold of Caesar Augustus. The Franks had to ravage the countryside for their supplies.

Their foragers brought in word that an armed host of Córdoba might be on the way to relieve Saragossa. It disturbed Charles that he would have to give battle with a river and a hostile town at his back. But his paladins had no doubt of the outcome. The young Roland, who guarded the Breton March, reminded him that they had come far to do this very thing—to master Spain.

The captive war leader, Ta'laba, smiled when he sighted Charles. There was something hidden in this antagonism of the countryside. Its people seemed to look on the Franks as barbarians come to conquer them. That had not happened in Italy. Rome had welcomed them. Remote and powerful, Córdoba would never suffer them to remain——

Brooding, Charles tried to understand what was happening. Breathless midsummer heat descended on his camp. Then came tidings that he had least expected, from the north.

Far distant, on his Rhine frontier, the Saxons had attacked priests and taken to pillaging.

His armed host had waited too long on the Ebro. It had found no visible force to oppose it, yet it gained nothing while it exhausted its supplies. Charles, who had come with such expectation, became perplexed.

Stay, Sulaiman urged, and Saragossa will yield. But Charles, no longer had faith in him. A trap seemed to have been baited for the Franks. Giving way suddenly to his suspicion, he ordered Sulaiman chained and his sons put under guard. When the Franks searched for the Slave they did not find him.

Charles ordered the transport wagons loaded, and began the retreat up the river. At Pampalona, he ordered the walls torn down.

No one tried to prevent the destruction of the defenses. The captive Ta'laba, when he rode by, said that the Christians were quick enough to break down walls when they faced no foeman. And Charles realized that his long march had yielded nothing more than the demolition of a hill town, and a few captives put in his hands.

His great array climbed to the pass of Roncesvalles no longer looking for renown, and his liegemen thought only of returning to their homes.

Charles ordered the outland folk to march with him in the main array, with William of Toulouse and the Provençals taking the advance. To his own Franks he gave the task of bringing up the baggage train and guarding the rear of the host.

No sign of an enemy appeared on the plain below. With his standard and accompanying dukes and bishops, Charles climbed up from the lowland heat, into the cool mists of the ravine. His column thinned out, to pass through tree growth and rock summits. Over the divide it passed, to descend and halt for the night within the hills of Gascony.

There were no tents, because the rear of his host had not come up with the wagons. But his liegemen slept easily on the grass through the mild August night. It often happened that the wagons did not keep pace with the horsemen.

The night was clear, without mist. It never left Charles' memory, the fading of the starlight before dawn, the stirring as if many around him had risen very early to look to their horses. They gathered around him, waiting, although he had not summoned them.

It seemed then as if his Franks of the rear guard had come in with the train. He wondered why he had heard no creaking of the wheels.

So he heard the tidings that his Franks who held the rear would never join him. Not one of them lived that morning.

Although no survivor could be found to tell the tale of the disaster, the story was clear to the eyes of Charles and his array when they rode back to the pass of Roncesvalles that morning.

The attack had come in the narrowest part of the ravine, where the trees screened the slopes. There, like a broken snake, lay the empty wagons of the transport, careened and smashed by heavy boulders, dislodged from the crests above. The scattered loads had been plundered, and all horses and oxen driven off except injured beasts that bellowed their pain.

Among the wagons lay the naked bodies of the Franks. They were all there on the ground, with the wounds that had killed them clearly visible. Vultures flew up from them. Knots of them lay in clefts or caverns where they had fought as long as they lived. Invisible hands had carried off their garments with their armor and weapons.

Their foemen, living and dead, had vanished. The attackers

had been swift and sure of foot. No trace of them remained except brown bloodstains and footprints.

Charles' attendants found all of the paladins who had commanded the rear—the scarred body of the Count of the Paladins, of Eggihard the Seneschal, of the warrior Roland, and the others. The ground by each one told the manner of their last struggle to experienced eyes. After the surprise of the crashing boulders had come the swarm of lightly armed mountaineers, catching the Franks out of ranks as they toiled beside the wagons in the narrow way where war horses could only plunge in mad pain. Then the rallying of survivors to the blast of horns—the back-to-back struggle of the last on their feet.

To mock the grieving warriors of the main array, a great curved horn, edged with silver, lay in the ravine, dropped by the victors or thrown away because of its weight.

In fury, Charles' men drove their horses at the heights, following the tracks of the assailants. There were no roads. The trails crisscrossed and disappeared into gullies that seemed to lead nowhere. Observers who climbed to pinnacles could see nothing moving in the chasms beneath.

Before dark Charles called them back from the pursuit. On those heights his liegemen could not keep together, and darkness might expose them to fresh attack. From evidence along the tracks, the Provençals of the border told him the foemen at Roncesvalles had been the mountain Basques.

But why? Why had the hidden folk of the Pyrenees assailed the rear army of the king? They must have judged by his actions that he had meant to set up his rule over them.

Ironically, his veteran Franks had been slain by the Christians whom he had expected to liberate from the pagan Moslems.

There was more than one riddle left unanswered at Roncesvalles—as the chroniclers named the pass of death. The sons of Sulaiman, the hostages, had disappeared. They had not been slain with the others. Had the savage Basques spared them, or had Arabs joined the ambuscade to free the hostages? Charles could not know.

He ordered graves to be dug for the mass of the Franks. The bodies of the leaders were wrapped in mantles to be carried on to their homeland.

After the senior bishop of his court had stood before a mighty boulder and said the burial prayer, Charles gave the command to resume the march. Nothing remained to be carried back except the bodies of the leaders. By sunset the last Frank rode from the pass.

Outwardly, Charles did not grieve. He reorganized his column for the journey down to the Garonne, where Hildegard waited with the women. But the memory of the ravine was a scar in his mind—the warning horn on the ground, the bald rock of the prayer by the shrouded forms of Roland and the bravest of the Franks. He did not willingly speak of it again. Nor did he ever again set foot within Aquitaine.

Those who wrote his royal annals made no mention of the disaster—merely telling of the taking of Pampalona and the march to Saragossa and back, as if it had been a triumphal parade. An obscure writer, however, who paid no heed to court or policy, said bluntly, "That year 778 the lord king Charles crossed into Spain and there endured a great misfortune."

After generations a chronicler of St. Gall wrote, "There is no need to name the dead at Roncesvalles for they are known to everyone."

No, the memory remained with Charles all his life. By fireside and hostel door the story was retold; it followed pilgrims a century later on the road to the shrines of Spain. With time the grieving altered insensibly into joy of the heroism and a legend of courage was formed around the name of Roland. In it the mountain Basques became Charles' enemies, the Saracens.

After three centuries the legend found its voice in the immortal *Song of Roland,* in which the Christian knights of *Charlemagne* withstand the paynims of Moslem Spain. Like an echo there still endured in the song the grief of the king.

The Charles who rejoined Hildegard, after she had given birth to twins, had changed from the buoyant Arnulfing who issued the glad call to arms that Easter.

At Auxerre he heard the full tidings of the calamity in the north, where, in his absence, the newly baptized Saxons had risen under the urging of one named Witukind. Down the right bank of the Rhine to the Moselle the Saxons had swept, burning Karlsburg ("Charles' town") sparing neither women nor children.

Charles gave no evidence of his dismay, but he realized how foolishly he had been mistaken. His impulsive plan of conquest had collapsed like a child's sand castle. His hope of a united Christian army had proved to be no more than a wishful dream. The very men who heard him urge it, in his council, were buried because of it. What had the aged Sturm called it? "Because of one terrible power." The power of Charles' will and word over so many people.

From that hour the big Arnulfing no longer deceived himself. Long afterward the shrewdest chronicler of his life would say, "For he had trained himself to bear and endure whatever came, without yielding in adversity, or trusting to a deceitful chance of fortune in prosperity."

Charles had the honesty not to deny his responsibility. And in his self-humiliation, unexpected strength showed. The one thing that seemed not to occur to him was to give up his purpose. If it took long years and different methods, he would make amend for the disaster at Roncesvalles, and he would remedy the failure on the Rhine. If these combating nations could not be brought into a single Christian folk under his own peace, he would not cease from striving to accomplish it.

In this tragedy of 778 he showed his first quality of greatness, an untiring determination.

95

It must have surprised those close to him when he released Sulaiman ibn Arabi, freely, to return to Spain. The consequences in Spain were not encouraging. Sulaiman was assassinated. After a while the true master of Spain, Abd al Rahman appeared in the north with his host, seizing Saragossa from the rebels, sweeping up the Christians along the line of the Pyrenees, subjecting the Basques, taking the spoils to enlarge his mosque of Córdoba, leaving only the Asturias free of the Moslem rule. The great emir claimed one last thing from the Christians, the release of his captive commander, Ta'laba. Charles released Ta'laba.

Abd al Rahman, not he, had been the victor in Spain. Charles understood that clearly, realizing his own failure as leader and king. It was necessary, he decided in his brooding, for the king of Frankland to become a different and wiser person. To do that, he would need the aid of other and wiser minds. He would have to find new teachers. It did not seem to occur to him that this was an almost impossible task. He simply set about doing it.

Another thing Charles did, beyond belief. The chronicles of the Franks do not mention it, but an Arab historian relates: "*Karlo,* king of the Franks, a powerful despot of that nation who had hostile dealings with Abd al Rahman the First for some time, came to understand that the emir was gifted with manly distinction. He sought better terms with the emir, offering him alliance by marriage and a truce. Abd al Rahman answered him favorably on the matter of the truce, while the marriage proposal was heard of no more."

Charles, then, wanted peace along the Pyrenees, and the truce with Córdoba held there for ten years. On leaving Aquitaine, not to return, he gave to William of Toulouse the duty to preserve and fortify the frontier, to unite Gascons and Provençals in an army of his own. This he gave to the youth who had least to do with the disaster at Roncesvalles.

Then in a manner peculiarly Charlesian, he bestowed on Aquitaine—where he had first galloped into war—a nationality of its own. When he next visited Rome, he took with him a three-year-old child, survivor of the twins born at the Garonne on southern soil. This boy was baptized by the name of Louis (Hludovic). He was given the title of king of Aquitaine, and a destiny still more strange.

The child Louis was to be raised at the court of Toulouse to learn the Romana speech of the south and the way of the Aquitanians so that in time he might be fitted to rule them.

In this manner Charles began to atone for the misfortune he had caused in Spain. He never denied his responsibility for calamities.

That year he rode north into fresh misfortune. Hildegard wept because one of her twins went to the mercy of God. She had doted on the two babies, alike in every feature. It seemed to Charles that little Hildegard could console herself because the one boy of the twain survived, but she grieved for the death of the other child. So she had little strength to comfort the women of village and manor who wailed their heroes lost at Roncesvalles.

Then drouth dried up the cultivated lands; even in the forest, streams sank to muddy pools. When the harvest dwindled, ignorant families ate their seed grain; they slaughtered livestock for meat during the winter. Once the royal court halted for the night at a bishop's palace, where the dirt had been swept hastily from the courtyard, and the filth from the hall to prepare for the king's coming. Charles had set his mouth for the taste of roasted venison or at the least broiled fish from the streams. But there was neither game nor fish set on the table. The lay brothers fetched in platters of dark cheese, of a kind unknown to him.

Doubtfully with his knife Charles sliced off the dark rind to get at the white meat beneath. Behind his high seat stood his host the bishop, anxious as a servant. "Lord king," he murmured, "why do you cut that away? Truly, it is the best part of this cheese."

Reluctantly Charles chewed the severed rind, and exclaimed that it went down like good butter. Did the bishop's hall have much of this splendid cheese stored away? When he heard that his host had tuns of it, he commanded two wagons to be loaded with it, to take on the road with him.

Hildegard assured him that the women of the hamlets were gathering acorns that should have gone to the pigs, because famine would follow the drouth. Charles sent his messengers, his *missi*, out on the roads with orders to the abbeys and manor houses to give out grain, seed, and cheese from their stores to families of the slain warriors, to widows, orphans, and the poor. All these last were, by God's providence, the especial charge of the king.

Yet, beyond his sight, he could not tell if his orders were obeyed. Inexorably, famine gripped the lands. There were no traders' caravans as in Spain, to bear to one hungering county what another could supply. At the gray church of St. Denis by the dusty road where he halted to visit Pepin's tomb, Fulrad told him that the famine was sent by the Lord in wrath for the sinful waging of war.

That night after grumbling Peter of Pisa had read to him about the sorrows of the Trojans after the burning of their city, Charles lingered, wakeful by his candle. He did not fall asleep easily until the middle of the night, and then usually woke restlessly before dawn. To occupy the lonely hours when his servants stretched out to sleep beyond his curtain, he made a habit of studying, taking for textbook the copy of the Gospels begged from Hadrian.

Being alone, he could use his finger to trace out the letters that ran together without separation between the words in the ornate Roman script. Holding the folios close to the candle, he searched for a remark of Paul the apostle that had caught his fancy. He found the small cross he had made opposite the line, and repeated under his breath the Latin words while he tried to think of their meaning: "But God hath chosen the foolish things of the world."

Such words he could not understand very well. Still, he

fancied that Christ had favored the dumber animals, riding an ass, watching doves, and tending sheep. These were hardly the wise, cunning animals like foxes that made their holes——

As he struggled to think of the Lord turning to foolish things, he gained a conviction that the words themselves, however well spelled and clearly read, signified little unless their *meaning* was revealed. At that moment he became impatient with the repetitions of Fulrad, whose mind was bound up in his monastery, and with the prating Peter, who strung words together like the silver beads of a necklace.

Charles' reaction to his mistakes and the calamities that followed was to resolve that he must have better teachers. During the famine he began his search for schoolmasters who could explain the meaning of things.

Such enlightened men, however, could not easily be found. Old Sturm felt his death near and went into retirement at Fulda, whence the bones of Boniface had been carried away as a security measure during the Saxon rising. Fulrad, although hale enough still, gave less thought to his duty as archchaplain than to the atonement of his sins and the glory of his name. Of the remainder of his clerics, Charles had little hope. He complained that their emptiness of mind was only equaled by their sloth of body. Once at evensong in a Mary church he noticed a strange monk, who arched his throat and worked his lips around his open mouth, pretending to sing out the words that he could not remember properly. Charles, who tried to mute down his own shrill voice in such chanting, observed how the others nudged each other and grimaced mockingly at the stupid monk. After the last *in saecula saeculorum amen* Charles strode over to them, and lashed the mockers with his tongue. And he praised the red-faced monk for trying so hard to carry out his task.

Then Hildegard came to him and knelt down as she always did when she expected to win something from him. She said she had heard he wanted a new archbishop, for teaching, and would his generosity bestow this post on a poor young clerk who had served her faithfully? Charles did not try to explain that he was searching for a teacher for himself; he bestowed on Hildegard's client a bishop's domain.

At the same time, he realized that Hildegard was changing. For one thing she ceased to be motherly in love to small Pepin Hunchback. She seemed to dislike the crippled son of another woman. She spoke much of her own five sons and daughters, carefully tutored by Peter of Pisa in the Palace School. Often he found time to sit with the royal children during their lessons in grammar and rhetoric, and he thought they learned less because they cared less, than the common children of the Palace School. But Hildegard wept at his outburst of wrath.

"My lady and love," he assured her, "your offspring have in their minds only rabbit hunting or daisy chains, as the case may be. The churls listen and learn because their bread and silver depend on their knowledge."

"No! They are more afraid of you. Charles and Carloman and Louis and Rotrud and Gisela are diligent and gentle. You expect too much of them. Besides, your way of living takes them forever footing from hall to *Hof*. When have they been allowed to hold two Christ-tides at the same place?"

"At Worms."

Then Hildegard, whom nothing could content in these hard days, besought him with fresh tears to give up his mad wandering as she called it, and to abide each winter at the palace of Worms, or Ingelheim, or even Theodo's Villa. The children needed more home space and peace of mind. So his Swabian wife expressed her longing.

That boon Charles could not grant her. For one thing his growing court would eat up the harvest and stores of a single palace in a season; for another, he had to journey where he was needed. Nor would he hear to leaving his queen behind to settle down.

"The mother of kings," Angilbert, who had a mind to poetry, summed her up.

Between them, Hildegard and Angilbert brought home to the preoccupied Charles this thought, that his sons would rule in royalty someday. But what would they rule, and in what manner? Charles himself was the first Arnulfing to have kingship thrust upon him. This thought was to lead him to action very quickly.

One thing marred his joy in all his children. The oldest, the pale crippled boy, deserted school after Hildegard withdrew her love from him. At least so Charles heard from Master Peter. Whenever his father was absent, Pepin Hunchback would be off somewhere with friends. So far as Charles could make out the shy boy did not fare forth to hunt, or to swim. Neither in forest nor hall did he have a known haunt.

"He seeks a place and fellowship of his own," said Adalhard.

After Roncesvalles, Charles had called this twain, Adalhard and Angilbert to his council. His younger cousin Adalhard—who had dared once to call him adulterer—came forth from monastic quiet at Corbie, protesting that he had no mind to politics. Yet Charles persuaded him, as he persuaded others, to serve him.

While the vivacious Angilbert also meant to devote himself to the service of the Church, he could write good verse, and even read Greek—a language in which Charles could barely say thank you—so Charles nicknamed him Homer. Both these young kinsmen paladins could be trusted, and Angilbert at least could influence gatherings of chieftains, and find an answer to the knottiest problem. Yet Charles realized that these young paladins would be his helpers, and not the mentor he sought.

They preceived how the king, in his lusty strength, took no thought for the growing weakness of the pallid queen, who still had to follow him about from pillar to post. But they said nothing of this to Charles.

"You cannot change an aurochs into an ox," Angilbert assured his peer, "by telling him to become an ox, content in a stall."

The royal huntsmen never tired of telling how Charles had faced the death-dealing aurochs. "As our God-protected master grows in girth, and I swear to you that his girdle reaches eight spans around," quoth Kerold, "he grows in mightiness. If he is angered, his eyes flame like carbuncles, his brows draw down like storm clouds. What terror comes from that look of his! As for the power of his hands, he can bend three iron spikes with them. With one hand he can lift a man like me—ay, with shield and haubergeon—from the ground to the saddle of a horse."

It so happened that Charles was coursing a stag with dog packs in his Ardennes preserve—that lay nearest the Rhine—and the horns of his huntsmen were sounding merrily, when he beheld a lovely vision in the forest. A damsel it was, not shrinking and shy but full-blown with hair flowing in the wind, golden and bright as the treasure of the Nibelungs. Reining in her horse, this Rhine maiden gave him the right of way, crying after him, "Swiftly you ride, valiant king!"

Kerold told him that this was a proud maiden, Fastrada, of high Rhineland lineage, and lands that ran with his preserve. Turning home late after the kill, Charles did not find Hildegard waiting to welcome him in to the gate of Düren's castle. The queen was busied elsewhere. It came into his mind then that Hildegard had changed much from the lissome thirteen-year-old, bright of eye, who had handfasted him at the fair.

That year he was kept on the Rhine by the need to avenge himself upon the Saxons.

By breaking the faith they had sworn at Paderborn, by slaying the very priests who had baptized them, by overrunning his new frontier, these pagans had set at nought his labors of six years for his conquest and their salvation. As he had done so many times before, he restored his frontier, but searched in vain, with anger in his heart, for a Saxon army to destroy in retaliation. As before he encountered unarmed villagers, willing to give hostages and accept baptism again.

"A faithless and foresworn folk!" he stormed at his paladins.

Adalhard looked at him oddly. "I say the Devil inspires them. Certainly something does."

"Find the force that drives them on," observed Angilbert in his turn. "Destroy it, and then Your Clemency can make abiding peace with them."

Charles vented his exasperation on the poet priest. What force impelled a whole people—nay, many peoples banded together—to die gladly under the Frankish swords, chanting their own courage, and then in another season to submit like dumb animals to punishment?

"Usually it is a leader conspiring against you," said Angilbert. "I think the Sachsenführer is the one named Witukind. If so we must find him, and solve the problem by burying him."

"How?"

Angilbert could only suggest that they pay or torture some Saxons to lead them to the invisible leader, who might be a pagan priest, a fey man, or a simple intriguer.

Over the mystery of Witukind, Charles brooded. He had sacrificed his pride to gain a truce on the Pyrenees, yet he could not pacify the trans-Rhine front. And all around him, like wolves waiting in a ring, dwelt other pagan enemies, the Dane folk on the sea border, the Wends, Slavs, and those dreaded horsemen of the east, the Avars. Like wolves crouching in the darkness of the night, frightened by the fire of a civilized man, they waited for the fire to go out or the man to come forth among them, to join together and rip the life out of him and eat his flesh. Wolves did not act together except when, by instinct, they rushed on their quarry to make a kill. Now it seemed that there was a human being, Witukind, dwelling among the wolves, directing them when to rush out and when to hide in the coverts.

The peasant blood in Charles that made him feel at home in the forest enabled him to comprehend the instincts of animals.

More than that. When he lay awake at night, in a half dream, he went back to the grove of the Irminsul. He ordered the great tree that was also a god to be hewn down. Yet in his drowsing memory only the tree trunk crashed down to the earth. Above it survived something huge and deathless, its hoofs sunk in the earth, its head against the stars. This god remained there still, overlooking the Saxon wilderness.

When Charles threw off his sleeping robes and called for a lighted candle, the half dream left him. Opening a Mass book on the table, he peered at the written lines, pretending to repeat a Pater Noster, but seeking some omen to guide him in the words where his finger fell. The words never explained the mystery of the Saxon forest.

One evening Charles departed on foot from Düren, taking with him some house churls carrying a beer keg. Although the ground was hard with winter cold he did not keep to a road but followed a network of animal trails to a grove where the star gleam showed him the hut of the venerable scops. The two of them sat drowsing over embers of charcoal, and they complained that he had brought them no alms for years.

Without their harp the singers looked like any other hairy derelicts of the woods. When Charles filled their claws with silver pence, they ceased grumbling; when they guzzled down the beer, their tongues wagged. Charles praised them for foreknowing happenings, and foretelling disasters.

Shrewdly the old connivers blinked at him, making no response until the beer was drunk. Then Charles asked these forest-wise scops to foretell when he would vanquish his Saxon foemen.

These connivers licked their chops and said that they had hungered long. Charles promised to send them a saddle of swine on the morrow's morn.

One said he fancied venison more, like their dear chief,

their battle-bold king. Their warrior leader, he prophesied, would prevail over the Saxon folk when the blood of the last human sacrifice dried in the ground.

That angered Charles. The pagans slaughtered oxen or human captives to pour out the blood like wine to their gods. It was evident enough that when they ceased to do so, they would be Christians, and his subjects. "You tell me what I know well enough," he retorted. "And by the same token I know more. The Saxons will not yield until the Saxon leader is slain. Tell me where I can hunt down Witukind, and I will ask no more of you." When they said nothing, he added, "And I will give you the venison."

He could not tell if they recognized the name of Witukind, or if they merely connived for meat. The one who had filled himself with most of the beer nodded his hairy head and spoke out. "Wonder-wielding king, you will not find that man of strife in hamlet or hall. Now the knowledge comes to me that you will find Witukind afar where the land ends, and the air and sea water join together, and all else is hidden from your farseeing eyes."

Hearing such nonsense, Charles clenched his fist to strike the cunning scop. Then he stayed his hand and laughed. "Now it is not hidden from my eyes that both of you are bold in lying."

He left the drunken scops without expectation of finding a place where the land ended and the sea mingled with the air.

The next summer, of 780, the chronicles relate, "Over all Saxonland Charles the king stretched his powerful arm."

Charles, however, did not manage to do that. He was seeking the trail of Witukind. Starting forth early with his levy of arms, he forged slowly through the embattled wilderness, burning habitations as he had done before, slaying or enslaving captives, feeding off the villages, seeking out resistance where swarms of swordsmen ran from the forest at his fires of evenings, or hidden machines launched massive javelins and stones at his marching column. He did not believe any longer that fear of him would bring the Saxon folk to submit.

By seeking out resistance, the Franks hoped to keep on the track of the invisible Witukind. Charles and his paladins reasoned that Witukind withdrew before them to far sanctuaries, either among the Danes or the wilder tribes of the Baltic's edge. It so happened that his pursuit this time took Charles past the streams of the Lippe and the ruins of Paderborn, through the barrier of the Teutoburger Wald, down to the Weser. If Witukind was actually ahead of them, he must be going toward his haunt of the Baltic coast.

Refusing to turn back, Charles followed up the Weser to the Ocker stream, and then crossed into the northern plain. There he was setting foot where no civilized man had gone. No Roman legion had seen these marshlands. One happening encouraged him. The priest who brought him word of Sturm's death was a younger man, a tall Anglo-Saxon, Willehad, who had vowed to carry on the task of the martyred Boniface. What educated and devout missioners came over from the isles of Britain—Boniface himself and the learned Irish Columban! Now, walking beside Charles' war horse, this Willehad said he would build his church beyond the Weser.

Many of his Franks, however, did not possess Willehad's high heart. They fared slowly into the mists of the flooded plain, where boats often had to carry the loads of the wagons.

They came thus to the land of the Slavs, tribesmen with braided hair and pagan soothsayers for priests. They had never sworn faith to Charles, nor had he a quarrel with them. He took hostages from the wild folk, and forbade his liegemen to kill, to plunder, or to take women. His column needed no order to keep well closed up in this unknown land.

Still Charles led them north and east, as he thought. Mist veiled the sun, and a strange thing happened. During the midsummer nights a faint light persisted. When the king waked and looked out from his pavilion, he could see the dew shining on the iron helms of his guards. Almost as soon as full dark set in, the dawn came. Willehad, who had dwelt among the pagan Frisians, told him that farther to the north, beyond the cold sea and Scandia, at the last land, called ultima Thule, daylight lasted for twenty-two hours in midsummer, and the night darkness lasted as long in winter.

Charles did not understand how that could be. He had been taught that to go north was to go "toward the dark" and to go south in the direction of the Middle Sea was to go "toward the light." Surely the sun itself circled over the flat plain of the earth there in the south! How then could this unearthly light prevail so far to the north?

Willehad, intent on preaching the Word to the chieftains who came to greet the Frankish king, could not tell him. Nor could these Baltic barbarians tell Charles anything of the invisible Witukind.

Still he pressed on through the wind-driven mist. It seemed in some way familiar to him, as if in another time he had dwelt in this gray land. Adalhard reminded him of the tale that the Franks had once made their home here, on the coast.

Then his outriders led him to an odd thing. Above a marsh inlet projected a dragon's head. It was carved out of the wooden prow of an empty longboat, thrust so far into the rushes that the water beneath could hardly be seen. Whoever rowed this craft had vanished.

Dismounting, Charles tasted the water. It had a salty tang. Under his feet the ground mingled with the sea. And he remembered the words of the scop, that he should seek *afar where the land ends, and the air and sea water join together.* Surely all else was hidden from his eyes in the mist!

Had Witukind been in the dragon longboat?

Turning east, Charles came to the flooded Elbe. This he knew to be the east border of Saxonland. Beyond, in their clearings, dwelt only the savage Slavs.

Up the Elbe Charles led his war bands. This river would

become the eastern frontier of his domain when he had sub-jected the Saxons.

Faring homeward at the summer's end, he thought about the dragon ship in his path, so far inland. Surely the empty ship had been a sign, but the meaning of the sign had not been revealed.

At his side thoughtful Angilbert hummed verses that Charles could not quite catch. It provoked him when he heard Latin he could not understand.

"*Regis regum rectissimi,*" Angilbert murmured. "Of the king most righteous, the day of mastery is at hand. Day of wrath and vengeance, day of clouds and shadows——"

It seemed to Charles that his comrade was singing his com-ing to the far border of Saxonland.

"—of mighty thundering and straining anguish, when love of women will cease, and the desires of the world will end, when man strives no more with man."

Then Charles recognized it as the song of the Irishman, Columban, of the Judgment Day of the Lord.

He reached the Rhine in the corridor where the gray river narrows between close-pressing peaks, one of them shaped like a dragon's head, the Drakensberg. There at last he had tidings of Witukind.

While Charles had been searching the east border, the Saxon leader had roused resistance in the west. This ceased, and all became quiet at Charles' home-coming. Yet Witukind had been before him at the Weser.

So the mystery of the invisible leader was in part made clear. Witukind kept ever to a remote fastness, where spies and messengers brought him word of the march of the Franks. From his hide-out, Witukind sent directions as to where the Saxons were to assail the Franks, and where to abide in peace. Every movement of Charles was reported to him while he remained hidden. It would be no easy task to draw Witukind from his fastness.

While the Saxons appeared to have submitted to his power

that autumn of 780, Charles no longer believed they meant to keep the peace. They would not do that until he destroyed Witukind.

Then, when everything seemed to demand his presence on the Rhine, he journeyed forth from Worms to spend Easter in Rome.

The annals of the monks explain what Charles did that year at Rome but not why he did it. Yet the known facts of his journey make up a pattern—broken but recognizable—when pieced together. And this pattern reveals a change in his ideas.

Apparently the king of the Franks, and of the Lombards and Patrician of the Romans, started forth on what was, for him, a pleasure trip. Taking only part of his army, he rode easily with Hildegard and the baby Gisela and his younger sons, Carloman and Louis, down to Pavia, where he inspected the palaces and enjoyed the warm baths. Clearly he expected no conflict other than the courteous contention he had been carrying on by letter with Hadrian. For Charles, always particular about the *meaning* of a title, had decided in his own mind what Patrician of the Romans signified.

That title may have been bestowed as a gesture of courtesy by earlier Popes. Charles now took it to mean the protector and therefore the temporal master of the Romans. He, and not Hadrian, would rule the dissevered portions of the historic peninsula.

The determined Hadrian, however, hardly conceived of the barbaric Frank as master of Italy.

"We pray you to remember, most loving son," he wrote, "your extreme kindness to us when you hastened to the thresholds of St. Peter and Paul. Then you said to us that you did not come in quest of gold or jewels or titles. You said that you and your God-protected army had endured labors only to insist on restoring the rights of St. Peter, on exalting Holy Church and making sure of our own safety."

But Charles had discovered through his *missi* that proud cities like Ravenna, duchies like Benevento, and far communities like the Venetian isles refused to subject themselves to Rome. He also learned that the boundaries named in his donation of rule to the apostolic lord embraced most of these stubbornly resistant entities.

Evidently at this point he urged his duty as Patrician. For the diplomatic but unyielding Hadrian replied, "The dignity of your patriciate will always be faithfully upheld by us . . . so in like manner the patriciate of St. Peter, your protector, fully conceded in writing by your father the great King Pepin and confirmed by you, must remain inviolable."

Hadrian also invoked the now famous "donation of Constantine" the manuscript now established as a forgery, but which must have seemed authentic to minds of Hadrian's time. By this document Constantine the Great appeared to have pledged to St. Peter the disputed bulk of Italy.

No match for Hadrian at this courteous controversy, the blunt Arnulfing complained that he had reports of Christians being sold as slaves from Roman ports to Saracen markets. This implied that he held authority over such ports.

"Never has any such deed been done with our consent," Hadrian blazed back at his powerful friend. "It is indeed true that the unspeakable Greeks have traded in such fashion along the Lombard shore. We have neither ships nor sailors to catch them at this. . . . But the Lombards themselves, we are told, have been forced by hunger to sell many families into slavery. Other Lombards have gone out to the Greek slave ships of their own accord because they had no other way to keep alive."

The famine that took such toll in the north had entered Italy as well. Charles heard of villages deserted by their inhabitants, of towns devastated by earthquakes. "Since the coming of the Franks, disasters have multiplied."

So Charles arrived with very young children, a small escort, and his own compelling personality to make a change in such conditions and such a situation. Throughout the plain of Lombardy he decided disputes and issued edicts for the government of the cities. For Italy, unlike the tribal north, seemed to depend on the cities for aid. And Charles demonstrated that he would be in reality king of the Lombards, without interfering, otherwise, with the life of the cities.

This accomplished, he proceeded in state down to Rome for the festival of Easter 781. After seven years Hadrian faced him again.

Nothing is told about their meeting. This time, however, the barbarian Frank ordered the ceremonies, while keeping in devout attendance on the distinguished defender of Rome. With him, like a gusty wind, he brought tidings of his expanding frontiers, of the thrusting back of the pagan borderlands of the Saxons and Slavs.

"Lord save the king," Hadrian prayed, "for, behold, a new and most Christian Emperor Constantine has arisen."

The watchful Roman nobles were treated to an unexpected ritual, when the king's young sons were baptized. Hadrian himself stood at the fount, while the name of Louis was given the three-year-old boy. In the case of the four-year-old Carloman something very unusual occurred. Hadrian bestowed upon him the name of Pepin.

This meant that Charles had put aside Pepin Hunchback from any succession. The new Pepin, Hildegard's son, would take the cripple's place. Evidently Charles had yielded so much to his wife's pleading.

Then upon Louis Hadrian bestowed the crown of Aquitaine, naming the child king. Upon the new Pepin, an impulsive, quick-tempered child, he bestowed the crown of the king of the Lombards.

As Louis would be schooled within Aquitaine, so the little Pepin would abide, after a few years, within Italy, guided by a Frankish counselor. His edicts, however, would be issued by his father. Thus a titular ruler had been given the restless Romans, while Charles would rule from afar.

111

Hadrian took it in good part, saying that he was now co-father with Charles. Such a crude plan had every chance of failure. Moreover he now looked to Charles, not to Constantinople, for aid to his city of Rome.

After that Charles fairly surprised the Romans with a new ceremony. From the sea unexpected guests arrived—two majestic officials of Byzantium, the Treasurer and Chamberlain of the court of Constantinople. Beyond belief, they explained that they made request upon the king of the Franks to pledge his daughter in marriage to the young son of the *Sacred Basilissa*, Irene, empress of the Romans at Constantinople.

Charles had not explained in Rome, it seems, that he sought this betrothal of his eight-year-old Rotrud to Constantine, surviving heir of the ancient Caesars. Readily he agreed to it.

The amazed Hadrian watched the exchange of pledges between his barbarian friend and the ministers of the fabulous court of the east. These two Byzantines produced a third, Elisha by name, who was to accompany Charles henceforth, to initiate Hildegard's daughter "in the speech and writing of the Greeks, and the customs of the Roman court." Elisha was a polite old eunuch.

Charles had planned a distinguished career for still another of Hildegard's children. Hadrian did not hesitate to give his blessing to the betrothal—although he may have regretted fleetingly invoking the name of Constantine the Great in his debate-by-letter with the Arnulfing. It so happened just then that better relations seemed to be opening between Rome and Constantinople.

"Now I am truly the godfather of the children," he commented amiably.

How had the king of a tribal folk on the Rhine negotiated such an understanding with the court of far Constantinople? Had some merchant of Frankland carried his message to the palace above the Golden Horn? There is no knowing.

But why? Why had Charles attempted a fantastic thing? There may be a clue in the chronicle of the Arab of Spain, who declares at that time *Karlo* "sought better understanding with the emir and an alliance by marriage and a truce."

If the landlocked Frank reached out for better relationship with these two culture centers of the outer world, did he make any third gesture of the kind? A glance at his royal annals for that year 781 shows that he sent two *missi* with envoys of the Pope, to Tassilo, duke of Bavaria, to remind that enlightened prince of his oath of loyalty sworn long ago to Pepin the king and to Charles the *great* king—*"Caroli magni rex."* Tassilo was asked to send hostages and present himself at the court of Frankland.

Charles had by no means forgotten Tassilo's scarlet cloak or his desertion in the face of the enemy. And, in a fashion of his own, the powerful Frank attempted to carry out Bertha's project of a dozen years before, of allying himself with other distinguished princes, in peace. Just possibly, his children might reign in the courts of Christendom, if not in Moslem Spain.

By luck or foresight in that year the throne of the true emperors at Constantinople came within the grasp of Irene, an extraordinary woman, the mother of the boy Constantine, who sought support in the west for her rule. Thus the unlooked-for request of the barbarian Frank had been granted.

Hadrian realized that, while he had imposed somewhat upon the ignorance of Charles at their first meeting, Charles was now imposing on him. He had denied that the title of Patrician held any claim to authority over the city of Rome, yet the massive Arnulfing quartered comfortably in a palace of the dead Caesars certainly exercised authority.

"He has taken under his scepter," said Paul the Deacon, "this city of Romulus."

Paul the Deacon had a quick mind and a mastery of classic Greek. In the mild south of Italy he had devoted himself to writing and devotion from afar—within the cells of Monte

Cassino on its height—to the brilliant duchess of Benevento. A Lombard, he sought in Rome from Charles the release of his brother, a Lombard captive to the Franks.

His meeting with the impetuous lord of Frankland may have brought his brother's freedom, but it ended in the learned Paul's agreement to join Charles and teach Greek at the palaces on the Rhine. In Paul, Charles discerned one acquainted with the meaning of civilized life.

At last Charles left Rome, taking Paul the Deacon along. With music playing and banners flying, he paraded to the north, inspecting the monastery of Mount Soracte, pausing to have his daughter Gisela baptized, deciding disputes while he admired the statues in turbulent Florence.

There perhaps he felt the craving to carry away with him some of these wonders of a lost civilization. Yet it was at Parma he found the greatest spoil of his journey. Here a forty-five-year-old Briton rose from a bed of fever to greet him, not with obeisance but with high good humor. Alcuin, a Celt who quoted Cicero, had made pilgrimage from his beloved school at York. Smiling, he answered Charles' questions.

"Why did you rise to greet me even before you saw me?"

"Because I saw Your Excellence walking where you did not exist."

"How?"

Pointing out the pool in the courtyard Charles had crossed, Alcuin said, "I saw your image in that water."

"Now I have often seen that, yet I did not think of it." Pleased by the riddle, Charles asked expectantly, "How did you understand who I was?"

"Who else would walk alone before all others?"

Calling for bowls of wine, the inquisitive Frank settled down to ask more questions. The tall, fragile Briton protested that he was no more than a deacon. In spite of his fever, caught in the marshes of Rome, he relished the clear white wine. Charles craved for Alcuin to be master of his School of the Palace. Alcuin explained that he had the mission to bear back a bishop's pallium with him, and he could never live out of sight of the Channel.

Charles carried him away with Paul, after bestowing on Alcuin two monasteries facing the Channel, where pilgrims from Britain landed.

Soon the gentle Celt was calling his master David. Charles realized that in the scholar of enlightened York he had found his schoolmaster. Although Alcuin did not realize it as yet, his mission would be not to instruct the School so much as to teach Charles himself the meaning of things.

Through the Alps they fared to the headwaters of the Rhine. Rejoicing in his new companionship, Charles dictated to Paul a loving letter to Hadrian, who might have many misgivings after his departure.

In reply, Hadrian protested, "We have rejoiced greatly at receiving your wise letter in which you say that your cause is ours, and ours is yours . . . we trust that this truth will become manifest to all men."

As always after a successful journey, Charles stopped by the way at Prüm, in respect to his lady mother. Bertha, although aging, had filled the retreat with her good works, gathering in full crops after the lean famine years and demanding more good river land for her monastic domain. There at Prüm she ruled over an empire in little. Charles gave her the land holdings, having few other riches to bestow on her.

When tales were told by the fireside after the Christmas snow, Charles bethought him how little he actually held in his gift, how few were his own people, the Franks, how dark and dull their minds. He had beheld beauty, and found inventive minds in Florence and Parma. In those last years of ceaseless faring forth, he had come to realize his own incapacity, and the futility of trying to make a whole out of a nebulous Frankish domain that rested on no more than the loyalty of certain men to himself, their king.

Alcuin had taught him to reason about that. "Memory,"

Alcuin defined, "is the power of the mind which recalls the past. Intelligence is the power to understand the present. Foresight is the power to perceive what will come to pass."

Humbly, in the presence of such wisdom, Charles reflected that he had a good memory, to start with. By degrees, and constant labor, he might gain some intelligence.

Lacking available hours during the day, he made use of his waking hours at night by keeping writing tablet and pen underneath his pillow so that by lighting the night candle himself he could try to gain the skill of writing letters with his clumsy fingers. He could practice at that time without being disturbed in his effort.

Meanwhile he absorbed learning with his ears, as it was difficult to glean it from written pages with interwoven letters and obscure meanings. If the letters were clear to the eye and the meanings to the mind, it would be simple enough.

Listening to the amazing tales of the scholar from Monte Cassino and the schoolmaster of York, he felt proud and exultant. He remembered how his ancestor Arnulf, although named the Eagle-Wolf, had been a stalwart and bold bishop of the town of Metz. Surely that ancestor had achieved things more amazing than finding that ring again in a fish. He might even have brought about, in a humble way, a miracle.

Longing to give new honor to his one notable ancestor, Charles let out his voice and told how in the reign of the celebrated Dagobert, Arnulf had in reality been the soul the people revered.

"When my ancestor Arnulf, the archbishop, wished to lay aside his episcopal dignity and fare forth into the wilderness, the king Dagobert himself and his queen besought Arnulf with tears not to depart from them. And the Austrasian folk, all of them, the lame and the blind and the orphans and the widows of the town of Metz, crowded around the gates and begged with doleful voices that Arnulf would not leave them to go into the wilderness. But Arnulf reminded them gently to trust in the Lord of Glory, for even Lazarus, miserable as

116

he became, was yet carried by the angels into Abraham's bosom.

"Now the people were mourning and Arnulf was preparing to fare forth into the wilderness when the Lord wrought a marvelous thing in the town of Metz. It might be called, in some wise, a miracle. The night before the day of Arnulf's going forth, the warehouse of Metz broke out in fire. All the people ran to it but could not put out the flames. At that very hour, the horses waited at the gate to take Arnulf away to his retreat. 'No,' said Arnulf, 'take me instead to this immense conflagration.'

"So they did that. All the people knelt down while Arnulf raised his banner, which had a great cross on it. He raised this banner high in the very flames, which at once died down. Then Arnulf and all the people sang matins together, and he went back to his bed to sleep, and not to leave his town of Metz."

It warmed Charles' blood to behold Alcuin's gentle smile when the tale was told, and his own small children watched from the edge of the hearth. So eager he was in the telling, with laughter in his voice. It pleased no one more than himself. Nor did he realize that, with his mind of a boy, he had told them the things he himself would like to bring about.

But he knew that he could work no miracle. Although he had claimed great honors for Hildegard's children that year, he understood that he would never be a great king.

By their firesides his liegemen who had followed him to Rome told their listeners how the king had reigned in Rome with glory. At hostels by the roads of that winter-bound land pilgrims told how they had seen the great king pass by. In the writing chamber, by the light of the wall embrasures—for candles were forbidden near the precious parchment—monks wrote what they had heard of *Carolus magnus*. In the southland of Aquitaine, whither he had not journeyed again, Provençals and Gascons asked in their mincing speech where *Charlemagne* might be.

117

Chapter V

ALCUIN AND THE REBIRTH OF MINDS

MASTER ALCUIN found much to wonder at in a nightingale.

"Such a small brown body," he observed, "such a tiny throat. But what a swelling of harmony in it! All night its music rings for me, and I marvel not that the angelic choir of heaven gives forth continual praise to the Lord, when I behold in such a tiny thing so much of grace."

As the gentle schoolmaster of York took pains to study a songbird—and he marveled as much at a cuckoo giving voice to the spring—so he attributed quite naturally its rare music to the benevolence of the Creator. The frail and middle-aged Alcuin could not pretend. His reverence came from instinct; his verses were one long prayer; the man himself felt a joy in life that was known in another day to Francis of Assisi.

He met grief with uplifted head, and without set, consoling phrases. When he missed the particular nightingale singer, the companion of his sleeping chamber at night, he said, "Whoever stole you from that broom bush envied me my happiness."

The hardship of the northern winter he dismissed lightly. "A time for reveling, and firesides," he described it, "and tranquil sleep."

Liking clear wine and stimulating talk and walking through

animal pastures, he shared many of the likings of the king of Frankland. Hildegard he called "the sweet queen."

The mind of Alcuin of York influenced events in Frankland almost as soon as he became the mentor of Charlemagne.

It is well now to speak of Charles, son of Pepin, as Charlemagne—the name bestowed on him in memory by the peoples of the west. To most of them he was still Charles the king, yet in some measure different from his father, or other princes of the barbaric realms. This Charlemagne strode among them in his rough Frisian tunic and trousers; he twitched his ears when he roared in laughter at their jests; he expanded his nostrils and blazed in anger at their misdeeds. His dominion might extend no further than his ruddy presence, but in his presence men felt a strengthening hope.

Paul the Deacon, of noble Lombard family, homesick for his southland and Monte Cassino, could speak of "the quiet power of our lord the king."

While Paul felt himself to be a captive, Alcuin enjoyed his task of teaching the ebullient Frank. Yet the gentle teacher was by no means kindred in spirit to his pupil and master. Stubbornly Alcuin refused to speak the Germanic dialect of the Rhinelands, holding it to be allowable only to those who wished to pray and knew no other tongue. To Charlemagne's matter-of-fact mentality, he opposed a Celtic whimsicality. Nor would he consent, despite the king's persuasion, to accompany the armed host on a journey forth. He said his frail body was not fashioned for the back of a horse.

"But you have read," quoth his master, "how the queen of Sheba, a woman, journeyed to Solomon the king?"

"Ah, she came to his city of Jerusalem, and marveled much thereat. She did not follow him among the Philistines."

Usually Alcuin's answers satisfied the insatiate curiosity of the big Frank. Long hours of night riding had roused Charlemagne's interest in the behavior of the stars. (Lacking compass, time clocks, and maps, the Franks used the encircling stars for direction finders as well as time tellers.) Why

119

did all the star clusters move around the one called the Pole, near the points of the Wain? Why was Sirius visible only on the horizon down near Rome? What force impelled them to move, keeping to their appointed places?

Alcuin explained how the manifold heavens were raised above the flat plain of the earth by the Creator—first the zone of the air that they breathed, then of water, and of fire, of the mysterious Luna and the signs of the zodiac, up to the farthest stars and the heaven of saints and angels, to the ultimate heaven of the Lord Creator.

So he began his tutoring in astronomy. Where his science failed, as often happened, he quoted Virgil or Augustine fluently.

And Charlemagne went to school, with more than a boy's zeal, at forty years of age. He made rapid progress in Latin because his tutor spoke with the nicety of Cicero. He was fluent enough, but Alcuin warned him to use words rightly. *Ara* meant an altar; *hara* was a pigsty, and it would not do to confuse the two.

"Mistakes in words are dangerous," Charlemagne admitted. "But mistakes in meaning are more so."

He had a lingering fondness for the good round speech of the Rhineland. Why should the hot month of July be named for a dead Caesar, when it was obviously the Hay Month? Also, March no longer had anything to do with the Roman war god; it should be *Lenzinmanoth*, the Lent Month. Just as obviously, May should be *Wunnemanoth*, the Joy Month.

It pleased Charlemagne to rechristen all the months. "My people speak Latin badly," he observed, "and so they chant badly, and so also they pray badly because they use the wrong words."

"If your people have the right thoughts in prayer, do the mistaken words matter?"

"Yes, they matter."

Too well did Charlemagne understand that the thoughts of the Franks followed their cravings, toward fornification, foulness, luxury, idleness, quarreling, manslaughter, and drunkenness. His own thoughts tended that way.

With ferocious energy, availing himself of Alcuin's schooling, he tried to rouse the people near him from sloth of body and decay of mind.

With high good humor the Celt from York undertook the hard task of schooling a strange nation. There was no escaping the urgency of his royal master.

From England he obtained disciples to teach younger boys the first three steps of wisdom, grammar, dialectics, and rhetoric, with a smattering of mathematics. The remaining four of the seven steps or pillars of wisdom—algebra, music, medicine, and astronomy—he taught himself, with the Lombards, Peter and Paul, in the Palace School. This had existed before, of course, in chambers off the courtyards of Worms, Ingelheim, and the Colony. Since many of the nobles and clerics followed after Charlemagne's peripatetic court, this Palace School was often held in hayfields or wine cellars.

It began to be said in the land that Charlemagne the king, not content with his own folk, summoned in foreigners from Lombardy and Britain to teach them. This saying was to grow into grumbling.

The sagacious Alcuin borrowed a method from Pythagoras —he borrowed most of his ideas from others, notably from Bede the Venerable, his own spiritual master—in having a half-taught pupil debate a question with an untaught boy, while he confined himself to explaining what puzzled the lads.

Then, too, he enjoyed turning answers, which may have been difficult at times for him, into riddles and jests. In one lesson of later years Pepin (Carloman Pepin) asked the questions, and the master answered.

"What is air?"

"The guardian of life."

"What is life?"

"The joy of the good, the sorrow of the evil, and the expectation of death."

"What is death?"

"An unknown journey, the mourning of the living, and the fulfillment of the will of a man."

"What is man?"

"A wayfarer who pauses in a dwelling wherein he is host. . . ."

"What is the moon?"

"The eye of night, shedder of dew, prophet of storms."

"What is the sea?"

"The road of the daring, the border of all land, the receptacle of rivers, the source of rain."

At the end Alcuin posed riddles such as this. "I saw the dead bring forth the living, and the breath of the living devour the dead."

Pepin solved it. "By the friction of tree branches fire is produced, which devours the branches."

By riddles and argument the schoolmaster of York stirred the minds of the Franks to search for understanding. Of actual science—of the physics of Aristotle, or the geography of Ptolemy, or the amazing star data of Hipparchus—he knew little more than his pupils. The mystery of the greatest star, pallid Luna that swung across the night sky, need not be debated. The moon moved at the will of the Prime Mover. She would continue to do so until the sun became black as a sackcloth of hair and the stars fell from the sky like leaves blown from a fig tree, and the Dragon climbed from the sea to the land in the last day of human life.

That Day of Judgment, so well described by Boniface, might not be long in coming.

Alcuin's mathematics did not require intensive figuring on the part of his pupils. Their only figures were the Roman, ranging from I to IX, without zero, or minus quantities. To multiply anything like MCCXIX by a simple XIV was a hard task for fingers using a marker on wax tablets. Yet it could be done in the mind by thinking of the figures. The same was true of algebraic equations.

Here, too, the adroit Celt and his disciples made use of the ageless number puzzles:

A stairway has a hundred steps, with one pigeon perched on the first step, two on the second, and so on, up to the hundred pigeons on the hundredth step. How many pigeons are perching on the stairway? To find that out, remember there will be a hundred pigeons on every pair of steps, taking the first with the ninety-ninth, the second with the ninety-eighth, and so on. So you count forty-nine hundred and add the middle step with fifty and the last with a hundred. Now you know there are fifty hundred and fifty pigeons.

They were forced to do their own imagining because they had almost no textbooks. Very quickly Alcuin wrote out a simple grammar and Mass book. Skilled monks of the writing room copied these out, in new volumes. Alcuin also sent for copies of the history of Bede and the verses of Virgil, from his old library at York. But for the most part the Franks, adults and children, learned through their ears and kept notes in their memory.

They had to work without pictures. No statues had been made in Frankland for many generations. The paintings on the church walls showed scenes of demons with forked tails tormenting sinners in the flames of hell inside the jaws of an enormous dragon, or the blessed being herded by kindly angels toward a heaven above a rift of clouds. The sinners had no clothes; the blessed kept their garments.

Then, too, the sacramentaries Charlemagne had fetched from Rome contained a few pictures—of good St. John writing his Evangel with the help of a symbolic eagle, or a frightened St. Peter shrinking from a crowing cock. There were three cocks visible, to make clear that it crowed three times as explained in the Scriptures. Such fragmentary pictures the king ordered to be copied by his artists. Skillful hand carvers of the Rhine made faithful copies upon wooden doors and ivory plaques. Deft women embroidered them upon cloth banners or hangings.

Some remnants of Roman art could still be found—portions of mosaic paving displaying the gladiators, peacocks, and triumphal soldiers of the vanished civilization. Charlemagne liked well to tell his listeners how he had beheld at Parma and Rome entire scenes of ease and elegance, of martyrs hoisted heavenward, and the walls of Jericho falling before the blast of Christian trumpets.

He also added by degrees to the ancestral legend of Arnulf, who was born, as it seemed now, of a patrician family. After listening long himself to the adventures of the Trojans as related by Virgil, he remembered that one of his ancestors had been named Anchises, or something very like. Was it impossible, he wondered, that the earliest Franks who came in mysteriously from the sea might have been far-wandering Trojans, led by the Anchises, who was the father of Aeneas?

That explanation of the origin of the Franks he put forward only timidly, but the tale got around because the king had told it. Alcuin, who admired Virgil, would say neither yea nor nay to it.

"Do not look back, dear friend," he advised. "In your wisdom look to the future, for that rests in your hands, most Christian king."

Already the thoughtful Briton, accustomed to the strife of petty rulers of his island, sensed the power that might come out of Charlemagne, if he could be well guided.

But the barbaric Frank had gleaned a new idea from his lessons. The blessing of culture and magnificence, too, seemed to have come always from the east, whence the Trojans wandered grieving for their lost home, whence Paul had come to Rome. There in the east the splendor of all arts could be found still in Constantinople, and even the pagan Arabs had brought with them precious things of mind and body out of Babylon or Baghdad where the kalif reigned in a hall of gold, and fantastic elephants could be seen.

He had Paul the Deacon read Greek history to him, and enlisted the oddly robed Elisha to teach Greek to the other children as well as Rotrud. They found it very amusing to watch the polite Elisha greet Rotrud by prostrating himself on the matting as if he were looking for ants.

Alcuin evolved his Academy of the Palace after studying the habits of his master. The name Academy had a nice sound to it, being something new in Frankland, and Alcuin perceived clearly that the king would have demanded it in any case. This Academy offered not so much higher education as education to higher pupils—the six royal children, the paladins like eager Angilbert, and Charlemagne himself.

Between bouts of the fever that never left him, Alcuin guided this family circle with gentle raillery. Quickly he picked up the nicknames Charlemagne had bestowed. Angilbert became a youthful Homer within the circle, Alcuin himself "poor Horace" and the king "David, who was raised by the Lord above his enemies."

Turning over the School to his assistants, Alcuin took charge of the intimate grouping of the Academy whenever the king rested at Worms, Ingelheim, or Theodo's Villa. Very soon he found himself playing the role of master of ceremonies, while the Franks sang and enlivened the jesting with wine. Alcuin contributed bell ringing as his act. With small silver bells it was possible to ring the melodious peals of the great church bells. His jovial master insisted they must get a now organum from the emperor, or rather the empress Irene, since the old one had broken down at St. Denis and no one could be found to repair it.

He relished hearing the high voices of his children join in a Gloria. The oldest, Charles and Rotrud, were tall and strikingly handsome, at the age where he had fared forth into the storm to greet Stephen.

"I want my sons to be glorious as kings," he insisted, "to be good riders, good warfarers, good huntsmen and swimmers, and masters of knowledge. I want them to understand more than other men."

He himself had possessed neither title nor dignity, and little education at that early age. For his daughters, touched by the grace of womanhood, he craved more. They must study with the boys and learn as well the woman skills of spinning and weaving cloth; they must sing melodiously and listen well to the finest poetry.

When Bertha asked so often about the stars, her father believed she should learn the secrets of astronomy; when Rotrud's voice swelled above the others in the Gregorian scales, he was sure her mission would be to glorify singing.

Alcuin called them his doves. Slender Gisela with the luminous eyes he nicknamed Delia. Yet it seemed to him that their merriment came from healthy bodies, which they liked to adorn with silk streamers and even pearls from Spain. His Bertha kept her fine eyes ever on the magnetic Angilbert.

Often the long hours of the Academy by the palace hearth tired the gentle Celt, who had, besides, the task of copying books for Charlemagne's library, of carrying on the School, and his own ceaseless letter writing to distant abbeys, where the wellsprings of sacred knowledge had not dried up.

He wondered at times why the other older son, Pepin Hunchback, did not appear at the palace. He was told that the cripple attended upon his grandmother at Prüm in the forest.

In spite of his besetting weariness—of which he did not complain because it came from the frailty of his body—he conceived an admiration for his master that grew to love. Charlemagne never rested. The massive Frank labored over the mysteries of knowledge as he exerted himself with Chancellor and Seneschal in planning the stocking of farms, the storing of seed grain, the clearing of canals, building of new churches, and bridges to do away with fords and ferries.

When such a session was finished the king would hurtle away to hunt beasts in the forest.

Once Alcuin came upon him swimming the river with a score of companions, quizzing them on how the laws of the Saxons came to be as they were.

Again Charlemagne paced his sleeping chamber, dictating an angry letter to the archbishop of Mainz-on-Rhine, "I am surprised that while you labor, with God's aid, to win souls, you take no care at all to teach good reading to your clergy. All around you those who are subject to you dwell in dark ignorance. When you could enlighten them with your own knowledge, you suffer them to live in their blindness . . ."

Alcuin's pupil had learned to be eloquent in Latin. He never ceased his questioning: How were the texts of the Scriptures first written, in what language; how did different peoples come to have different laws; what was the origin of Roman law—of the ancient musical notation, the Gregorian chant; how did the Romans of old master the languages of the many folk they ruled?

More than that, Charlemagne wanted words explained in simple meaning. "You speak of justice? What do you mean by that?"

"Justice depends on three things, reverence for God, man-made laws, and the values of life. The end of justice is to preserve, not destroy."

"It is much easier to destroy than to preserve anything. What do you think a man-made law is?"

"Usually a custom of a people, a general habit they follow out."

"That can be evil. The Saxons offer human sacrifices. Do you justify that because it is their custom?"

"No. It violates a higher law, that of the equality of men."

"Equality?"

"A judge must be impartial, treating all men alike. So all men have equal rights, under a just law."

Alcuin dared to say that, knowing that a thief would have

his arm cut off in Frankland, while a manslayer might redeem himself by the payment of wergild. Property came before life, and rank before justice. And Charlemagne, like his father, held to personal law within his rule, so that Saxon or Bavarian or Lombard would each be judged by his own custom.

Yet they all had different customs. The Bavarians did not require oaths in giving testimony; Burgundians punished murder by death, instead of wergild; Alemanni set the price of a good hunting dog at twelve silver pieces—above that of an escaped slave. And all differed in the delicate procedure of trial by combat.

"Who could make a law to satisfy so many different folk?"

"You will find it written in the Scriptures." Smiling, Alcuin ventured to quote his master. "When you could enlighten them with your own knowledge, you suffer them to live in their blindness."

Alcuin had the courage to oppose his David the king. He could do that, diplomatically, because he understood the mentality of the Frank so well. In wrestling with the ceaseless problem of making just laws for people who had different concepts of laws, Charlemagne did turn to the Scriptures, as his mentor advised. Yet he found most satisfaction in reading the words of Paul of Tarsus, the sinner of noble birth. This Paul did not try to brush aside the earthly ties of human beings—their love of women, their superstition and seeking after an unknown god. His own Franks much resembled those congregations of the sagacious Paul. Why Paul had taken pains at the house of Lydia to baptize all who came to her river, even the prison keeper terrified by the earthquake.

Reading about that, Charlemagne longed for an understanding woman to minister to him, for a house as fine as a Roman palace, and a church ample as the great Sancta Maria's, by a river where all common folk would throng to be cleansed of their sins.

Whenever Alcuin had an hour to repose, before dawn prayer or when the members of the Academy slept after a good noon dinner, he sat at his writing stand, talking to distant friends by letter.

Increasingly couriers and wayfarers brought in to him carefully folded and sealed packets. Eagerly the schoolmaster caught up such gifts, asking in a breath whence they had come, and how fared the sender?

Once his master heard him chanting in the courtyard: "It's come, it's come! So long I've waited for this page, sweeter than the taste of honey, worthier than a shining jewel."

There below Alcuin stood transfixed, hugging the missive, lifting it to pry away the seal carefully, glancing avidly down the written lines.

After tasting the joy of such a message, Alcuin would tell his king how matters went in Lindisfarne across the sea or in far Aquileia, beyond the Venetian isles. Charlemagne was not slow to make use of this increasing news service; when he rode afield, he had Alcuin inform him minutely of happenings in the Rhinelands, especially within his family. He also requested Hadrian henceforth to send him weekly news of Rome, which gave the gossip of Italy as well.

Later, when Charlemagne managed to get another organ from Constantinople—to be copied by his craftsmen, so that other churches than St. Denis could have organ music—he obtained from the east a remarkable means of sending brief missives on wings through the air. It was so simple and practical that his Franks managed it easily. Strong-winged pigeons, accustomed to a particular home, could be taken in wicker cages far afield and released to fly back with the speed of the wind. The difficulty lay in finding a fabric to write on light enough to be bound to the messenger pigeon's claw. White floss silk, bought from African traders, served best.

By keeping up this gay converse afar between David and "poor Horace," Alcuin was drawn into a responsibility he had not anticipated. He became, perforce, the adviser of the king, and so, in time, the unofficial minister of Frankland.

That in turn was to have consequences unforeseen by

either. Dwelling ever in hall or abbey, Alcuin formed only mental pictures of distant people; Charlemagne, making his endless rounds of rivers and highways, became obsessed with the actual needs of varied folk laboring to draw their food from the earth. Alcuin urged what should be done; his pupil knew what could be done. For the present, however, they agreed well enough.

Alcuin welcomed the rare visits of the royal lady, Gisela, sister of the king, who had retired from the age to become abbess of Chelles. The sturdy Arnulfing found that his grave and silent sister brought the cloister into the merriment of his hall. Still, he enjoyed gifting her with land, and rare gold. It pleased him to aid Gisela in her service to the Lord, while he followed his own whims.

It irked him that Hildegard, who belonged to him entirely, should plead excuses to be absent from the joyous instruction of the Academy. His wife could not say the simplest thing in Latin, nor would she make any attempt to answer riddles about the stars that his daughter Bertha guessed at once.

Alcuin listened in silence to his complaint about Hildegard's sloth of mind. "She is good and simple," the Celt said briefly. "And such as she are the chosen of God."

It reminded Charlemagne of something he had marveled at, without understanding. Something said by Paul. *For God hath chosen the foolish things of the world.*

After she gave birth to a girl child as Christmas began the year 783, Hildegard kept to her sleeping couch. After the king went forth to the Field of May gathering, Alcuin sent a letter by the hand of a disciple who rode fast as a *missus*. The missive began by telling how green was the grazing and how good the plowing, and it told the king that his sweet queen had died.

Charlemagne postponed the expedition against the Saxons for long enough to entomb Hildegard. For her tomb he selected the basilica of St. Arnulf, most notable of the churches of Metz, and he ordered Paul the Deacon, not Alcuin, to write the elegia to be carved in the stone. He instructed the Lombard poet to be sure to include the phrase "mother of kings."

Hildegard had been twenty-six years of age; she had given him nine children, of whom six survived. The youngest daughter had died soon after her mother, and Bertha, his own mother, followed them to the grave, in her case a tomb at St. Denis. Charlemagne meditated upon the women who had gone from his side to the grave or cloister. Where were Gerberga, his brother's wife, outcast by him, and Ansa, the notable wife of his enemy Desiderius? He could not remember where Desirée was buried.

Before he left to join the waiting army, he paid for perpetual lauds to be sung, day and night, for Hildegard and his mother.

When he returned from the expedition that fall he wed Fastrada, the proud Rhine maiden who had crossed his path in hunting. Her golden hair gleamed like fire in the sun, and her glowing eyes challenged him to possess her.

That summer of 783 he locked himself in a death struggle with the Saxons and the invisible Witukind.

For Charlemagne, king of the Franks and of the Lombards, Patrician of the Romans, and conqueror—to all appearances—of the pagan Saxons, found himself defeated, after eleven years of his striving, by these inflexible kinsmen and foemen.

He had tried punishing them, and converting them; he had made generous truce with them; he had threshed through their lands as a winnower threshes loose grain with a flail. He had built hamlets and churches, headed by the eager mission of Willehad. Both Hadrian and Alcuin praised him for "subduing the savage pagan race, and bringing their souls to salvation."

And the last year had brought new disaster upon him.

Why and how?

Alcuin could not tell him. Nor could the leaders of his

army, who had joined the ghosts of Roncesvalles. Alone, he faced the mystery of a people who could not be mastered. Carefully he went over in his mind the extraordinary happenings of that last summer.

First, the undefinable stirring of the Saxon forests. Then his swift move to show his authority, without conflict. His assembly at Paderborn—as in the other year leading to disaster beyond the Pyrenees—at the rebuilt churches. His summoning thither of envoys from Siegfried, king of the Danes, and from the Avar khagan to impress the Saxon chieftains.

In some manner it failed to do so. For after Paderborn came attacks on villages of converted Saxons, and hunting down of missionaries—Willehad fleeing out of the forests, crying that all who bore the name of Christian were doomed —Willehad, the zealous, escaping to Rome to seek peace for his soul, while his brother missionaries lay in their blood like slain animals.

Witukind! The Sachsenführer abiding far from Paderborn, yet sending his voice thither, among the chieftains. Perhaps by spies who rode in with the cavalcade of Danes. The voice of Witukind calling on the Saxon folk to rise and avenge the old gods.

But why? Why, at the very moment when Charlemagne's power lay over their lands, with his armed host journeying north to quiet the Elbe frontier? With no visible sign of war behind them?

Charlemagne thought about that army of his, pushing unaware through the forest roads as his host, four years before, had climbed to the Pass of Roncesvalles. Brave officers led it —Geilon the Constable, Adalgis the Chamberlain, and Worad the Count Paladin. They must have moved warily, crossing the Weser with scouts posted on the heights around them.

Surely they sighted the Saxons thronging to the ridge of the Süntal, above the river. They should have waited for the supporting army that old count Thierry had gathered on the Rhine to hasten to their aid. Perhaps they did wait, until they heard the trumpets of Thierry. Then they rushed headlong, with the paladins leading and the Frankish chivalry pressing after, each man eager to be first to mount the Süntal, only to find the Saxons waiting there in ambush. There the Franks tried to flee, each man for himself. Old Thierry saved some survivors, only to be slain himself.

Then Charlemagne took command. It was too late in the autumn, the grass dead, the frosts gripping the land at night. He led all the horsemen he could gather back to the Weser, ranging up the river, hunting fleeing Saxons into the hamlet of Verden hemmed in by pine growth. Four thousand warriors and more he caught there, demanding that they yield up to him the leaders of the Süntal ambush, and Witukind. They would send no one to seek the chieftains, and he ordered their deaths. In one day the four thousand were slain, kneeling by the river. . . .

After that the silent resistance spread to other folk. The royal annals relate "as far as the seacoast the Frisians abandoned the Christian faith and began again to sacrifice to their idols."

In his brooding Charlemagne became convinced that he had been wrong. From the day of seeming triumph when he overthrew Irminsul he had carried out what he planned, yet had gained nothing. The Saxons, like the Northmen, were survivors of the Germanic race, bound to the worship of Thor and Balder. Like the Franks of an earlier age. Now there was something in him and in his people to which the Saxons would not give true allegiance. Yet with the Danes and Northmen of the sea they would get drunk and draw blood from veins, to become sworn brothers. Why?

He was close to the solution of the mystery. But it struck him then that if he acted toward them like a Dane or other pagan, they might be brought to agreement with him.

His soothsayers, the aged scops of the grove, had vanished or had ended their mean lives in the forest. Yet he had been careful to order some older scribes to copy whatever ancient legends they heard. He wanted to preserve both the speech and the song traditions of his ancestors. Now he turned to a manuscript of Saxon laws and studied them patiently.

They all told of payments and punishments for injuries. "For striking a highborn man, XXX silver pieces . . . If the tunic or shield of another is cut by a sword, XXXVI pieces of silver to be paid for composition. . . ."

It seemed as if the greatest amends were to be paid when the prospects of vengeance were greatest. For slaying a runaway slave, a small sum made amends. If the Saxons needed to have laws of that nature given them, he could inflict punishments of the kind they understood.

So Charlemagne drew up his *Edict for the Saxon Lands*. It explained the punishments clearly.

For conspiracy against the king, or breaking faith with him and his Christian people, the penalty was death.

Churches must be honored like the pagan shrines of yesterday, and the right of asylum respected. Worship of springs, trees, and groves was forbidden.

Failure to baptize children entailed a fine of 120 silver pence from nobles, 60 from freemen, 30 from serfs. Failure to keep the fast during Lent might be punished by death.

That, too, was the penalty for making human sacrifice, burning bodies of the dead, entering a church by force, or setting fire to it, or stealing from it, for refusing baptism or killing a bishop or a priest.

The only appeal to mercy would be full confession to a priest, and penitence.

These laws would give to Saxonland the material and moral order it needed. Or so he thought.

Within a year after the *Edict* was made known, the Frisians in their mound villages and the Saxons as far as the Elbe rose in revolt.

Then, the royal annals say, Charlemagne led in his Franks to "strip bare the country, tearing down fortified places, scouring the roads, mingling slaughter with burning."

He did not understand that these stubborn pagans fought not against himself, but against the kind of Christianity that had been imposed on them. They had found it described clearly in his *Edict*, and were determined to die with swords in their hands.

During these years, 783–85, he never left Saxonland. He placed his oldest son Charles among the leaders of one army; Easter and Christmas he celebrated in the road camps; he summoned his bride Fastrada and his children to his new home in Eresburg, whither Alcuin would not venture.

It would have been better if he had not brought Fastrada to the war.

Names in that age often described a person, at least in the Rhineland. Bertrada (Bertha) meant the Glowing, and Fastrada meant the Unyielding. Charlemagne's bride, then, was a hard woman. Like Bertha, she became proudful when she became queen, consort of a mighty monarch.

The spoiled daughter, perhaps the only child, of a Rhineland count, Fastrada rode forth with Charlemagne, looking upon her court and people as so many servants of her will. Handmaidens slaved to embroider satin and purple silk for her gowns. Handsome she may have been; the court annals say she was "proud, arrogant and cruel." Of all those close to Charlemagne, she was the only one to enforce her will against his.

Perhaps like the legendary Brunhilda in yielding her body to a man she felt the need of taking vengeance by making other men suffer. Certainly, being a noblewoman of the Rhine, she hated the Saxons. It thrilled her to hear of the massacre at Verden, where kneeling warriors were slain like cattle marked for slaughter.

In bringing her to Eresburg in the Saxon fastness, he may have enjoyed her companionship, but the garrison and the throngs of Saxon captives driven into the log palisade hardly did so. When her royal husband absented himself with an expedition Fastrada could wage her own peculiar warfare on the defenseless families, pagans and Saxons, at the mercy of her armed guards. That excited her more than riding down a wearied stag for the kill.

Fastrada's tormenting had consequences beyond the citadel of Eresburg. She seized an opportunity to humiliate the Thuringian nobles near at hand behind the Frankish armies. Perhaps Fastrada had a feud of her own with the Thuringians. One of them had pledged his daughter to wed a Frank but refused to send the girl when bidden to do so. It was a slight matter, of which Fastrada made much. Demand went from her to the barbaric nobles beyond the Hessian plain to produce the woman or stand in disobedience to the king her husband.

As a result, the Thuringian chieftains conspired to kill Charlemagne.

In that year and a half when the Arnulfing moved into Saxonland with his family and armed host, his power as well as his life was at stake. Revolt simmered from the Thuringian mountains to the seacoast, where the Frisians fought for their gods, and the Bretons in their peninsula defied the king.

To Charlemagne it must have appeared as if the lacerated Saxons were pulling down with them the rude, weak structure of his rule.

What did he have to rely on? The hardiest of his paladins had been lost in that senseless charge against the Süntal. The most sagacious survivor, William, son of Thierry, was holding the line of the Pyrenees. Another, steadfast and loyal duke, Gerold, brother of the dead Hildegard, held the Bavarian March not far away at the headwaters of the Rhine. Gerold, devout and unquestioning as Roland, could not be called to his aid because the Bavarians under Tassilo were allying themselves to the dreaded Avars.

Along the sea to the north other dangerous foemen roused, where the trans-Elbe Slavs gathered about their soothsayers—Witukind had been among them—and the Dane king took to warfaring by ship. Witukind and his lieutenant Abbion had promised the Dane king great glory and spoils if he entered the rivers to ravage Frankland. And Charlemagne knew that he had no force to check those berserk fighters in their dragon ships.

He understood his own failure as a battle leader. His dominion consisted of no ordered nation; it was guarded only by the force of those loyal to him, the faithful as against the unfaithful. Usually in other expeditions he had been careful to summon forth only the closest neighboring people, the east Franks, Thuringians, Swabians, to go against the Saxons, or the Aquitanians and Provençals to go against the Moors of Spain. It was hard in a single summer's campaign to draw armed forces from more distant lands; also the neighboring warriors naturally had greater zeal in pushing forward their own frontiers.

Now neighbors of the Saxons were rising in revolt, and he dared not draw on the garrison forces of the Brittany, Aquitaine, or Bavarian fronts to swell his own armed host. To lay bare a border at that moment would be to invite new invasion, and on the most critical border, Bavaria, such invasion was preparing, while Tassilo and the Avar khagan watched his defeat in Saxony. In Italy, where Hadrian hailed him as a second Constantine, he had his few counts and their guards as a token force. No, he could depend only on the few thousand horsemen from the homeland farms of the Rhineland—those who had survived the Süntal.

And these Rhinelanders were losing spirit, believing that the invisible Witukind prevailed over their king by a wizard's power. Faithful counselors like Adalhard anticipated that two women were the bane of Charlemagne—his wife Fastrada, and the Bavarian queen, sister of the dead Desirée. After long years that ill-fated Lombard bride would have her vengeance.

If Charlemagne were slain and the brittle hegemony of the Franks broken down, western Europe might become, as it had been in the last century, a vortex of warring, tribal folk. The new frontier of the churches would vanish in flames.

No one realized this better than the wearied king of Frankland. He had no illusions as to his ability, or the extent of the danger confronting him.

So, with despair in his heart, Charlemagne acted with the daring of a great king. From the moment of his awareness of the crisis, he abandoned all his old plans and habits—going bodily with his family among the Saxons, keeping the field without truce, in winter as well as summer. He marched in as if to final victory, rebuilding the churches of Eresburg, restoring the dwellings of Paderborn. To the news center of Rome, he sent couriers speeding with reports of conquests, and urgent command for the fugitive Willehad to return to the Saxon mission.

Willehad found the palisade and huts of the frontier town rife with Charlemagne's activity, thronged with monks who sang Te Deums as they labored. It was as if the king had taken over the task of the missionary. Willehad's zeal flamed again.

"Where did you mean to build your church?" his master asked him.

Willehad remembered that journey to the misty shore. "Beyond the Weser," he responded. "But that is not possible now."

"In a year we will build it there, beyond the Weser."

Instead of sending out his paladins to war, Charlemagne took command himself, with his standard. Caught with a small force in the forested heights of the Teutoburger, he did not try to retreat but led his riders to attack. Unskilled in battle, his presence seems to have steadied the wavering Franks, and the Saxons were driven from their heights. Another battle he fought in a ravine called the Narrow Way. Again the Saxons tried to withdraw and were punished terribly in their flight. So long as he lived, Charlemagne never took command of another hand-to-hand battle.

He survived. In the hard winter he sent forth from Eresburg small mounted detachments that swept the roads and
raided the stored food of villages. It was a hunger year, and
foodstocks failed in Saxonland. He ordered grain to be carted
and meat herds driven from the Rhine for his garrisons. He
sent his twelve-year-old son Charles with one of the raiding
armies, to make show of the king's confidence.

Flooded valleys held him back from the line of the Weser;
he left Charles there in command, and circled east through
the Harz to reach the northern plain. He led his host through
swollen rivers, chanting praise to the Lord. Such rapid raiding gave the impression of great forces entering the Saxon
forest.

Swimming the horses through rushing rivers, dragging
wagons across flooded marshes, he reached the hinterland of
the Weser and drove back gatherings of Slavs, telling his
followers that the Saxons must be guarded against the
demon-worshipping pagans. (His army lost at the Süntal had
been on the way to do that.)

"Our most glorious king," Kerold related to his messmates,
"came once to such a flood that his war horse balked at the
water. It is God's truth that our giant king, loftier than Atlas,
who holds up the sky above us on his shoulders, sprang down
from the saddle and swam that flood, pulling the war horse
after him."

Such tales grew in the telling and reached all the Saxon
hamlets. Charlemagne encouraged such omens of victory.
There is a legend that he took two Saxon swordsmen of noble
blood into his personal guards. After a while he noticed that
the berserk fighters became bored by standing at his pavilion
entrance. He took the risk of asking them to serve within
his tent, if they wished. (They had pledged fidelity to him.)
They answered that they would obey him.

After one evening of waiting on him, fetching his letters
and wine and candles, the two warriors rushed forth to the
encampment beyond the king's dwelling and lashed out with

their swords until they were slain with those who fell to their swords. In this manner the warrior Saxons wiped out in blood the infamy of acting as servants.

Whatever actually happened, the incident is typical of the stress of those days when Charlemagne tried to win men from their old traditions. In the end he won his victory.

The chronicles do not explain how he won it. The Saxons had been beaten back to the forest wastes before. This time the Franks had food to give them. Yet it seems as if Charlemagne, abiding among them, gained their admiration as well as their fear. The warrior race needed to respect a leader, to submit to him. The big Frank who hunted and raided their valleys, holding freedom or captivity in his gift, was obviously something different from the lord of the Rhine who had drawn up the *Edict for the Saxon Lands*. Just as obviously, their leader, Witukind, had kept too long in hiding among the Danes. Witukind had failed this time to cajole or deceive the inflexible king of the Franks.

Then Charlemagne staged one of his persuasive shows. Incredibly, he held his spring assembly at rebuilt Paderborn, welcoming Saxon chieftains to wine and meat and song, as if he had been in power there all along. No missioners preached in this meeting of chieftains, and the harassed Saxons gorged themselves with food.

To them after the feasting, he explained one simple fact: the conflict was ended. He made one request: that Witukind and Abbion should be brought in, to be baptized.

This time the Saxon chieftains sent for their leader. In his covert beyond the Elbe, the Sachsenführer demanded hostages to be given by the Franks for his security. Charlemagne sent over the hostages, and Witukind and Abbion, who had lost the confidence of their people, walked into the Frankish lines without followers to guard their backs. A *missus*, Alwin by name, led them to the small river Attigny.

"And there," the annals relate, "were baptized the aforesaid Witukind and Abbion, with their companions; and then all Saxony was subjugated."

Charlemagne made the most of this performance. Acting as godfather himself, he presided at the baptism, giving a Christian name to Witukind, and baptismal gifts of gold and embroidered garments. With high good humor he feasted the leaders of the rebellion of six years, and escorted them a way in honor upon their road home.

By so doing he destroyed all power of the crafty Westfalian over his people. After humbling himself before the Frank, Witukind could never bid another Saxon to draw his sword against Charlemagne. He went back to such dishonor that even his death is hardly mentioned.

At Rome, Hadrian ordered three days of prayer and thanksgiving for the victory.

With the Saxon race subdued, and a cathedral rising to the treetops at Eresburg, Charlemagne turned his attention to "The conspiracy of the Thuringian counts and nobles," as the chronicles name it. He lost not an hour in leading his veteran host across the Hessian plain. His horsemen covered the roads of the Thuringian hills.

The leaders of the conspiracy could not withstand such force; they fled to sanctuary in the abbey of Fulda. After ravaging their home estates, the king arranged through the abbot of Fulda to send the outlawed nobles to plead their case before him at the palace of Worms.

The pleading of the conspirators might surprise modern minds. They were careful to explain the truth. They had agreed, they testified, to kill the king and in any case to join the Saxons in revolt. (Fastrada had been diligent in laying the evidence of their crime before her lord.)

"If my comrades and associates," declared the Graf Hardrad, "had carried out my plan, you would never have come back alive over the Rhine."

After hearing their case so truthfully stated, Charlemagne

granted them his mercy. All the conspirators were sentenced to journey under escort to the tomb of St. Peter, or other noted shrines, there to swear fidelity to him and his sons.

Charlemagne's remarkable mildness in such a case may have been instinctive with him. His physical power and health usually made him gentle in dealing with the weak or unfortunate. His cruelty, as at the village of Verden, sprang from his anger. Although he had no private illusions about his birth, he now assumed all the attributes of the early Merovingian rulers. They had been absolute monarchs, under the will of God, over all their race and subjects; they had been the final judges, the interpreters of God's will. They had been, in a word *sacred* in person as well as authority.

His subjects voiced no empty phrases when they addressed the monarch of Frankland now as "Your Clemency" or "Your Security." In his mercy lay their security.

Moreover, by long and hard experience, Charlemagne was becoming the most astute schemer of his time. By christening and rewarding his very dangerous antagonist, Witukind, he gained more than the most arduous campaign could have won. A Witukind slain, sword in hand, during battle would have become a heroic legend, splendid enough to inspire future generations of muddled, dreaming Saxons to do likewise. In fact Witukind actually was made into a sort of legend. You can read how this Witukind, like a William Tell, devoted his life to the freedom of his people, which was hardly the case. But during his own time Charlemagne contrived to free himself from the danger of such a legend. Unfortunately he did not foresee the danger that would arise from his own missionaries; Alcuin warned him of that, too late.

Nor in his pacification of the Thuringians could the king subdue Fastrada. Just what happened remains obscure, yet Fastrada unmistakably gained her personal vengeance. The annals say "Only three Thuringians lost their lives; they resisted arrest with their swords and were cut down after killing several men." Worse befell the penitents journeying to the shrines; some of them were taken from the road and blinded; others found themselves exiled from their home-lands, and their properties accordingly confiscated to the king and his queen. The laconic record states that this was due to "the pride and cruelty of Fastrada the queen."

Meanwhile Charlemagne was able to send part of his forces to Audulf, warden of the Breton March (as Roland had been). That same year of 786 the Franks overran all the peninsula of Brittany, and reduced the rebels to their loyalty and tax payment again. Legend relates that these same Bretons had migrated from the island of Britain to escape the barbarians, and they still resented authority. On the coast above the mouth of the Rhine the Christian Frisians subdued those who had turned pagan. So in the west Charlemagne regained control of his borderlands. But he had escaped narrowly with his life from disaster in the Saxon forests.

While he prepared to move to his endangered eastern front, Charlemagne returned eagerly to Alcuin's schooling at the Rhine palaces. There another friend, the homesick Paul the Deacon, begged leave to depart to the peace of his Monte Cassino "under Benedict's beloved roof." Reluctantly, Charlemagne let the Lombard scholar go, on two conditions. First, Paul was to write out a book of Homilies—words of the Fathers for all the days of the year; second, Paul was to carry certain messages to his friends the Beneventan duke and duchess. For Charlemagne planned to make use of them, as well as of Hadrian, in his own venture to the eastward.

At the same time the first political venture of gentle Alcuin failed unexpectedly when it opposed one of Charlemagne's personal prejudices. By then Alcuin had become the mentor of all Frankland, dispensing—as one of his letters declares—"the honey of the Holy Scriptures, the old wine of the classics, the fruit of grammar, the dazzling splendor of the stars."

His enthusiasm delighted the equally industrious king. During his nights at Eresburg, "David" had advanced in astronomy, to the understanding of eclipses, as propounded by Alcuin (who had read up on the rudimentary science of Pliny the Younger). After following in his mind the course of sun and moon through the signs of the zodiac, the Twins and the Archer and others, Charlemagne became dissatisfied again with dead classic names.

The Bear that revolved around the fixed north star hardly resembled the bears he had hunted. It looked much more like a Wagon or Wain, with shaft pointing outward toward the guiding star. So he named it the Wagon.

But Charlemagne's chief readjustment of science was the naming of the winds. Poets like Virgil spoke only of four winds, and wrongly. Perhaps in Rome the west wind had been "mild Zephyr" but here on the Rhine it was certainly the battering west wind from the sea. Furthermore, how could there be only four winds when they came from all directions—or at least twelve directions? If the sky itself was divided into the twelve zones of the zodiac, and the winds came from the sky, they must be twelve in number. Charlemagne named them accordingly, methodically, *nordroni-nordostroni, ostnordroni-ostroni* (north-northwest, westnorthwest), and so on around the circuit of the sky. (Seven centuries later the Flemings of the coast still used the Carolingian wind names, and after that navigators setting out across ocean put these names into the boxes holding the new compass.)

From the most interesting sky Charlemagne's avid curiosity turned naturally to the earth. No doubt that blind wandering folk singer, Homer, had described the earth as he imagined it, and that emperor's poet Virgil had told much about the Middle Sea with its islands. But Virgil, who seemed to understand farming well enough, always ended up by praising the Romans. Augustus, the emperor, may have gifted him with gold armlets and drinking horns to do that. The

Romans however were dead and vanished as their broken-down aqueducts that marched uselessly by the roads. The coming of the Lord Jesus, true Son of God, had changed their world into something different.

The reality of this modern earth bemused Charlemagne. He could fully comprehend only what his powerful hands could grasp, his eyes behold or his ears hear. Moreover, being forest bred, he believed that all the manifold things of the earth—all the products of six days of Creation—had their uses. Dead branches on the ground kindled flame if rubbed with vigor; they supplied fuel to the flame, which in turn cooked the meat of dead animals. Continually he tried to discover the uses of earth's products. African traders assured him that even the fantastic, giant elephants served to uproot trees or push over stone walls. He longed for such a beast, to clear a path through the forest.

But what was Africa? Alcuin had less to tell him about the shape of the earth than about the vault of the sky, and this exasperated the big Frank. Alcuin's books maintained that Africa had been populated by one of the sons of Noah, and had been the granary of Rome, the home of the divinely wise Augustine. Nothing was said about its shape, except that human life did not exist beyond the burning heat of its desert, save along the river Nile which must flow out of the Mount of Paradise somewhere in the east where the sun rose daily from its wet bed in ocean.

Once Charlemagne had seen a picture of the created earth, painted on a wall of the Lateran palace. Hadrian called it a *mappa mundi* or tablecloth of the world, which made no sense, although the knowing shepherd of Rome explained that the famous cosmographer, Cosmas, had proved by the Scriptures that their earth had the shape of a table, with Jerusalem in its middle.

Yet Charlemagne remembered clearly how the Lateran picture map revealed the vastness of the earth, extending to the Ethiopians behind the African coast, and to *Babilonia,* or

Baghdad and the Persians at its eastern edge. Apparently he himself had wandered close to its northern edge, where mist covered the sea of the Normans or Northmen. Beyond that lay the cold of eternal ice under the north star.

As the king of the Franks longed for a road-breaking elephant, he craved a map picture on a wall of his own, perhaps at Ingelheim, where Fastrada liked to dwell. Then, too, he thought how, if he possessed a dragon ship like the one waiting empty in the mist he might fare forth from the Rhine upon the open roads of the sea—if he could arrange a truce with the Northmen and Arabs whose fleets ranged the seas, taking spoil from all other craft. He could not resist telling his children a wishful tale of a voyage they would make with the paladins and swordsmen on great longships to Jerusalem.

"We will abide there on Sion," he explained, "and look into the cavern of the Lord's cradle, in Bethlehem, and after that we will have peace, with no more journeys to make."

The children believed he would take them there, except perhaps for the smiling Bertha, who kept her thoughts to herself.

It was Bertha, through no fault of her own, who stirred up his anger against Alcuin. That master of learning never cherished Frankland as his home; he became eager to visit again the libraries of York and Lindisfarne, whence he borrowed the finest illuminated Mass books, to be copied for Charlemagne's library. Alcuin hinted that maps also might be found across the Channel, painted by enlightened Irishmen. Still, the king refused to grant his tutor leave to depart.

The diligent Alcuin, however, kept up correspondence with Offa, king of Mercia, the most notable of the many barbaric kings of Anglo-Saxon Britain. To Offa, Alcuin extolled the generosity and power of his king David, seeking to join his two masters in comradeship, if not in alliance. Useful exports arrived from the British coast up the rivers of Frankland—when traders could slip past the voyaging Northmen—

exports of wool and dried fish and bejeweled covers for the sacred books.

So it happened that Offa agreed to kinship by marriage. But when this distant lord of Mercia suggested that a daughter, Bertha, betroth herself to one of his sons, Charlemagne fell into ill-humor, exclaiming that Bertha was too young to be given in troth. Nor should she, in any case, give herself to a barbarian.

"Yet the little dove must wed," Alcuin protested. "Is she not being schooled for that?"

Inexplicably, his simple statement roused anger in his lord. Charlemagne bade him attend to the girls' minds and never again bespeak their marriage. Henceforth no more British woolgatherers, or fisher folk would be allowed to land on Charlemagne's coast. At the same time he sent Elisha, the Byzantine half man, away from Rotrud's side. He said the besotted court of Constantinople had slighted his daughter, which may or may not have been true.

Alcuin said no more of the matter, believing this anger to be a mood of his master. Yet it proved to be Charlemagne's willfulness. He craved to hear the singing voices of his girls, and to watch their slight forms riding easily after him upon a journey. He would not forego this enjoyment of his, and upon one excuse or another, he kept them from marrying, although Rotrud and Bertha were old enough for a man's embrace.

Perhaps because they solaced him in his weariness, perhaps because Fastrada laid her dislike upon these girls of Hildegard, Charlemagne kept them ever more closely at his side. It began to be said that he doted with incestuous eyes upon his daughters.

Among the paladins Angilbert, for one, became the champion of a daughter, Bertha. Being the tutor of this girl, Angilbert could walk with her alone; as he had felt for her mother, the man of poetry yearned toward the joyous, handsome daughter.

"She is a dove," Alcuin agreed with him, "but a crowned dove."

"No," cried Angilbert, "she will never, by the king's ban, wear a crown. To please him she is to be a song, a gladsome sight, a dove within a cage."

He could not speak his mind, as Adalhard had done in years gone by, to the lord of Frankland. Nor could he continue with good heart to teach the girl to draw melody from harp strings or sing lauds with lilting voice. Being the older of the two, and deep in love, Angilbert imagined her to be condemned without mercy to virginity, like her aunt Gisela, and to servitude, like Hildegard, her sweet mother.

Bertha herself had no such misgivings. She made a face to tease him, she danced backward in the path before him, and when he kept his moody silence, she asked gently, "What makes you sad, my friend?"

Then she embraced him with the strength of her young arms.

In later years when Charlemagne asked his chaplain paladin to describe Bertha in verses, Angilbert wrote: "She shines like a flower from the wreath of her handmaids. In the music of her voice, the light of her face, the pride of her step, she mirrors the image of her royal father."

Charlemagne was well content with the verses.

Chapter VI

DANGER IN THE EAST

As the year 786 ended, he moved to free his eastern frontier, although it did not appear possible to do so. In the autumn discussion his paladins protested bitterly. Gerold, brother of Hildegard, Keeper of the Bavarian March, told how proud Tassilo meant to remain independent in his Bavarian mountains, and would make fast alliance with the powerful Avars if attacked. Already Tassilo had slain the Frankish count, Keeper of the Italian border.

"For that," Charlemagne insisted, "he must stand before the court of Frankland to be tried."

He would not forgive his cousin Tassilo the old crime of *herisliz,* or his new treachery—as Charlemagne conceived it —of making compact with his enemies when he appeared to be worsted in the Saxon war.

The honest Gerold described how Tassilo lay secure behind the natural defenses of the Bavarian Alps, beset with ravines and lakes, stretching back to Salzburg and the headwaters of the Danube—Avarland. By now Tassilo had the strength of a great king, and he was not to be tricked.

"We have friends among their churches. Send greetings, good Gerold, to the bishop of Salzburg, with word that we will visit them before the next Christmas."

The steadfast paladins had no heart for that. Well they understood Charlemagne's jealousy of the wealthy and proud

149

Bavarians, of their royal house, the Agilulfing, older than the rising Arnulfings. Tassilo's queen had been a sister of Desirée. Would the blood feud with the Lombard dynasty never be buried in true peace?

The Seneschal, Audulf, fresh from his grim struggle with the Bretons, told his king how the Franks themselves were loath to ride forth so soon again. They had paid a heavy price to win victory over the Saxons. For two years they had been kept from the seeding and harvesting of their lands; they had lost kinsmen and war horses, if they survived themselves.

"Hard bears the burden upon those who are most faithful. It takes the labor of three peasants in the home fields to keep one foot fighter at the war; it takes the yield of a farm to outfit an armored rider. The *fideles* who obey your ban are beggared; those others who make excuse to abide at their homesteads reap gain and goods thereby. Ay, they can well afford to pay fines. Do not summon the faithful to a levy of arms this year."

"The ones protect the others!" The king blazed in anger, and fell silent.

His paladins told the truth. He could not face a new disaster, like the Süntal.

"How if we make a journey," he asked, "without battle?"

It seemed to them as if he were voicing one of those British riddles of Alcuin. They could not think of any answer.

When they left the council table, Audulf asked Gerold bitterly, "Will Almighty God make the Avars refrain from battle, or change the consummate Tassilo after thirty years into a loyal vassal? Tell me that, brother!"

For a very good reason Charlemagne dared not tell them what was in his mind. He held still to the vague thought of years ago—of gathering together a mighty Christian nation, within secure frontiers. After Roncesvalles, he made no mention of a Christian army. Yet the Frisian Christians had remained loyal, against their pagan kinsmen. By that test they

were as much the king's *fideles* as the nobl[...]
land.

But his nobles would never admit that. N[...]
outfit themselves and leave their families to r[...]
if he told them the truth in his mind: We Franks[...]
We will die out if we do not take in other natio[...]
a single Christian folk that will live.

He realized now that this had been the plan of Pepin.

From his new learning he derived some comfort. Had not
Augustine predicted that after the ruin of Roman rule would
come the refuge of God's dominion? Had not the astute
Hadrian summoned the people to prayer in all Christian lands
after the Saxon victory and peace?

Charlemagne took hope from that. After the council he
sent forth his paladins to summon his Franks of the Rhine
not to battle but to make a long winter journey. Then he
summoned the faithful among the Alemanni, Thuringians,
and Saxons to gather by early summer at Gerold's post, the
Bavarian frontier.

Having misled his officers, he next prepared to trick Tassilo
by the aid of Hadrian, a firm friend to the Bavarians.

To Tassilo he sent a mild bidding to come to Ingelheim
to answer charges of desertion, oath breaking, and disloyalty.
Such a summons the resourceful Bavarian would have little
trouble in evading.

Instead of waiting for the response of his hostile cousin to
this overture, the burly monarch of the Rhine called upon
his most faithful seigneurs, the East Franks, to muster their
veteran horsemen and ride forth with him again. To ride
now, at the coming of winter. This time, he promised them,
their journey would end in no battle.

The oldest of them remembered that first winter march
over the Alps and doubted his word. All the signs pointed to
war in Bavaria. But on the upper Rhine, Charlemagne turned
toward the pass of the Mount of Jove, leading to Italy.

At their moodiness he laughed. "What terror do you see on

151

road?" he challenged. "You will feast at Christmas in the Flowering City, you will make your peace where the tombs of the apostles wait in Rome, and you will be the guests of the fair, rich duchy of Benevento."

His merriment shook them from their foreboding. "Such peace and joy," they grumbled, "we have never known."

"Then come with good will and you will know it now."

With this spearhead of warriors he climbed up to the snow pass. His family and his clerics did not accompany him. No wagon train creaked after the swift-moving horsemen. Pepin Carloman, the ten-year-old king of Italy, joined him.

He did not take Fastrada, this time.

As Charlemagne had promised, they passed by Pavia and reached the garden-like Florence in time for Christmas. There he ventured to write to Alcuin, "We are on the way to settle the affairs of Lombardy."

Those affairs were not so casual as his words implied. Storm clouds overhung the contested peninsula, restless as rumors of revolt came down the roads from the north. The defiance of the Bavarians re-echoed in southern Italy. There waited a power untouched by war, the Beneventans, secure in their fortress city, with an impregnable refuge at Salerno, crowning a height over the southern sea.

This duchy of Benevento occupied the true boot of Italy, with mountain ridges and ports facing historic gulfs, with the Roman pleasure resort of Capua, and the smoking pinnacle of Vesuvius—in close touch with the fleets, the merchants, and the spies of mighty Constantinople. Something of Roman leisure and culture endured there, where Greek churches towered over vineyards, and courtiers amused themselves with backgammon and racing.

Its elderly duke, Arichis, knew the courtesy and trickery of an elder day. A Lombard, he made his land the last refuge of Lombard liberty, beyond the reach of the barbarian Frank. With his back to the sea, the bearded and fastidious Arichis could invoke the power of the sea, if he threw open his ports to the Byzantine fleets. And he was doing so now.

Hadrian's messages to Charlemagne gave warning of that—how Arichis claimed the monasteries of St. Peter, how the duke was mustering armed forces, strengthening the walls of Capua and Salerno, trimming his hair and beard in Byzantine fashion, accepting gold-woven robes, a sword, and a scepter from the Byzantine *strategos* at Sicily.

From the sea itself came warning—how a forgotten son of Desiderius besought the empress Irene for a fleet of dromonds and an army, to make a descent upon Italy, to win back Ravenna, city of Byzantine Caesars. Arichis soon would be master of Naples——

Perhaps Charlemagne seized upon these tidings to break the betrothal of Rotrud, openly, with the son of Irene. But he had set his mind against the marriage. To his thinking the Beneventans were invoking the Empire as the Bavarians turned to the Avars when they fancied him to be crippled by the long ordeal of Saxony.

And here, too, a daughter of Desiderius opposed him, in the person of the high-spirited duchess, who would not believe the Lombard cause to be a lost cause. Charlemagne wasted little thought upon Arichis but wished he might know how strong was the will and the courage of the duchess. He remembered very well that she was the benefactor of Paul the Deacon who had tutored her. "Lovely and steadfast," Paul admitted her to be——

Riding at ease, with his armed host following, Charlemagne took the road to Rome, to allow his men to make pilgrimage to the tombs of the apostles. Except for this steady march, we know little of what actually took place, in the shifting kaleidoscope of intrigue, rife with rumors.

Evidently Charlemagne avoided Bavaria, where he was expected, to appear in Italy, where he was not looked for. Yet he is listening all the while for tidings of Tassilo. He makes display of a peaceful journey, yet he has a striking force at his back.

At Rome, Hadrian welcomes him anxiously, with banners and urgent requests to take the field against the not-to-be-mentioned Lombards, to seize the port of Gaeta before it is too late. The astute Hadrian warns that Arichis is fortifying Salerno as a bridgehead to the sea, whence will come the Byzantine fleets, to restore Lombard rule in Italy. Charles the king must press on to Salerno.

But war seems to be far removed from the mind of the journeying Charlemagne. To Rome hasten envoys of Arichis, with rich gifts of heavy gold, with easy talk of allegiance to be rendered the Frankish king and his notable son, in Rome.

Charlemagne accepts the gifts but not the promises. Distributing gold to his followers, he continues on from the tomb of St. Peter to Monte Cassino on its solitary ridge. Here he embraces his old schoolmaster, Paul the Deacon, asking for news of Paul's friends and their affairs. The burly lord of Frankland creates a stir in the quiet cloisters of Benedict. He admires the library, asks eagerly if the Pleiades can be seen on the horizon. By Paul he sends greeting and announcement of intention to pay a visit to Duke Arichis.

From Cassino, he moves on, to camp around the palatial city of Capua, over the gray river Volturno. The Franks do not loot Capua. Quartering themselves outside the gates, they strip food and fodder from the countryside in the lean month of March.

He hears that Arichis, with his duchess and court, has fled from Benevento to safety in Salerno. Messages of greeting and bargaining pass between them while the Franks eat up grain and meat "like locusts." Their force is too great for Arichis to meet in the field. He has no word from his brother-in-law Tassilo, nor any sight of a Byzantine fleet heading in. At best, he can only try to defend the half-finished walls of Salerno.

Surprisingly the lord of Frankland agrees to a bargain. He will not cross the Volturno, or require Arichis to kneel before him; he will accept the sworn allegiance of the duke of Benevento, with tribute of seven thousand gold pieces a year. But Arichis must shave off his beard and dress his hair in the style of the Franks as evidence of his good faith. (What will his duchess think of that?)

As surety, Arichis will yield up his son Grimwald and twelve lords of Benevento, to be hostages. With joy Paul welcomes the agreement between the Lombards and his former master. He has warned Arichis of the savagery of the Franks in ravaging a country. (In fact Charlemagne has trouble holding back his henchmen from looting Capua.)

Then to Capua come two distinguished envoys from the court of Irene. With all their elaborate courtesy they ask Charlemagne whether or not he means to wed his daughter to the young emperor. He responds that he does not mean to do so.

At drowsy Capua the tidings for which the king had been waiting reached him. Tassilo had replied cleverly to his summons; instead of venturing out of Bavaria himself, he sent two bishops, one being Arno of Salzburg, to Rome to beg Hadrian to arbitrate the quarrel between the two royal cousins. A shrewd request—because the Pope desired above everything to keep the peace. Charlemagne saw in it the hand of the Lombard woman who hated him.

Swiftly he took his following up to Rome in time for Easter, bringing as gift to Hadrian the keys of Capua, and the restoration of monasteries to Papal rule. Mildly he faced the Bavarian bishops. Arno he knew to be a man of conscience, friendly to him. Hadrian urged Charlemagne to exert himself to keep peace between Franks and Bavarians.

"That is exactly what I wish to do."

Declaring that he had never wanted war with their duke, his liegeman, he asked only that the two envoys sign their pledge of Tassilo's loyalty, as sworn so often before to his father, to himself, and his sons.

Yet if the envoys did so, they would be pledging the loyalty of Tassilo as subject, to Charlemagne as king. Arno felt that he could not, in conscience, do so.

"We have no authority so to sign for our lord the duke."

Instantly then the Frank appealed to Hadrian's judgment. Was not Tassilo guilty if he refused to affirm the oath of loyalty he had given once? Hadrian could not deny it, and Tassilo was not there to argue it. Having just beheld Charlemagne's humbling of the proud Beneventans without conflict, Hadrian issued his judgment of Tassilo in strong words, which bear the impress of Charlemagne's persuasion.

"Anathema upon Tassilo the duke if he refuses to affirm his sworn allegiance. If the duke opposes a hard heart to these words of the sovereign pontiff, Charles the king and his armed host will be innocent and absolved of all sin, even to slaying and burning, in acting against Tassilo and his confederates."

With this moral quittance in his hand, the king of Frankland took his leave of the anxious Hadrian. Arno and the other Bavarian envoy hastened back to the Alps with a new burden on their conscience. Yet Charlemagne made no immediate move to enforce Hadrian's mandate against Tassilo. Instead, he led his liegemen with his son Pepin northeast toward the Adriatic coast and the once imperial city of Ravenna.

At Rome he had admired Hadrian's new buildings—notably the finely designed Romanesque churches of Sancta Maria in Cosmedin, close to the ancient ruined Forum, and the larger shrine of St. Peter in Chains. Hadrian was rebuilding Rome in marble, and Charlemagne wished he had such architects at Ingelheim, or Worms.

At Ravenna waited an able soldier, Eric, duke of Friuli, guardian of the mountain barrier beyond which the Avars roamed. There, too, waited the count of Verona and other

Franks. Charlemagne bade them muster their forces, to greet their king, Pepin. By so doing he collected a small but handy army at Ravenna.

And there happened something unexpected. Charlemagne fell under the spell of the dead city. In some strange way it seemed to be familiar, although he had never laid eyes on it before.

Apparently forgetting the Bavarian crisis, and Grimwald and the reluctant hostages of Benevento's good faith, he quested through the crumbling walls of Ravenna like a stag-hound on a scent. The round, moss-grown mass of Theodoric's tomb, the octagonal, domed Vitale with the mosaic portraits of Justinian and his empress Theodora, the lovely purple interior of the tomb of the unknown woman, Galla Placidia, that gave him the feeling of entering under the night sky, besprinkled with gold—all these he scrutinized, storing away their details in his capacious memory.

Taking the palace of Theodoric for his quarters, he paced the courtyard across to the domed cathedral, sitting there to study the long colonnade of multi-hued marble pillars, and the wall plates of shimmering alabaster.

Whenever he entered this otherwise abandoned palace, he passed the giant statue of Theodoric, the Gothic king, the one man who had united Italy under a firm hand. Theodoric the Goth, the ravager, had become in this magnificent bronze effigy Theodoric the Great, friend of humanity. Charlemagne was impressed.

Another circumstance struck him forcibly. Rome, for all its amazing sights and towering skyscraping structures, was still the creation of a pagan world that the Frank could not understand. While Ravenna was built by Christian hands in the days of the early Fathers. Moreover it bore the handmark of strong-minded rulers, Theodoric and Justinian—it had become a monument to their lives. Charlemagne had read the Fathers—or had their pages read to him at dinnertime—and by now he could appreciate very well the manifold problems

157

of divided Italy which Theodoric and Justinian had solved, although in different ways. While he inspected their handiwork eagerly, he questioned the Ravenna clerics about their lives.

But for the most part he absorbed Ravenna with his eyes. To his followers it seemed to be both cramped and damp, surrounded by reedy marshes. Charlemagne, however, had himself rowed through the muddied canal out to the abandoned port. There he came to the Adriatic, the waterway of the east, of the Venetian isles, the Istrian mountains, and the outposts of Constantinople.

With his keen eye for country, he realized why Ravenna seemed familiar. Its waterways and marshes and the unbroken green of its plain stretching to distant hills resembled the resting place of his early years, Aquis Granum.

The contrast between this miniature metropolis of Christian palaces and churches and the hostel-sprinkled wilderness of Aquis Granum must have impressed him. Ravenna enclosed the monuments of centuries. His green valley held only abandoned barracks of the Roman Sixth Legion and his own hunting villa.

In another year the Frank would ask the Pope's consent to remove the marble wall slabs, the pillars of the palace, and even the bronze statue of the Goth, to transport to Frankland. No matter if it was a herculean task to cart such massive segments of civilization over the Alps.

Meanwhile Charlemagne had overstayed his time in Ravenna. Heading back toward the familiar passes, he took his war band swiftly into the Alps. But he left Pepin behind with Duke Eric and a serviceable army mustered in Friuli.

By July, Charlemagne was back on the Rhine, calling for a council at Worms. As soon as his clerics gathered in the great hall he yielded to the temptation to tell them of the notable sights of his long journey. "Rejoicing and praising God's mercy," the annals state, "the lord king related to his clergy and best people all the manifold things he had encountered upon his journey."

Apparently he occupied the minds of his councilors in this fashion, while he made certain that Tassilo had sent no response to Hadrian's demand. For he acted without further discussion. In fact, he had made all his plans, and needed only to send orders by speeding messengers to his wardens—to Eric now waiting in Friuli and Gerold quartered with the army of former rebels, Thuringian and Saxon, on the Bavarian border. The orders were to march at pace into Bavaria, toward the objective of Salzburg.

Leading out his Frankish horse again, Charlemagne embarked men and beasts on barges to be rowed up the Rhine. Soon he was on the Lech, hurrying toward Augsburg (Augusta). From the south and the northwest the two other armies drove in, to gain the high valleys of Bavaria before the autumn storms.

Stunned by this unlooked-for invasion from three frontiers, Tassilo and his queen could muster no force to resist. The Bavarian host had not been summoned to arms. Its mountain warriors, on foot, could not close the valleys to the speeding horsemen of the Frank. Bishops of the churches, told by Arno of Hadrian's fiat, would not preach resistance to Charlemagne.

Despite the tears of his Lombard queen, Tassilo could do nothing but submit to the man who had outmaneuvered him. This he did in his courtly manner, riding forth with unarmed servants bearing gifts of gold and jeweled regalia.

"He placed his hands within the great king's hands," the annals say, "and rendered to him in obedience the duchy which he had received from Pepin the king."

Charlemagne remembered clearly how this same Tassilo had ridden off from the sick Pepin in the Gascon land, thirty years before. He asked if it was true, as he had heard, that Tassilo possessed a splendid scepter. (Which no vassal might have.)

159

From the gifts the proud Bavarian drew a gold scepter surmounted by a miniature crowned head. "I had it made," he said evenly, "for you, my cousin."

With the tribute of Arichis, and the rich gifts of Tassilo, to reward his armed hosts, Charlemagne turned back to the Rhine, where Fastrada waited at her favorite palace of Ingelheim. As he went, the October storms set in.

His horsemen branched off to their homes with a brief word to the hostels on the roads. "Peace and joy." The king had kept his promise to them. They had made a long journey without a battle. But they did not receive the awards of gold and spoil they expected from the king. Fastrada attended to that.

～ While Christmas was celebrated with peace and joy by his subjects, Charlemagne did not expect that happy state of affairs to last out the winter.

By the speed of his horses the lord of Frankland had wrung enforced submission from the cousin who hated him. Tassilo had tasted independence for thirty years; he had sons to inherit his throne. He had a wife who would never kneel to an Arnulfing. His Bavarian armed host remained intact.

Just as clearly as Charlemagne himself, the sagacious Agilulfing understood that the issue between them was not who carried a mandate from Hadrian but who would rule Bavaria. The gifting of a little gold, the lip service of a new oath, and the handing over of a dozen hostages amounted to no more than a forced gesture. Tassilo would resist with arms, and Charlemagne had no least wish just then to deal with another Witukind.

But how would the proudful Bavarian resist? By calling in the Avars, the natural enemies of the most Christian king of Frankland.

With so much clear in his mind, Charlemagne spent the winter months in letter writing, or rather dictating, with a purpose. The missives told of his responsibility for guarding

the borderlands of the Christians, against Slavs and Avars.
To Alcuin he put the question, was it not their task to expand
the frontiers of Christendom? Was not Willehad, kinsman of
Alcuin, consecrating his new cathedral at Bremen (Brema)
on the far bank of the Weser? Alcuin wrote, rejoicing, to
Arno, the "Eagle of Salzburg," that the glorious king had it
in his heart to overthrow the "Huns who are enemies of the
Lord." At Salzburg the stout Arno dwelt near indeed to Avarland.

Pilgrims from the Rhineland carried the same message
along the roads. At Ingelheim, Charlemagne rested quietly,
hunting as always, while he awaited human game to come to
the lures he had set.

What he anticipated was happening. Nagged by his wife,
Tassilo summoned his vassals to arms. On the Danube, the
Avar khagan, disturbed by the sudden advent of the Franks,
sent envoys to question the Bavarians. Tassilo asked the aid
of the pagan horsemen, to hold the mountains of Bavaria
against the lowborn, inflexible Frank.

Instead of finding himself at the head of an army, however,
the lord of Bavaria met obstacles he had not anticipated. His
seigneurs, who had no quarrel with the impressive Charlemagne, protested against breaking the pledge of the last
autumn. (It bound them as well as Tassilo to Charlemagne's
service.) His bishops would not go against Hadrian's will.
Especially Arno—who had supported his duke loyally enough
at Rome—cried out against allying themselves to Hunnish
pagans, despoilers of churches.

Some of his seigneurs rode down the Rhine, to lay their
case before the king. Immediately Charlemagne summoned
Tassilo to appear before the general assembly that June at
Ingelheim to answer charges of rebellion and disloyalty.

There was nothing else the Agilulfing could do, because
the Avars would not move to aid a monarch deserted by his
army. So unarmed, with his family, Tassilo came to his trial.

To his surprise he found himself not before Charlemagne's

161

court, but facing the assembled lords of Frankland, Saxony, Lombardy, and other lands. In the great hall of Ingelheim the charges against him were voiced by his own vassals.

Charlemagne made no accusation. In fact, while the high lords debated, the restless Frank went from the hall to make the rounds of the crowded courtyard, discussing crops and horses and game—anything but Tassilo's case—with the waiting counts and chieftains. He acted like the host of a vast gathering of guests.

Within the hall, however, a Frankish duke voiced Charlemagne's thirty-year-old grievance against Tassilo. "For desertion of his lord Pepin the king while the aforesaid lord was marching against an enemy."

Tassilo understood that Charlemagne had insisted on that charge, and that he himself would be condemned by the assembly.

When he was bidden to speak for himself, the duke answered with pride and eloquence, taking pains to tell the truth and the whole truth. He had conspired with enemies of the king; he had wished to take the life of his lord. His wife joined him in that. He had broken his sworn loyalty, because:

"If I had ten sons and they were all hostages, I would lose them rather than endure the shameful terms of that oath. I would rather lose my life than continue to live by it."

It was a courageous and honest speech, satisfying to the judges of that high court. So unanimously they sentenced him to death. Although they did not mention his family, Charlemagne could easily extend the sentence to the wife and children.

Instead of doing so, Charlemagne commanded that Tassilo enter a monastery, "there to make amends during his remaining years, for his sins." His sons would follow him to the cloisters and his wife would take the veil.

So with calculated mercy the unpredictable Frank answered the appeal of the proud Bavarian for death. Tassilo begged that he should be spared the indignity of having his long hair clipped there, at the assembly. Charlemagne allowed him to be shaved at the monastery.

The rule of the Agilulfing family was ended. By easy stages the upstart Frank moved into their palace city of Ratisbon (Regensburg), and inspected his new domain within the Alps, taking over Tassilo's properties, exiling his closest companions. Arno was consecrated archbishop of Bavaria.

Although he seldom wore, or took in his hands, the regalia of royalty—except to impress strange ambassadors—Charlemagne sometimes sat in audience with the scepter made with such artistry for Tassilo. Either something in his conscience troubled him or he wished to impress his new people again with the justness of this seizure of power. Because after a few years he had Tassilo, now a tonsured monk, come before him to state again that he relinquished all claim to Bavaria to Charlemagne, his rightful lord and king.

Meanwhile, on the Italian front Charlemagne had won a more remarkable victory without a battle. Kerold and the old troopers called it "a bloodless victory, or almost bloodless."

Look back at the calendar of that last crowded year, 787–88, when the Frank and his henchmen covered two thousand miles in their saddles.

On August 26, 787 died the elderly and resigned Arichis, duke of Benevento, and his peace died with him. His duchess exercised a woman's privilege of ignoring the family pledge to Charlemagne, and rallying the forces of resistance with courage. Urgently she wrote to Frankland begging the release of her son, Grimwald, hostage to Charlemagne and heir to the throne of Benevento. She invoked her mother love and the need of his leaderless people. (By then Charlemagne was hastening from the Rhine into Bavaria.)

At last the Byzantine fleet appeared off the coast. It brought an army of invasion, led by Adilghis, son of Desiderius, brother of the duchess. Again she begged for the return of Grimwald.

163

From Rome the alert Hadrian also besought Charlemagne not to release Grimwald. The duchess, reported Hadrian, had gone on pilgrimage to the shrine of St. Michael Archangel. Shrine, forsooth! The invasion fleet was next door at Taranto and she was concocting plans with her brother, and the *strategos* of Sicily and the officer of the empress, to wrest southern Italy from "God's apostle and your royal power, and mine." Hadrian stormed in anxiety. "Come quickly! *Do not let Grimwald escape you!*"

But Charlemagne did nothing of the kind.

That early spring of 788 while he wrote so many letters to Bavaria, the master of the Franks kept the youthful hostage at his side. Grimwald, little older than Pepin, ate at the king's table, rode with him to hunt and to the trial of Tassilo in June. Charlemagne treated the youth like a son of his own.

Then, with Tassilo disposed of and his hands free, he released Grimwald. There was a pledge at their parting, the boy promising to fulfill the duties of vassal to king, to stamp his coins with the image of Charlemagne, to shave, except for his mustache, in Frankish fashion—a point that seemed firmly imbedded in Charlemagne's mind—and to remain loyal to his king. He also promised to tear down the new walls fortifying Salerno (where the Byzantine fleet had put in).

So Charlemagne gambled on a boy's admiration. That September Grimwald rode back across the Volturno a free man, to be greeted by the acclamations of his nobles and the embrace of his mother, and the plan of battle of his uncle, Adilghis.

From that explosive southland, Charlemagne's envoys wrote in quick foreboding: "At the Beneventan frontier, we found no loyalty in the people toward Your Excellency."

Bitterly Hadrian exclaimed. "At Capua, in the very presence of your envoys that Grimwald congratulated himself, saying that you, his king, ordered all the people to obey him. And the Greek nobles at Naples howl with insulting laughter, saying, 'Thank God! All the promises to the Franks are gone with the wind.'"

In spite of such prodding, and prediction of disaster, Charlemagne (then occupying Bavaria) did nothing about the new Italian crisis. Perhaps he counted on the friendship of Paul the Deacon, now at Grimwald's side.

By autumn the Italian front was clouded in rumors, the Byzantines landing on the Adriatic shore, the Frankish envoys riding for their lives——

Through the rumors broke the news of the battle. On the line of the Volturno, by Mount Vulture, the expedition of the Empire met stunning defeat, losing four thousand soldiers, and their Byzantine commanders the *strategos* and the sacellarius. Among its leaders, Adilghis alone escaped to sea, not to return again.

Fighting thus against his uncle, Grimwald gained this victory, aided by the loyal duke of Spoleto and a single Frankish count. In keeping faith with the lord of Frankland, Grimwald had gone against his mother's prayers.

Adilghis vanished from the historical record; the Lombard cause was lost in Italy. There the absent Charlemagne ruled in the person of his son Pepin. The great cities, like Benevento, Bologna, and Verona, left pretty much to their own devices, gained a certain sturdy independence. (In coming centuries it would grow into the self-rule of mighty Florence and Milan under their ducal families of the Sforza and De' Medici.)

What had happened to Charlemagne's early oath at the tomb of St. Peter, to restore the bulk of the lands to the Popes? It was not kept. With the years he seems to have decided to award many church properties to the apostolic lords, but not the mundane rule. Perhaps he realized that Hadrian lacked the physical power to hold great territories in that age of violence. In any case, he himself held the mastery, with the sword.

Hadrian, although growing old, ceased not to protest

against the broken pledge and the loss of "the patrimony of St. Peter." At the same time the redoubtable champion of St. Peter appreciated the protection of his unusual "co-father." In truth, Charlemagne brought with him the boon of the king's peace.

In the months after the victory beneath Mount Vulture, Hadrian had reason to appreciate that. From their fastness on the Danube the Avars, unacknowledged masters of the east, emerged to attack savagely.

With so much disturbance in Christian lands, the watchful Avar khagan seized the opportunity for profitable raids. Warily probing, his horsemen drove at the Bavarian highlands and down through the Carinthian Alps toward the fertile Po valley.

Along the Danube headwaters the Warden, Gerold, threw back the invaders. Down in Friuli the experienced Eric mustered his Frank men-at-arms to beat them back from castle and abbey and mountain pass. Against the danger of the Avar attack, the Christian guarding forces united with good will.

Charlemagne could not have anticipated the time of the Avar move, but his frontiers were prepared for it. By a remarkable tour de force in those two years, he had turned the rebellious Bavarians and Beneventans into allies who warded off the assaults of the Byzantines by sea, and the pagan nomads by land. The headlong Churl who stirred up bitter strife by driving his Lombard bride, Desirée, from his side in a fit of anger had become the astute statesman who set free his potential enemy, Grimwald. The unhappy chieftain who blundered toward his first passage of the Alps at Mount Cenis and lost the best of his army at Roncesvalles had taught himself in some manner the most difficult art of carrying on a war without battles.

He was trying to train his oldest son, Charles, to lead armies, while the other sons of Hildegard, Pepin and Louis, gained recognition, if not precisely honor, as kings of Italy and Aquitaine.

Danger in the East

Now, as the year ended, Charlemagne sent out his word to Arno of Salzburg and the keepers of his far frontiers. He would come himself to protect them against pagan Slavs, Bohemians, and Avars. That word he meant to keep.

Slowly, with the persistence of a peasant, the monarch of the Rhine was working his way toward a new dominion. It was, in his mind, a dominion on earth resembling the city of God as described by the inspired Augustine. Its subjects became the *fideles,* the faithful, whether Breton, Thuringian, or Saxon.

"Your subjects," Alcuin acknowledged now, "are the Christian people."

Wide lay the borders of that nation-to-be. Far could its frontiers be pushed, to the edge of the Frozen Sea, and to the unknown east beyond the Adriatic. The first step would be to thrust it beyond the Avarland. At Ratisbon, court of his brilliant cousin, Tassilo, Charlemagne prepared for that step into the east.

As the year ended, however, he went elsewhere for the Christmas celebration. Without pausing at Ingelheim, where Fastrada had settled down in luxurious quarters, he embarked on the Rhine, drifting down with the wind to the broken paving of the disused Roman road leading to his valley of Aquis Granum.

At that road junction, while he swam in the warm sulphur water and hunted boar in the groves, he held the song and feasting of the Nativity, to the surprise of his paladins and members of the Academy. For he had not held Christmas there for twenty years—not since the year of his father's death.

Above the valley rose a pleasant hill. Its slope overlooked the huddled hamlet and Roman ruins. The afternoon sun warmed it. Wandering over it, Charlemagne selected a site for a palace like that of Pavia, with a colonnade stretching to the spot where a cathedral might stand, a small one but dedicated to Mary. It would be shaped like St. Vitale's at Ravenna.

While he wondered who would build it, he took joy in the bright glances of the village maidens, in awe of the king. They were filled with warmth and laughter, unlike the haughty and demanding Fastrada. This valley seemed to him to be an ideal spot for his new city.

A letter from Hadrian increased his delight. "It's come—it's come at last!" he cried. "Sweeter than honey."

The letter said: "We have your bright and honey-sweet missive, from the hand of Duke Alwin. In it you express your desire that we grant you the marbles of the palace in the city of Ravenna, as well as the mosaics to be found both on the pavement and on the walls of the churches. Willingly, we grant your wish, because by your royal efforts the church of your patron St. Peter daily enjoys many benefits."

Now he needed only somebody to design his capital buildings, and materials for the walls better than Roman stucco or Frankish log and thatch——

Long afterward an old soldier told the merry monk of St. Gall about Charlemagne's way of building what he wished:

"Why, the most inventive great king said to his men, 'Let's not be charged with idling away this day; let's build us some memorial of it. Let's make haste to build us a little house of prayer, where we may pay heed to serving God.' As soon as he said that, his men charged off in every direction, collecting lime and stones, with wood and paint, and skilled workmen to use them. Between the fourth hour of that day and the twelfth hour, aided by the men-at-arms and nobles, they all built such a cathedral, complete with walls and roof, with fretted ceiling and frescoes on the walls, that no one who saw it thereafter believed it had taken a day less than a year to build."

Chapter VII

THE TREASURE OF THE AVARS

ABOUT THIS TIME a cleavage began to open between Charlemagne and his Franks. Although he had managed to subdue the savagery of his pagan borderlands, he
found himself less able to tame the savagery of his own
people. In winning over the Italians and Bavarians he had
used patient persuasion; in his homelands he acted with
brutal determination.

For that Fastrada got the blame. "Our king, usually so
merciful, became cruel and demanding under her influence."
Perhaps. She could enforce her will against his. Yet the revolt
of the next years was caused less by her personality than by
his inability to rule his growing dominion beyond the area of
his own presence.

Cracks of the cleavage showed first within the Rhinelands,
with the old grievance of the veterans who returned to barren
fields and penniless homes. Their neighbors who evaded the
king's ban at least had grain stored up and fat herds. Moreover, the faithful who had crossed the Alps this time did not
get the spoil of the early years of the Lombard victory. It
seems that the bullion and gifts of Tassilo and Arichis went
to Fastrada's "gift" and this queen did not believe in handing
out treasure.

Then the inflexible king called out his armed host the next
year, 789, to ravage the Slavs across the Elbe, where the clay

169

and thatch villages yielded little payment to loyal men-at-arms. Many liegemen pleaded sickness or poverty, to abide on their farms. Some disappeared into the trackless forests, to swell the numbers of masterless folk who hunted their food and looted their silver.

Against all these deserters Charlemagne laid the charge of *herisliz*.

The difficulty was to catch the absconders. His dominion's being portioned off by vague landmarks among dukes (military managers), counts (administrators), and bishops of the dioceses—as well as the heads of the numerous abbeys and monasteries—offered convenient sanctuaries in these wildernesses of forests that the king was trying to turn into cultivated land. Distant hamlets, ruled by vicars or "hundred-men" might have use for a footloose swordsman or plowman, especially when he came with a gift in his hand.

Over all Frankland unwritten tribal custom still held good —that a warrior was a free man, and a free man could not be hired or compelled to manual labor, but gave or accepted gifts in noble fashion and worked with his hands only when so inclined.

Against such customary sloth and misdemeanor, Charlemagne laid his anger. His edicts compelled "The counts and hundred-men to render all justice, to make use of agents they trust not to oppress the poor but to hunt down thieves, pilferers, mankillers, lechers . . . Those given the power to judge shall judge rightly, without taking thought of gifts, flattery, or personalities."

The trouble lay in the personalities, as Charlemagne understood very well. A warrior habitually carried weapons; it would be a personal insult to try to take them from him. And especially after returning from a campaign, he was apt to use them when drunk or offended or otherwise roused to righteous wrath. Charged with bloodguilt, a Frank would claim his right to pay wergild, a noble would demand to be judged by his peers, and a Thuringian noble might claim kinship with the queen, while a peasant might be crucified for theft.

Alcuin's suggestion of abiding by Holy Writ had not served to cure this endemic puzzle of the laws. A criminal could appeal to God's will, in demanding to be tried by ordeal of fire, water, or boiling pitch.

With all his energy Charlemagne fought this evil of personalized law, for which his ancestors had been responsible. If it could not be cured by the *words* of Holy Writ, he decided, it might be healed by the *sense* of the Scriptures. Christians, then, should accept as laws what Paul and the apostles *meant* them to carry out in life.

Of course the final appeal was to Charlemagne himself, or in his absence—and he was usually far distant from the scene of a crime or dispute—to the Count of the Palace. Yet he had inherited a rudimentary method of projecting his royal presence elsewhere by the *missi*, or king's spokesmen. They explained his wishes, which really amounted to carrying out his orders.

Now Charlemagne attempted to gain control over his subjects by sending out new envoys with greater authority, the *missi dominici*. "To speak with his word and carry out the will of God, and order of the king."

Charlemagne used that phrase with no hint of vanity. Being a king *gratia Dei* signified in his mind being a ruler with the duty of carrying out God's will. The phrase came to mean other things later on—in fact some historians point to Charlemagne as the first of the French kings (or German emperors) "by the will of God"—but in his time it meant a great responsibility. This responsibility he laid upon his new envoys, who were virtually viceroys. "I wish that they give example of the right-doing they demand in my name."

These *missi dominici* were to accept no gifts, and take account of no personalities. They were to carry out God's intent, through man-made laws, and they were to report to him personally. Since the most bitter quarrels arose between

171

clerics and laymen, Charlemagne usually appointed them to travel in pairs, a duke to go with a bishop.

They were, above all, to help preserve the king's peace. "All who disturb that peace shall be arrested." They were to compel counts and prelates to aid "the Lord's poor." They had authority to discipline local rulers who erred. "On Sundays and feast days every one should go to hear the word of God . . . Counts must hold their spring and fall tribunals, and not go off to hunt or pursue other pleasures . . . Drunken men must be kept out of court."

This bold experiment in delegating authority did not accomplish what Charlemagne hoped. It, too, depended on the incalculable of personality—whether the *dominici* had integrity enough to refuse gifts. Reporting as they did, in these troubled times, to the king's ear, they tended to inform him chiefly concerning the loyalty or disloyalty of his officers.

They became, in fact, something of a security police. And he had need of that.

Even before the great drouth, times were hard. Probably Charlemagne began to realize, if he did not fully understand, how his nascent western kingdom had been cut off from the trade channels of the outer world. His sallies out to Saragossa, Benevento, and the Baltic shore had given him glimpses of merchant caravans and seafaring shipping. His growing Frankland was still encircled by the trade-and-raid fleets of Northmen and Arabs; he possessed no gold coinage like the Spanish dinar or Byzantine solidus.

Ingeniously enough, he tried to compensate for poverty. Letters from Hadrian thanked him for gifts of "serviceable horses" but asked for better ones, and tin to repair St. Peter's roof. Charlemagne gave out what he had, to St. Peter.

To support his silver coinage, he demonetized foreign coins and gold, while increasing the weight of his own cruder money—the silver denier. At the same time he tried to set up standards for weights and measures.

172

Although he lightened the road tolls for foreign merchants they seldom ventured up the Danube, or from the Venetian isles, where rumor related that silk, spice, glass, and the splendors of the east came in by sea. The silver, timber, and rough wool cloth of Frankland did not tempt them. Charlemagne's fit of temper had rid him of the traders from Britain.

The few imports that seeped into Frankland were luxuries that did not affect the economy of village life.

In fact his economy was a makeshift, intended to feed and arm his subject peoples. It startled him to discover, when he examined them carefully, that his Carolingian royal seals had been stamped from a gem intaglio of an Aurelian emperor of Rome, and of the Egyptian god Serapis.

Somehow, with Fastrada at his side, he felt himself to be lacking much that he had never missed in the lifetime of Hildegard. When Meginfried, his industrious Chamberlain, increased the crop yield of Charlemagne's villas, and suggested that they could serve the needs of other court dignitaries as well, he gave an order against it. "The villas are to serve the king alone, and no one else."

No monarch of that day insisted more firmly upon his personal prerogatives. His liegemen did not object to that; they rather admired him for it. His Frankish seigneurs, however, began to be dissatisfied with his benefices—his grants of cultivated land for livings. A Rhineland count would be given a hamlet, with a church and farms in "conquered" Saxonland, with the duty of keeping the peace, arresting fugitives, paying the king's tithe and the church tithe. This Frank would naturally use his beneficial power to enlarge his property by taking in more fishing streams and hunting forests. Very soon he would look upon such an estate as his own, to bequeath to his sons, while Charlemagne insisted that the benefice remained in the king's gift, to bestow on the officer who took the count's place.

Then, too, the granting of land estates to local lords had a consequence unforeseen as yet. The seigneurs' men-at-arms and peasants were bound by oath to obey Charlemagne and his royal sons. Yet they depended upon their seigneur for the necessities of life—a mill to grind their grain, seed for the next planting, animals for plowing, and above all protection against the raids of neighbors, or hungering bands from the forest. So necessity bred in them a second loyalty, to their landlord. Especially when that lord was a battle-bold leader, these henchmen felt themselves bound faster to him—the more so if their farmlands lay distant from the Rhine—than to an unseen king who spoke Greek and passed his summers in Rome, or Ratisbon.

Charlemagne, who understood his people, may have sensed the danger of this divided loyalty. Men who evaded pledging themselves to him, on one pretense or another, were hunted down or exiled. At the same time his ceaseless journeying took him hobnobbing among towns and border wards from Bononia (Boulogne) on the Channel to Monte Cassino. Yet he could not possibly visit all his new dominions; he was forced to rely more and more on his *missi dominici* and his few staunch local leaders like Gerold and Eric—"mighty in war and uplifted in spirit."

Nothing, however, could quite take the place of his own merry, demanding presence, and high-pitched exhortation to better things. In Aquitaine, where he had not set foot for a dozen years, matters were not going well. Louis, the king, was still a boy, and capable William of Toulouse, the Warden, had increasing difficulty with the Moors beyond the Pyrenees.

Charlemagne himself had trouble of a different kind with the great assembly of his Christian peoples.

In the year 790 something unheard of happened. Charlemagne did not journey forth that summer.

The autumn assembly was held, where he waited, in the ancient city of Worms among the vineyards, far up the Rhine and close to the Bavarian frontier. In fact, some of the meetings of the lay and clerical lords of Frankland took place in the fields, so great was the gathering.

The older Franks resented the presence of outlanders, Lombards, Bavarians, and Saxons, who were greeted by Charlemagne with the same honor as the Rhinelanders. In their eyes the national council of Frankland had changed into a very Babel of strange folk, speaking every language, but all intent on pressing claims to notice and reward upon the king, who should have listened first to the needs of his Frankish nobles. So these older Franks tried to consult apart, for mutual aid.

"No stranger came near the place of their meeting," wrote Adalhard, cousin of the king (his words survive in the manuscript of Hincmar, archbishop of Reims) "until the results of their deliberation were laid before the great king, who then, with his wisdom bestowed by God, replied with a resolution which all obeyed."

Charlemagne, then, did not interfere with the arguments of his nobles, but said his say after they were done. And the king's word was obeyed by *all*.

"While these discussions were carried on away from the presence of the king, he went himself into the midst of the multitude, accepting presents, saluting the men of most note, singling out those he had seldom seen, showing courteous interest to the elders, playing pranks with the younglings—doing pretty much the same with the clerics. . . .

"However, the king proposed to the lords, lay and ecclesiastical, the affairs to be discussed by them. If they desired his presence, the king joined them and stayed as long as they wished.

"The king also had another custom—to ask each man to report to him about the part of the kingdom that one had come from. For all were required, between the Assemblies, to inquire what was happening throughout their neighborhoods, seeking knowledge from foreigners as well as inhabitants, from enemies as well as friends, sometimes making use of agents without troubling too much about how these got their information.

"The king wished to know whether in any corner of the kingdom the people were restless, and whether they had made a disturbance. He sought also to know of signs of revolt, and whether nations still independent were threatening the kingdom with attack. If disorder or danger manifested itself, he demanded particularly what was the cause of it."

So Charlemagne, while playing his usual role of charming host, gathered in the newest intelligence reports. He had a way of keeping his own decisions back until the end of the varied councils. Without thought of irony, the notaries at the assembly wrote down its resolutions as made by "the Council and the king himself."

That autumn he was preoccupied with the loyalty question because he sensed restlessness in the heart of Frankland. And he meant to summon all armed strength to move against the Avars, before the eastern pagans could attack Bavaria or Italy again. Along those frontiers his *missi dominici* were actively negotiating with the Avar chieftains about the borders—either to make test whether the Avar khagan would agree to peace, or to delude him into thinking the Franks wanted peace.

It was dangerous to match wiles against the pagan nomads. Charlemagne realized that he would need the full support of Lombards, Bavarians, and Thuringians in dealing with them. Thus the assembly of 790 enabled him to discover whose loyalty he could rely on, and what strength would muster at his summons.

He needed more than the force of his own Franks.

Einhard, the Dwarfling, relates: "He liked foreigners and took pains to protect them, even when they came to the kingdom and the palace in such a multitude they seemed to be a nuisance."

176

The Treasure of the Avars

This Dwarfling had become the butt and the joy of the Palace group. Tiny in body, he scurried about carrying pens or wine for the great scholars. "Like an ant," said one. Alcuin christened him Nardalus, the Dwarfling, but added gently that he had a fine spirit in his small body. Since he was skilled only in metal working, this nineteen-year-old monk from Fulda also gained the nickname of Bezaleel.

Answering to all his names cheerfully, the youngling Einhard hid his ambition to write like his master, Alcuin. At the same time, then and thereafter, Charlemagne became the object of his hero worship. In the observant eyes of the new scholar the massive Arnulfing was not only a majestic lord but a magnetic human being with reassuring foibles and fancies.

Years afterward Einhard described him, as he had been in the full tide of his energy.

"He was large and strong and of lofty height. The upper part of his head was round, his eyes very large and lively, nose a little long, and hair light, and face laughing and merry. Standing or sitting, he had a stately air, although his neck was thick and somewhat short, and his belly rather prominent. His step was firm, his bearing manly, and his voice clear, yet not so strong as you would expect from his size. . . .

"He went by his own inclinations rather than by the advice of physicians, whom he almost hated because they wanted him to give up roasts, which he relished, and to eat boiled meat instead.

"Charles could not easily deny himself food, and often complained that fasts injured his health. In eating he was moderate, and more so in drinking, for he hated drunkenness, especially in himself and his household. Rarely did he allow himself more than three cups of wine at a meal. He was fond of the roasts his huntsmen brought in on spits. While at table he liked to hear reading or music—reading aloud of the stories and deeds of old time. Yet he was fond as well of St. Augustine's books, and especially of the one titled *The City of God*.

177

"In summer after the noon meal, he would eat some fruit, drain a wine cup, put off his shoes and clothes, and rest for two or three hours. In the night, he had the habit of waking and rising from his bed four or five times. While dressing he would give audience to his friends, yet if the Count of the Palace told him of a lawsuit that needed his judgment, he had the parties brought in at once, and gave his decision. Wherever he might be, he would hear such a case."

To the studious Einhard, his king's ability to order affairs as if in judgment seat, while going about other matters appeared marvelous, as did his ready answers.

"Charles had the gift of quick speech, and saying everything with clearness. He was so eloquent he might have been a teacher, yet he held those who taught him in great esteem. With the deacon, Alcuin, the greatest scholar, he labored at studying rhetoric and especially astronomy. The king learned to reckon, and investigated the movements of the star bodies with a knowing scrutiny. He also tried to write, and used to keep tablets and blank pages in bed under his pillow, so he might train his hand to shape letters in hours of leisure. However, he began so late, he did not succeed in that . . .

"He used to wear the national—that is to say the Frank—dress. Next his skin he put on a linen shirt and linen trousers, and over these a tunic fringed with silk. Wrappings, held tight by bands, covered his legs, and shoes his feet, while he protected his chest in winter by a snug jacket of otter or marten skins. Over all he flung a blue cloak, girding on a sword that usually had gold in the hilt. He only carried a jeweled sword at feasts, or welcoming a strange ambassador. On high feast days he put on embroidered clothes, and fastened his cloak with a gold buckle, and wore as crown a diadem of gold and jewels."

While Einhard waited on his hero, another dwarfed figure appeared at the court at Worms. Pepin Hunchback left his haunt of Prüm to find the palace alien to him. Fastrada of the shimmering gold hair ruled the women, attended by ladies more splendidly robed and jeweled than his mother had ever been.

Women, in fact, filled the king's house, now that Pepin's half brothers held courts of their own in distant lands. Even the oldest, handsome and dull Charles, had been made duke of Maine by the river Loire (for Charles had not come up to his father's expectation as a battle leader).

After evensong when the king dismissed his paladins, the women buzzed about him on the palace lawn, like flies around a honey jar. They all flashed in new finery, as if each one held rank, bestowed by Charlemagne, and wore such finery to please his eyes.

The hunchback's father sat at ease on his field bench, on a tapestry woven with his name. *Carolus Rex*. A cross separated the words. He never tired of the girls' harp twanging and voice shrilling. They behaved like peacocks, conscious of their finery, dragging their trains over the wet grass after them. Rotrud had her straw hair bound with a purple fillet, and a gold chain around her neck.

The hunchback watched and listened, from the ground by the cup bearer's tables, where he might pass for one of the serving youths waiting to be called forward. Yet he was ten years older than these girls of Hildegard. Bertha, he noticed, kept back in the shadow of the colonnade, holding hands with the chaplain, Angilbert. She pulled an ermine cape over her white shoulders when the night dew fell. Candlelight flickered on gold, in her diadem, and gilt on her slim girdle.

When his father called her, Bertha came forward to give her song to the harp. "Across the hills—and through the valley's shade—they come, the tired travelers—with script and staff, they come—seeking peace beyond the hills—in the valley of Christ's peace."

So Bertha sang, tunefully, knowing well the words that Angilbert had written. Her father beat time with his heavy hand. This was his hour of rest and merriment.

The hunchback spied upon the splendid women. Crouched

179

in his corner, he noticed how a strapping woman-in-waiting kissed the king's hand secretively as she brought fruit to his bench. His hand caressed her leg.

They were wanton, these women, in pressing around their master, who gave out silver-set gems with open hand. Pepin wondered if Fastrada the queen observed their antics. He could not read her face.

Her brats in the sleeping chamber were all girls, with a hint of gold in their baby hair. Pepin thought that Fastrada might glitter like soft gold, yet her spirit might be hard as the rough stones of his cell at Prüm. Would a stone hurled against her head slay her?

Kneeling by the wall of the royal chapel at Mass, the hunchback heard the priest pray at the end, turning from the altar "For Charles the king, for his sons *Pepin* and Charles, for Pepin, king of the Lombards,and Louis, king of Aquitaine, for Fastrada the queen——"

His name came before hers, in the family. He had reached man's age without other title than a name mumbled in prayer. Pepin did not have the strength to dash a rock against the proud head of the queen. Yet he had friends who warned him, new friends who sought him out, who shared wine with him and listened courteously to his words, as if he had been favored and honored by his father. They warned him to speak no ill of Fastrada.

"There was one Hostlaic," whispered his friends, "who declared that Kriemhild, the Burgundian queen, had no greater longing to behold the bloody death of brave men than Fastrada, who slew the Thuringian nobles with her tongue's evil speech. This saying of Hostlaic's came to the notice of Fastrada, brought by her women spies. Truly, then the queen expressed great kindliness toward the before named Hostlaic, and gifted him with cakes prepared by her women. When this Hostlaic fell ill, she expressed her sorrow, and visited his bedside, vowing that she would summon her own physician to attend him. When she did so, the aforesaid physician found that Hostlaic departed from life unconfessed and un-blessed. My lord, do not speak an ill word against Fastrada."

Whether his friends spoke the truth, Pepin did not know. They took him to the table of a seigneur who gave him the high seat of honor. The maidens of this house brought wine first to Pepin. Around and below him sat mighty men, Thuringian comrades of the dead Graf Hardrad—Bavarian lords who had served Tassilo. They toasted the hunchback as the first-born and heir of the king. If God willed that the king should perish in the march to Avarland, his son Pepin should, in right, rule Frankland. So they said to him.

The hunchback hoped that a stone would crush Fastrada.

"In Holy Writ it is told how Abimelech, the son of Gideon by a concubine, slew with one stone his father and his seventy brothers," a priest of Bavaria related.

"Now it grieves me," observed another, "to hear it said at court how Himiltrud, the noble mother of Your Excellency, was only a concubine and no wife wedded to your father."

Pepin's anger lay against Fastrada and her court of women, not against his father.

"So long as Charles lives," they told him," she will go her way without mercy."

"After the death of Gideon, Abimelech reigned in glory."

Such feasting and talk left an impress on the mind of the hunchback. Better for him if he had stayed within the gardens of Prüm. He found himself a man grown, yet a stranger at his father's court. The other dwarfman, Einhard, gained esteem from the king by his prattle. Charlemagne was absorbed in gathering strength to attack the Avars. Alcuin, who would sit in talk and kindness with the hunchback, had finished a great Mass book with clear, good writing, for the king. So pleased was the king, Alcuin gained leave to visit his homeland of Britain.

Pepin's new friends banded about him in conspiracy. They carried small stones in their hands as a token of recognition, when they met. All of them were kind to Pepin Hunchback.

They showed him how to avoid the spite of Fastrada, by feigning sickness. Because he lay alone in a hostel by the river, he escaped the observation of the queen. His companions could visit him there, bringing royal gifts, and promising him that royal dignity would come to him.

For the king was riding forth to Ratisbon, to gather there the armed host of Frankland. If he ventured on into Avarland, anything might happen, even his death.

But certainly, said Pepin's friend's, Fastrada would be left behind, as at Eresburg in Saxonland, and her cruelty and pride would anger many bold lords. Then the nobles could rise against her, and Pepin could claim the throne, because he was worthiest of the sons of the king.

Pepin liked to watch these strange lords kneel by his bed. Not for many years had Pepin received such attention.

"Against the Avars," wrote Einhard, "the king made his greatest preparations, in the highest spirits."

After thirteen years Charlemagne was attempting what he had failed to accomplish in Spain—to lead a *Christian* army far against dangerous pagans. At Ratisbon (Regensburg) he proclaimed that he had decided "to call the Huns to account for their misdeeds against Holy Church and the Christian people."

To the Franks the mysterious nomads appeared to be Huns because they had drifted out of the unknown east. They had settled beyond the Danube on the debris of Attila's Hunnic domain. Moreover these squat horsemen with broad bony faces and hair plaited behind their ears seemed to be blood brothers to the disintegrated Huns. They had forced their way over the grass highways of the steppes, driving other people from their path, dwelling with their herds in the Hungarian fastness, where Christian missionaries had never set foot.

In that wilderness their khagan ruled a city hidden in the forest. Arno of Salzburg said it was called the Ring, being encircled by earth mounds where the pagans buried their dead. No one could understand their speech. (They were the first of the Mongol-Turk horse nomads to arrive in Europe.)

Kerold and the troopers, however, had plenty of gossip about this Ring. "Wide it is," they related, "as the land between Tours and the lake of Constance. High is its wall, of oak and yew logs—seven cubits high, and just as wide. Firm it is, with stones and binding clay. Within it the folk have their dwellings so close together that a man standing in one doorway can call to another in the next door. Thus, when the trumpets of the khagan peal from his vast palace of logs, their pealing summons may be heard for twenty leagues within this Ring, and the men all call from house to house, 'Take arms!'"

While not one of the Franks had seen the Ring, they understood very well just what it was like. Above all, they had heard the tale of its treasure. In old time the Goths had sacked Lombardy, and the Vandals had ferreted out the hidden riches of Rome, but they had passed on their way quickly enough. For two hundred years the Avars had raided all the Christian frontiers, carrying off the precious vessels of the churches, laying tribute on the emperors of Constantinople, besides gleaning ransom money for all their multitude of captives.

This treasure of theirs, after so many years, must be greater than the hoard of the Nibelungs, guarded by the wiles of the Rhine maidens. In fact, the more the henchmen discussed it, the more the treasure of the Avars came to resemble the gold of the Nibelungs.

Charlemagne did not deny this rumor of the treasure. A multitude of stark seigneurs, swordsmen, and peasant spearmen turned out to follow him to Avarland, to find the treasure. But, except for the mountain Bavarians, the king summoned only riders to his standard. No peasants could stand against the Avars, who moved like a storm cloud on their horses, tireless and ferocious.

The king's summons went far, even to Louis and the liege-men of Aquitaine. And he had reason to regret that soon enough. All that summer his war bands thronged the roads to Ratisbon, on the headwaters of the Danube. He decided to thrust three armies of great force, as in Bavaria, against the hidden horsemen. First, the Lombards and Italian Franks started up through the passes of the Carinthian Alps toward the Danube. Eric the count and Pepin the king led them.

Charlemagne led his own Rhinelanders down the right bank of the Danube. On the left bank young Thierry, the count, and Meginfried the Chamberlain brought on the Saxons, Thuringians, and Frisians.

On the river itself went Gerold and the Bavarians, floating down an armada of small craft laden with supplies. Where the river Inns joined the Danube this triple array halted for three days to sing litanies beseeching the Lord's aid "to preserve the army and chastise the Avars."

Then they descended the wide river that wound between forest walls down to the spreading valleys of the Avars. Although they found no roads the Franks forged ahead along the river trails, while Gerold's flotilla kept in touch with both banks. They came to village sites, finding only stray people and dogs. Burning the villages, and slaying what men they found in the forest growth, they quickened their march along the river.

All cattle and horses seemed to be gone from the hill pastures. After the autumn rains, they came upon networks of tracks, yet without other trace of the pagan horsemen. Charlemagne remembered how he had filed through the seemingly empty pass of Roncesvalles, where William of Toulouse had marked the emptiness as a bad omen.

Where the spur of the Wienerwald came down to the river (near modern Vienna) the outriders heard horns sounding. Ahead of them men moved through the forest mesh, shouting. They were the Lombards of Eric and Pepin the king.

These friends greeted the king's host with misgivings. Here

they had found barriers of felled trees and trenches above slopes of slippery clay. The place smelled of stale animals; the Avars had waited there to make a stand, but had gone east with their herds.

Down the river the Franks pursued, racing through the deserted settlements. They passed a great lake, with boats empty of men. October cold set in. Still the Avars escaped them.

At the river Raab Charlemagne camped in the mists. The Lombards had fought a battle, and taken captives and spoil. Luck seemed to favor them, because in the camp of the Franks an epidemic spread among the horses (which may have been poisoned by the natives). Daily more of the battle chargers died, until only a tenth of them survived.

With winter beginning and his horses decimated, Charlemagne gave the order to return, part of his host swinging south and part making its way north through Bohemia. The men returned safe, the annals say, "praising the Lord for so great a victory."

It was no victory. The pagan horde had escaped with its animals to the eastern plain, where lay the Ring, still hidden, with its treasure still untouched. Charlemagne needed that gold.

One thing he had done; he had marched into Avarland unchallenged. His Christian army had dispelled the old fear of the pagans and ended the legend of their power.

"Greeting and my love," he wrote to Fastrada from the road. "Thanks to God I am well, and safe. And I have glad tidings of my beloved son Pepin, who has taken spoil and captives from the Huns, who fled in fear at his approach. Now we hold a solemn litany to render thanks for our safe return. Our priests ask us to fast at this time, taking neither wine nor meat. All of us are giving alms, either of silver solidi or pennies, as we can afford. Each priest chanted fifty psalms, if he knew his psalter well enough. Then they walked with bared feet in procession.

"Now I wish you to consult with the clerics at home, to do the same. Yet be careful, please, not to do more than your slender strength allows you. It worries me that no letter has come from you. Please let me know how you fare, and whatever else you wish to tell."

He still held his Rhineland queen in affection, if not in love. Apparently he had lacked tidings from the palace at Ratisbon. His letter makes clear that he carried many sick with him in that retreat over the ancient Roman frontier road. Having lost most of their horses, his liegemen were forced to shoulder their packs and trudge afoot through the winter-bound valleys. They carried little spoil in their packs.

No rain or snow fell, and the beasts of the forest also were on the move toward distant water. The drouth continued. Smoke of burning underbrush covered the way, and at night fires glowed on the heights around them.

At the gate of Ratisbon, Fastrada greeted him without joy, saying that the coming of his hunchback son to court had been an ill omen. The hunchback behaved like a troll, hiding by the river, and habiting with night prowlers. And the half-pagan Bavarians were sacrificing slaves to sprinkle the human blood on their dried-up barley and cornfields.

Then Charlemagne heard how, during his absence in Avarland, disaster had struck in the Pyrenees. Louis, the studious, sickly boy, faced him with the lords of Aquitaine. They had marched east at the king's order, and when he had not needed their force, he had instructed them to await his return at Ratisbon. They told him of the slaughter and spoiling in southern Aquitaine.

At the March of the Pyrenees, his ten-year truce with Abd al Rahman had expired; the great emir of Córdoba died, and his successor summoned forth the Moorish host to a holy war. When Charlemagne disappeared into the east, the Moslems struck through the Pyrenees, sweeping on to Narbona, looting churches, enslaving village folk.

Before Narbona stark William of Toulouse made a stand

with old men and boys and peasants armed with scythes. Such fighters on foot could not stand against the Moslem horse. Then William held the wall of Narbona for a space, and again his followers were slaughtered. Narbona was ravaged. A third time he stood, before the gates of Carcassonne, and this time by his valor he slew the Moslem commanders and turned back the invaders. Yet Aquitaine grieved for its dead, while its army sat idle in Ratisbon at the king's bidding.

Charlemagne accepted responsibility for the new disaster. "The fault is mine, and no one else is to blame," he declared, and released the Aquitanians to hurry back to their ravaged frontier. His folly had undone the work of William, who had held fast to the Spanish side of the Pyrenees barrier, and now was forced back to the Garonne and his own city of Toulouse. Charlemagne praised the courage of this man who had turned back an invasion singlehanded.

More than that, when Charlemagne ungirded his sword with the gold hilt that night at his couch, he never put it on again to command his armies. Since thousands of Christians had died by his mistake, he would give command henceforth only to his masters of warfare, the valiant William, the good Gerold, and the sagacious Eric.

That night he lay awake long with lighted candle, turning the pages of Alcuin's Mass book, tracing out the words of prayer with his finger. He longed then for Alcuin, who was far away in Britain.

The night of the warning he was wakeful, listening for the bell that would call him to lauds. In midwinter the darkness lasted until the second hour of the day. His sandglass could not tell him how many hours had passed, when he heard the giggling and bustling of women in the antechamber.

Going to the curtain, he found a bevy of Fastrada's ladies half clad with hair undone, pushing at the outer door. "What are you after?" he demanded. (At least so the women told the queen.)

187

They thrust folds of their skirts into their mouths to stifle laughter, crying that it was a stripped, scraped, silly, and raving man trying to push through the door.

"What is he raving?"

"That he seeks your excellent presence. But he is quaking all over in shirt and hose——"

"Let him in and take yourselves out."

Remembering that he himself was in shirt and hose, the king of Frankland went back to his couch and candle. In came a heavy and shorn man, clad as the women said, panting and shivering with cold. "At each door," he cried, falling to his knees, "they tried to keep me from your beneficent presence—first the guards——"

"Now that you are here, drink wine, and speak sense."

The shivering man did that, speaking with the Lombard accent, giving his name as Fardulf, a poor deacon of St. Peter's church in the city, protesting that he had merely gone to light the altar candles for the dawn service when in the dark he had heard the armed men talking low at the very altar, talking of how they would cut down Charlemagne when he came as he did by custom to early prayer. They would make pretense of a drunken brawl and the blow would appear to be an accident.

Fardulf heard this because the swordsmen were cautioning each other how to act in the mock brawl. He hid behind the altar but they discovered him, stripping his robe from him and making him take oath that he would lie quiet where he was. Yet as he lay there, shivering with fear and cold, Deacon Fardulf bethought him how the conspirators would skewer him like a pig the moment the king was slain. He had crawled from the other end of the altar before they moved to the door. And he recognized some of the voices.

Charlemagne sent his palace guards to surround the church, to rouse Meginfried and Audulf, to man the streets at dawn with dependable Franks.

When the conspirators were caught in Ratisbon, the whole

of their scheme became known. They planned to slay the boy Louis with the king, while other armed bands attacked his other sons. Then they meant to bring forward Pepin Hunchback as the oldest son and true heir to the throne. It took weeks to round up all in the plot, at Eresburg and Pavia.

At an assembly of his liege lords in Ratisbon, the conspirators were tried and condemned to death. Charlemagne showed his mercy afterward only to Pepin, his son. The hunchback was sent under guard to his old cell at Prüm "for a little while." There he spent the rest of his life, alone, laboring in the gardens with his fancies for company.

Some of the accused cleared themselves by the will of God, after undergoing an ordeal. A few Charlemagne spared to go into exile. The rest died by the rope and the sword, or were blinded.

Although Fastrada could not attend the judgment hearings, she listened eagerly to the details of the deaths of the unfaithful liegemen. And she reminded the king how she had known that the troll-like Pepin, spawn of a concubine, would bring evil into the palace. How much more she had known about the conspiracy, he never could decide. For Fastrada was ambitious and her young girls could never inherit any part of the growing power of Frankland.

When it came time to reward the man who had saved him, Fardulf the Lombard, Charlemagne went to St. Peter's church to look at the altar where the deacon had hidden. It had the usual candlesticks, with a magnificent chalice on the altar cloth. Seeing this, Charlemagne was moved to give it to Fardulf—bestowing on the church another chalice of his own, instead. When he picked it up, admiring it, he noticed the inscription under the lovely inlaid figures—*Tassilo Dux Fortis*.

This chalice, finer than any Charlemagne owned, had been given by the "Brave Duke Tassilo." Replacing it moodily on the altar, he went to root in the chest where Meginfried kept gold armlets and such for gifts. A handful of these he bestowed on Fardulf. But he watched over the honest deacon, and in later years appointed him abbot of St. Denis. Charlemagne never forgot loyal service by an outlander.

It seemed just then as if Fastrada's prophecy of evil was coming to pass in Frankland. In the dry, baked earth the seed of the next spring's planting did not sprout, and hunger began along the southern borders. It entered the Burgundian land. The king warned his abbots and counts to send grain south by ox-cart, well guarded. At the Beneventan border there was conflict again.

For that year, 792, in the rising tide of tribulations, the royal annals relate: "The Saxons revealed what had been hidden this long time in their hearts. As dogs go back to their vomit, so did they return to the paganism they had spewed out of them. Again they forsook Christianity, lying to God and to the lord king who had so greatly benefited them. Joining with the pagans of other lands, burning down their churches, seizing or slaying their priests, they turned wholeheartedly to the worship of idols."

Beyond the Elbe the Slavs took to arms, and on the coast the Frisians revolted.

It seemed to the Arnulfing as if the Lord, as with Job, had sent many tribulations upon his land. With all his energy he fought against the creeping starvation and spreading unrest. When his villas and abbeys had no more grain to send to stricken areas, he ordered his officers to give out their silver coins, until the next harvest; he set a fixed price upon bread. Realizing his lack of transport, he hurried the building of wooden bridges over the river crossings, and even started bridging the Rhine at the Mainz junction.

On his journeys by boat, he had noticed how narrowly were separated the headwaters of the Rhine and Danube in his new highlands. He ordered the peasantry there to dig a canal to link up these great waterways. And, ceaselessly, he importuned Alcuin to return. Without his mentor, he felt hampered in his labors. Fastrada could not aid him with the famine as Hildegard had done.

The Treasure of the Avars

When Alcuin demurred at leaving his homeland, Charlemagne urged and persuaded him, and gifted him with the abbey of St. Martin at Tours, where the finest books were being copied in the scriptorium. The abbey, he wrote, needed Alcuin as much as his distressed king David.

"A friend such as he," the gentle Celt explained to his own people, "is not to be denied by one like me."

Even in his beloved York, Alcuin had missed the gay evenings of the Frankish Academy where observation of the stars was mellowed by the quaffing of wine. "Here the wine in our casks is all spent," he wrote to the Rhineland. "Only sour beer foams in our stomachs. Drink for us, then, and make your days joyous. But for my ills, good physicians, send two loads of wine, fine and clear. Send at least one!"

When Alcuin's tall, stooped figure appeared in the hall of Worms, Charlemagne ordained a night of festivity. King David had recovered his lost friend. He need no longer dictate his questions to scribes.

Master Alcuin brought gifts of rare books, and the copy of a map of the world, as well as the friendship of King Offa. It seemed to the sensitive scholar that the growing power of the Frank could protect and enrich the needy king of Mercia. To this hope he held more urgently, when he heard of the devastation of the Northmen who came from the sea to destroy the peaceful church and monastery of Lindisfarne. "Never since we dwelt in Britain have we suffered such terror from a heathen race. Never did we think such an invasion of ships would come to pass. Think—only think you of the church of holy Cuthbert spattered with the blood of its priests! Think of this glorious place ravaged by pagans."

In his grieving for the lost monastery, Alcuin cried out against the sins of the British princes. "Their fornication, adultery, and incest filled the land. Think whether such bad habits of theirs have not brought on us this unheard-of evil!"

With his own tribulations heavy upon him, Charlemagne wondered whether such sins did not bring such visitations.

Alcuin, in his sorrow, believed so. He knew of signs that heralded the disaster—blood falling in a rain on the roof of St. Peter's church in York. Then the wanton splendor of dress of the nobles, and the arraying of their hair, had mocked at God. "They stagger on, weighed upon by their extravagance, while others perish of cold. A Dives, robed in purple, sinks himself in joys and feasting while a Lazarus dies of hunger at his door!"

Humbly Charlemagne listened to such inspired eloquence. His own untaught mind could not grasp such swift elucidation of happenings. He could only visualize clearly the tasks to be done to meet need, the bridging of rivers, the seizing of draught animals to draw carts, the sharing of hoarded food. Alcuin beheld in him a power as a defender of Christians who, alone, could help the churches of Britain.

It did not occur to the Frank that he had taken many score of needed yoked oxen to draw the sledges bearing the marble columns of Ravenna from the Alps to the foundation of his new church at Aquis Granum. Or that Meginfried slaughtered many sheep and cows each day to provide four courses of meat for the throngs within his own palace. He had set his mind on the building of the great church, and he could not refuse food to the crowd of pilgrims and wandering folk that pressed into his gates.

Yet he wondered if there were not some clear sign by which God would give him evidence of approval as well as anger. Alcuin could tell him.

"You have named the signs of God's anger in Britain," he said. "What, then are the signs of his loving approval?"

Gently the Celt shook his head. "They are not to be named, but you will know them."

"How?"

"There was one who sought to find God present upon the earth around him. He searched and he saw only the water of the sea, the depths of the abyss, the four-footed running animals, the winged birds, and the multitude of creeping things. When he found no sign of God, he cried at all these things around him, 'Tell me something of God.' And then they all shouted together, 'He made us!' "

The famine spread from the south to the northern river valleys and forests. Charlemagne fought it by edict and by example. When multitudes of families forsook their villages to seek the king's villas he ordered them to be fed with game and stored-up cheese. Among them he rode, shouting his assurance that the Lord would not suffer his people to starve. Merry and sleepless, he cried at them, "Think—the Lord, who made you, will send food on the wings of ravens. So he did with Elijah."

It seemed as if the Devil had crept into Frankland. Armed bands raided homesteads to carry off food. Charlemagne gave out an edict never known before—that weapons could not be carried but must be surrendered to his officers, to be stored in arsenals. No weapons could be taken out of his frontiers to be sold to foreign folk or pagans.

His borderlands were in tumult again. He called on the wardens for greater efforts, and marked off every frontier zone as if it were a country in itself—the Spanish March, the Breton March, the Dane March (or Mark) the Elbe, and the great East March. No longer did he venture thither. Instead he sent the armed levies to the wardens, to William, Audulf, Gerold, and Eric in Friuli. They were more able than he to defend the Lord's frontiers.

Praising them, he told his liegemen the tale of *Eishere* (who never existed). "Why should I go to subdue pagans when I have nobles like Eishere to do it for me?"

The circumstance that no one ever met Eishere in person did not detract from the renown of this hero, who was described by the king himself. Eishere, it was said, not only swam foaming rivers, he forced a channel through the ice of mountain torrents. In himself he was quite an army, a terrible army. "Eishere mows down Bohemians and Slavs and Avars

193

as if reaping hay—he spits them on his spear like birds on a roasting spit. How did he fare against the Winides? Why, all you homekeeping sluggards ought to hear him tell about the Winides! When he came back from carrying seven or eight of them around on his spear, he said, 'I am tired of their squealing when I carry them around. Why should I have been bothered about such tadpoles? My lord king and I ought never to have been asked to weary ourselves fighting against such worms.' "

Against the Saxons, Charles the king's son was sent—with experienced commanders. "Take their leading families, take more than before, as hostages for peace."

The Avars drifted back to the ravaged valley of the Danube. Warily they sent envoys to discover what the Franks were doing, and what might be in the mind of the remarkable Christian king. Too long had these Avars lived by spoiling, off the fat of the eastern lands; their fierceness had died in them. Charlemagne feasted the envoys, and filled their arms with gifts of his remaining gold. He made them drunk, and baptized them, and sent them away honored and impressed. And in them he created a cell favorable to the rule of the mighty Christian king. As with the Bavarians, there grew up in time a party among the Avars favorable to Charlemagne.

"They will come into God's grace," he prophesied, and gave the mission of converting them to his old antagonist Arno, the Eagle of Salzburg.

To Arno the eager Alcuin wrote, "If God's grace is inclining to their kingdom, who dares refuse them the ministry of salvation?"

But Charlemagne also strengthened Gerold, keeper of their frontier, and started building stout bridges across the upper Danube, to open a new way for his horsemen to Avarland.

In these years of crisis his *missi dominici* rode without sparing themselves or their horses. For once they had no thought except to carry out the king's will. Not to do so meant

194

death. "Obey!" they cried at fox-hunting abbots, and tippling landgrafs. For once they carried the king's presence with them. "Rid yourselves of foulness and fine garments! Will you feast, when hunger waits at the gate?"

When these king's messengers met nobles wearing the fine new short cloaks, gayly striped—copied from the Basque— they told what Charlemagne said of them. "What good are these little napkins? You can't cover yourselves with them in sleeping, or shield yourselves with them on horseback from wind or rain."

Charlemagne rode in his faded blue wool mantle, with his daughters following in the armed escort. Their young Valkyrie voices rose over him at evensong. He rode with despair in his heart through a tortured land. His laughing presence gave strength to his weary people.

He told them their land would be blessed by the Lord after tribulations ceased. At Aquis Granum the springs kept the valley green and the crops growing. "Here is a sign of the Lord's loving mercy," he said.

At the rising walls of the cathedral church, he said it would not be dedicated to St. Martin, patron of the Franks, or to St. Arnulf, ancestor of his family, but to the most merciful Mother of God. It would be raised by them in thanksgiving, this Mary Church.

As his presence brought assurance, his detailed planning for a better morrow carried conviction. Human beings cling, unreasonably, to hope. And in that time of stress Charlemagne became the personification of their hope. Their future lay in him.

He turned aside from no obstacle because he felt a responsibility laid upon him to go on. He had changed in some way from the man who led the parade of power through empty Avarland. Lacking the ability of a great king, he played the part of a great king.

This had a certain effect on him. For the first time he realized that his proper place was in the center of things.

By remaining at the mid-point of his communications—such as they were—he would keep in touch with all frontiers, and send officers to remedy a far-off situation, whereas in his early years he had thought only of journeying there himself. So, to win success in Lombardy, he invited failure in Saxony; absent in Avarland, he had lost the line of the Pyrenees.

With the single-minded Frank such an idea had immediate consequences, although not what might be expected. No sooner had he perceived the advantage of a centralized personal government than he decided to confine it to one city. He would have, as it were, a Rome in Frankland.

Now the geographical center of his domain might have been at the Silver City (Strassburg) or even Geneva. Yet Charlemagne selected the still to be built Aquis Granum. Perhaps he was drawn to its warm bathing pools and hunting preserves; perhaps he was unwilling to move from his homeland of the Rhine-Meuse valleys. Whatever his reasoning, there is no mistaking his determination to make Aquis Granum his capital city, and so it became, under the more familiar names of Aix or Aachen.

To ornament his new city he requested permission from Hadrian to take out of Ravenna the great and unwieldy statue of Theodoric the Great. The royal annals say, of 794, "The king went back to the palace which is called *Aquis,* and there celebrated the nativity of the Lord, and Easter."

It is related also how Fastrada the queen died in that year, and was entombed with honor at St. Albans, in Mainz. He did not bury the woman who had caused so much strife at St. Arnulf's beside Hildegard. Her epitaph was written by a new friend, Theodulf the Goth, and it contained only cold praise. His liegemen of Frankland felt only relief at the passing of the conspiring queen.

Charlemagne never allowed another person to overinfluence him. He took in marriage Liutgard, a woman of simple mind, no older than Rotrud. The girl, who may have been his mistress, was carefully schooled by Angilbert in the duty of royalty, and taught to read with skill. She was gentle, and loved by Alcuin, who beheld in her "a woman devoted to God."

Perhaps the king beheld in Liutgard the image of docile Hildegard, the girl of thirteen who had handfasted him at the fair in Aix. For Liutgard's shy personality had been shaped in his homeland. And Charlemagne's instinct, just then, seemed to be drawing him back to the wellsprings of his life.

In the chaotic years from 792–95 he fought with all his strength not to conquer new domains but to preserve his original kingdom of Frankland, his heritage and his responsibility. He returned to the companionship of his Frankish liegemen, ignoring the demands of "the foreigners." Aix itself lay secluded in a valley filled with memories of the chanting scops, of his ancestral villas, and hunting. Charlemagne was thankful to preserve his kingdom. He was not to be allowed, however, to enjoy it.

He had set in motion forces that would oblige him, to move outward again from his Rhine-Meuse sanctuary. First the wardens of his marches restored peace of a sort along the frontiers. The Saxons were kept from combining with the Avars. And from Avarland came tidings so startling they seemed to be almost miraculous.

Pepin and his Lombard warriors fought their way back to the Danube. The Bavarian host crossed the new bridges to join them. Avar princes who resisted were wiped out. The nomads broke into factions, killed their khagan. Arno of Salzburg led in his priests, vowing to do as the first apostles had done, to "teach the untaught before converting them."

Savage Serbs and Croats harassed the weakening Avars. Through this disintegration, Eric of Friuli drove his armed host over the Theiss—where Charlemagne had not been able to go—to the heights beyond the Hungarian plain. A Slav chieftain showed Eric the way to the hidden Ring.

Into the earth mounds and log walls of the Ring Eric broke his way, seizing the treasure of the Avars.

In fifteen carts, each drawn by four oxen, Eric was bringing this treasure, with the submission of the Avars, to Charlemagne at Aix.

Nothing could have stirred the centers of Christendom more than the news. Alcuin, overjoyed, sent praise to Eric for "his arm, valiant against the foes of the Lord's name." To Alcuin it appeared that the triumph had been gained by the wisdom and force of his king David. "Surely Christ has brought beneath the feet of your soldiers the Hunnic peoples, so dreaded of old for their savagery and courage."

Theodulf, the Gothic poet, wrote exultingly, "He has come to Christ, this Hun with braided hair. He is submissive in faith, he who was so fierce."

Arno, the intrepid, sent his missions "around the lake of Balaton, beyond the river Raab, even to the Drave, where it joins with the Danube."

It seemed to religious souls that the hand of the Lord was manifest in the humbling of these most dangerous pagans.

So Charlemagne found himself hailed as victor in the one war that he had not led himself, and recognized as the creator of the "Christian army" that he had failed to shape in years gone by.

More than that, the Avar treasure proved to be rich beyond expectations. The diligent Dwarfling, Einhard, voiced his amazement. "No such spoil of money and treasured things was ever brought to the Franks in the memory of man. So much gold and silver was found in the khagan's palace, or taken from the camps in battle, that these Huns must have been years amassing it."

That was certainly true. Like Attila's Huns, the eastern nomads had hoarded their gleanings—fine church vessels and bullion bars, gold paid in ransom, and the richest stuffs given in bribes for more than two centuries. Out of Eric's oxcarts poured gold glass, Persian brocades, Byzantine pearl-sewn silks, crystalware, jeweled weapons, carved emeralds, sapphires, forgotten crowns and scepters, hangings of sheer cloth of gold.

The treasure yielded specimens of art never beheld before by Charlemagne or his goldsmiths and metal workers of Aix. The rarity and skill of all this eastern work caught Charlemagne's attention, and he set some of his artisans to copying it, if they could. Here, at one stroke, he obtained magnificent decoration for his new cathedral.

The bulk of the treasure he gave out generously, as he had not done in Fastrada's time. It rewarded Eric's followers and all who had proved faithful. It refilled the depleted chests of his churches, and adorned their altars from Ratisbon to Toulouse. It went across the water to the cathedrals of Britain, to Alcuin's joy. King Offa received a jeweled sword, with Charlemagne's friendship.

To this imperial bounty, Liutgard added her gifts. At Aquileia on the far eastern sea, Paulin the bishop learned in a letter from Alcuin that "My daughter the queen, a devoted woman, has dispatched two armlets of gold to you, asking you to pray for her."

For Hadrian, his critic and advocate, at St. Peter's, Charlemagne set aside fitting gifts from the Avar hoard. Then he heard that the aged Hadrian was dead. Charlemagne wept and wrote in mourning for "his sweet co-father" to the Pope succeeding Hadrian.

Despite their differences, during their unusual relationship, the brilliant Hadrian and the forthright king had sustained each other. Without Hadrian, Rome was to become a very different place.

At the same time Charlemagne lost the companionship of Alcuin. For the schoolmaster of the Franks, feeling his years, could no longer endure the ceaseless activity and festivity of the court. He begged leave to retire to his new abbey at St. Martin's, in Tours, and the king allowed him to go, knowing that Alcuin would still be within reach of letters.

Quartering himself in his half-finished palace of Aix, pacing through the unpaved courtyard leading to the side door of his Mary Church, Charlemagne found throngs waiting for his passing. When he climbed to the small gallery, folk from all the distant lands crowded into the space below to appeal to him.

They were his new subjects, the Christian people. But what, in reality, was Charlemagne?

After careful thought—for the letter shows the pondering of every word—he wrote to the new Pope: "I made a covenant of co-fatherhood with your blessed predecessor . . . it is our duty, with God's aid, to defend everywhere externally with our arms the Church of Christ from the invasions of pagans and the devastation of the unfaithful, and internally to strengthen it by our recognition of the Catholic faith. It is yours, most holy Father, to help our warfare with hands upraised like Moses in prayer, so that . . . the Christian people may win, always and everywhere, the victory over the enemies of the Lord's holy name."

It was a great responsibility that Charlemagne so expressed. It invoked no kingly authority or imperial power but laid down a task to be carried out. It called for the creation of a new rule in the west of Europe, the fulfillment of Augustine's prophecy of the coming of the city of God.

To make this vision a reality was a most difficult task. To carry it out, the barbarian Frank set to work with all his untiring energy.

Chapter VIII

CROWN OF EMPIRE

At the start Charlemagne found he had no aid from his clergy. Yet without the efforts of his priests, he could not influence the mass of his peoples.

The ancestors of the Franks had been handy with axes. Their broad-bladed axes served them well, to hurl at an enemy or to clear forests. Like their kinsmen the Danes and the Norse, these pioneer Franks could turn a strip of forest into a tillable field and build a house with a smoke hole in the roof and a beaten clay floor between the spring thaw and the autumn frost.

Naturally they sought the rich soil of riverbanks, adjacent to the easily traveled highway of the water, which supplied them with fish, to be salted and dried for winter food. Using axes and *scramasaxes,* they put together skiffs and coracles of dried hides readily enough. From Roman ruins they obtained bricks, iron joint bars, and possibly some lead pipe. A freeman's house sheltered his cow, pigs, and watchdog, or—if he were wealthy—his horse. His wife, if she were clever, might add woven wall hangings and white linen to their furnishings of cooking pots and spits, and the hand-hewn table or bed. An artistic husband might carve the bedposts or chair backs with designs of crosses, swastikas, or haloed saints.

Being in so far self-sufficient this freeman usually liked his farm to be independent of others, off by his own river and oak grove; he was quite willing to walk several leagues with his family to the neighboring village, to drink ale at a fair or saint's festival, to buy his wife a mantle clasp, or take her to communion. By Charlemagne's time this typical Frank was in the way of becoming a farmer more than a warrior, a villager instead of a clansman. He clung stubbornly, however, to his inalienable right to speak in a lawsuit, to drink more than his fill, and to keep his property for his sons. Urban life appeared to his independent spirit to be voluntary imprisonment; he had no notion what it would mean to be a citizen of a *state*. As for the Roman Empire, he understood it to be a legend like the feats of Beowulf, although it left vestiges like the broken aqueduct at the Colony from which good building stone could be carted up to the new monastery at Fulda, beloved of St. Boniface.

To the seigneurs, farmers, and serfs of nebulous Frankland, the churches and monasteries had become the dispensaries of all invention, science, and salvation. They had replaced Wotan worship—not entirely, however, and not everywhere— as the bridge to life after death which had formerly been found in Valhalla. Moreover, as the village hundred-man laid down the law to settle disputes, the village priest cured illness by the touch of holy relics, and gave souls to infants by baptism. The parish school might even teach sons of landlords and lay brothers how to work metal—Einhard had mastered this art at Fulda—make wine, shape letters, or intone a Pater Noster. An archbishop's school in a great city like Frankfurt (Frankonovurd) with more than a thousand inhabitants might perfect the brighter students in reading, along with ways to exorcise demons.

Too often if a church possessed a complete writing of the Scriptures, which was seldom the case, the precious bound leaves would be zealously encased in fine painted leather, or polished, jeweled wood, to be left untouched on the altar and properly venerated, but never read. When a shorn priest read aloud a psalm, he usually repeated what he remembered rather than what he saw in the interwoven letters that ran words together. As for the lay nobles, rarely could one sign his name. Charlemagne himself still made a large cross with a *K* and *R* at the ends. War heroes did not require an education, and a successful farmer used his leisure to brew beer or watch the girls dancing——

It will be apparent that Charlemagne was failing in his effort to restore the minds of his people. Outside of his own increasing children—now including Fastrada's flaxen-haired girls and Rothaid, who had no official mother—and the disciples like Einhard, the Palace School and Academy taught few younglings the mysteries of Euclid and the healing art of Hippocrates. Elsewhere the chosen few like Alcuin and Arno shed illumination by sheer force of personality. Charlemagne, however, refused to admit failure.

Since he could not reach the multitudes who now looked to him, he demanded that his churches do so. "Preach, or leave your benefice."

"There was a certain bishop," related the monk of St. Gall, who did not seem to favor bishops, "with carpets in his hall, and hangings on his walls, and a cushion upon his chair, and precious purple silk on his body, who ate of the finest morsels his pastry cooks and sausage makers could serve on a service of gold plate. Once the most religious emperor Charles ordered all bishops throughout his domains to preach in the nave of their cathedral before a certain day, or be deprived of their episcopal dignity. Well, this before mentioned bishop was alarmed because he had no learning except gluttony, and he feared likewise he would lose his soft living.

"So after the lesson was read on that festal day, he climbed into the pulpit as if he were going to preach to the people, who all crowded up in wonder at such an unheard-of happening. They all did so, that is, except one poor redheaded fellow who had covered his head with cloths because he was

203

ashamed of his red hair. Now the bishop saw him and called to the doorkeeper, 'Bring me that churl who covers his knob, there by the door of my church.'

"The doorkeeper seized the poor churl and dragged him up, because he struggled, fearing the terrible bishop would inflict a doomful penalty on him for standing with covered head in the house of God. But that bishop, bending down from his perch, now calling to his congregation and now bawling at the poor knave, began to preach as follows: 'This way with him! Don't let him slip! Willy-nilly, lout, you've got to come! Nay, closer.' Then he snatched off the headcloths and cried to the people: 'Lo here, behold all ye people—the boor is redheaded!' Then he went hastily back to the altar and performed the office, or pretended to perform it.

"When the emperor Charles, who knew his lack of skill, heard how he had made an effort to say something, to obey the order, he allowed that bishop to keep his bishopric."

Driven to expedients, the king of the Franks produced some ingenious aids to learning. When the new organ arrived from Constantinople he had it taken apart and copied, so that in his great churches "bellows of oxhide blew through pipes of brass with the roaring of thunder and clashing of cymbals."

"Sing truly the words that glorify the Lord," he demanded of the palace choir, and sang with them.

"Have the Gospels copied clearly, not by idle youths but by careful older men," he urged the writers of the monastic scriptoria. Massive, lengthy Bibles might be few and rare, but the Gospels, and especially the counseling of Paul—that grand preacher—spoke to everyone. At Tours, Alcuin labored nights with his writers, to spread the Gospels through the churches of the dominions.

Charlemagne's admonitions struck like the snap of a whip against ease and worldly sport in monasteries and nunneries. (Did he not have the same inclinations?) Abbots and abbesses are forbidden to keep hounds, falcons, or jugglers. No abbess might write or forward love letters. No monk might turn from his calling to filthy money.

To sin is human, he admitted, but to keep on sinning is diabolical. His belief held fast to fundamentals; he did not understand the ideals of Plato, or the temporizing of the philosophers.

"Preach," he stormed at his clerics, "how the impious will be cast into flames by devils. Declare, how the righteous will live forever with Christ."

They failed to do it. In their efforts, they mumbled catchwords, snatches of prayer, ejaculations to repent. Many of them were sons of lay lords, feeding themselves from the churches. Their narrowed minds could not take in the mystery of life, the immensity of divine power.

When he realized that, Charlemagne ordered the sermons to be painted on all church walls, showing to the eyes of all comers the dark red flames of hell, the joyful white and gold of the sphere of heaven.

And he preached himself. Faring from church to market place, and fairground, he gave forth the Word, from king to people. Believe and be saved. Salvation does not come from works alone, although those are good, but from faith. No circuit rider of later days voiced the Evangel with more persuasion and fury.

"Jesus Christ our Lord will reign forever. I, Charles, by the grace and mercy of God, king of the Franks and defender of Holy Church, give greeting and peace to all orders of ecclesiastical piety or secular power, in the name of Jesus Christ our eternal Lord——"

Shouting, holding congregations in fear and longing, he preached salvation through the darkened lands.

This is the paradox of Charles—*Charlemagne*. A half-taught brute, taking strange women as he lusted for them, gorging meat after sunset on fast days, tricking his friends, he contrived to master all who opposed him. That was Charles the boar hunter, the Arnulfing. Charles the Hammer did not have his force—Pepin the Short did not have his guile.

Yet that same man honored his father and mother, never blasphemed, gave away his possessions, championed "the Lord's poor"—and felt personal responsibility for all human beings under his rule. That was the *Charlemagne* who grew into a legend.

This dualism came, it seems, from a simple circumstance. The half-educated Frank believed every word of religion. When he read the first words of the letter to the Ephesians of "Paul, an apostle of Jesus Christ by the *will of God*," he believed that the same will of God had created him king. Being thereby leader of the churches of Frankland, he felt himself bound to preach, and, as king, to be first of the preachers. He said that very clearly himself at the head of the so-called *Carolingian Books.* "Having received from the Lord, in the bosom of the Church, the government of our kingdom, we must strive with all our force, with Christ's aid, to defend it and upraise it so as to deserve to be called by the Lord *a good and faithful servant.*"

Not pietism or a mere sense of responsibility made him say that. Other monarchs, as barbarian as Theodoric, the great Goth, or cultured as Marcus Aurelius had been moved by those impulses. His own son Louis would be known as Louis the Pious. Charlemagne differed from all of them.

He tried to carry out the bidding of the Bible—"with all our force." Above other needs he put the "gathering in the harvest of God's fields."

In attempting to do so, this peasant-born monarch gained an insight into the people around him vouchsafed to few in less stormy ages. He saw humanity as a whole. He saw himself as one man among many in distress which it was his duty to relieve.

From our vantage point of later years and greater sophistication, we realize that he attempted an impossible task. But in his mind the task was not impossible, if Christ aided him.

It was only necessary to find a practical way of doing it.

As he had taken to the saddle, when troubled in his youth, he rode the rounds of his churches now, to the pealing of the new organs, the orison of newly trained voices, with feasting far into the night and prayer at break of dawn—a manner of evangelizing that exhausted Alcuin, who spoke longingly of the great good achieved by writing, especially by such learned souls as Augustine and Jerome.

"Would I had twelve clerics as learned and wise as they!" Charlemagne burst out in reply. (So the tale is told of him.)

"The Lord God, who made heaven and earth," cried Alcuin in exasperation, "was content with two such men—and you ask for twelve!"

At this time the king was well content because an Avar *tudun,* a nomad prince, came in to make submission to the victorious Christian, and accept baptism—which the Avars realized went with submission. Charlemagne attended the baptism, and acted as godfather. (In his time such spiritual sponsorship carried much more responsibility than today.) He also rewarded the new Avar convert lavishly with Avar gold.

By then, however, Alcuin began to have misgivings about Charlemagne's method of mass conversion of pagans by force. Not that he questioned the king's right to subdue unbelievers by war.

It remained for Charlemagne himself to question that right and he did so very carefully. By canon law—the law he sought to enforce—it was a sin to wage war to gain territory or increase power. The blessing of Jesus Christ came with peace, not strife. Who could even imagine Christ the Lord returning again to earth in the carnage of a battlefield?

Believing that, or moved by instinctive strategy, Charlemagne led out his armed host not to war but to avoid battle if possible. Against the Christian Lombards he had the justification that he was going to the aid of the apostolic lord of St. Peter's; against the devout Bavarians he managed to carry

207

Hadrian's mandate, that the Bavarians would be guilty of sin if they resisted him. Even in pagan Spain and Avarland he contrived to avoid ordinary warfare. (Roncesvalles, the Süntal, and Narbona were fought far from his presence, although he accepted responsibility for them.) Both Einhard and the monk of St. Gall mention that his remarkable marches toward subjection were "bloodless—or almost so."

Many commentators, including Napoleon Bonaparte, have praised the Arnulfing for a military genius he never possessed. He did show consummate ability in gaining his objectives without battle. Judged by the standards of his time, he acted within his rights.

Against the Saxons, however, he used brutality. His persuasive strategy had no effect on the people of Irminsul.

Alcuin's misgivings were caused not by his king's campaigns but by his missionary efforts. The schoolmaster solved the riddle of Saxon resistance. It was caused by the priests who marched in with the soldiers, to baptize an ignorant people in rivers and demand Christian conduct straightway, with payment of tithes to the priests, under threat of damnation. All this might well cause the Saxons to turn back to their harmless, invisible gods of the forest. And if they persisted in doing so, what might be expected of the Avars?

In deep anxiety he wrote to his beloved Arno, head of the Avar mission: "Now preach righteousness rather than exact tithes. A new spirit in people needs to be nursed with the milk of apostolic kindness until it grows strong enough to take solid food. The tribute of a tenth, they tell me, is overturning the faith of the Saxons. It is better to lose tithes than faith. Why must we place a yoke on the necks of ignorant men that we and our brethren could not bear?"

It was one thing to write thus to the experienced Eagle of Salzburg, and quite another to admonish the determined Charlemagne. Yet Alcuin attempted it, through Meginfried, in stinging words. Let the clerics in Saxonland heed how they took money; let them be not so eager to exact tithes, inflict retribution for any offense, or demand what the untaught Saxons cannot perform. "Really, let them learn from the apostles to be revealers and not stealers."

Nothing came of this, and Alcuin dared remonstrate with the king himself. Carefully he began his plea by picturing what joy would come with the Judgment Day if throngs of Saxons followed the "most happy king" toward the throne of Christ. (An astute appeal to the heart of an evangelist.) But, continued Alcuin, despite the toil and devotion of the king, the election of the Saxons did not seem to have been, as yet, of God. So, "give to these conquered peoples new teachers who shall feed them, as babes, with milk. Tithes may be good, but it is better to lose them than to lose the faith of souls. Remember what St. Augustine taught. Let a man be taught and brought to faith, and then—and only then—be baptized."

Charlemagne went his way in Saxonland, unheeding. Grieving, the Celt wrote Arno, "What is gained by baptism without faith? A man can be driven to baptism; you cannot drive him to faith."

Yet, after twenty-four years' struggle, Charlemagne was bent on driving the Saxons to faith. His angered tenacity matched the Saxons' will to resist. He stormed against "Saxon faithlessness" when they fought for independence. When he had envisioned a Christian community, the Saxons had ceased to be Christians; when he sought, as he now did, to return to the hegemony of his grandsire, Charles Martel, of the Germanic, Rhineland peoples, across the Rhine itself stood the Saxons in arms against him. Within the heart of his domain—as he saw it—they joined their strength to the pagan Slavs and Avars.

Inexorably, during the years 794–98, he drove his armed forces back into the familiar roads of Saxonland, regaining Paderborn, wintering again on the Weser, until the army of his son Charles broke through anew to the Baltic shore.

But this time Charlemagne tried a new expedient. First he took one third of the men of the hamlets as hostages; then he began to uproot hundreds of families from their forests to resettle them in the Rhine-Loire valleys. Having failed to subdue the Saxons, he started to transplant them.

Wherever he failed, the tireless Arnulfing wrestled with failure and wrung from it a success peculiarly his own. His river the "swift, foaming Rhine" had never been bridged and —so his people said—could not be bridged. At Mainz his bridgework was swept away by floods. He sank barges filled with stones upstream, drove down wooden piers, anchored then to the shores with stonework, and bridged the Rhine.

His Franks had no skill at architecture. He gave one of them, Master Odo, the plan of Justinian's church at Ravenna, small and eight-sided. Master Odo did not succeed in building another St. Vitale, but the Mary Church stood entire and wonderful at Aix. It had hardly been built, as the old soldiers gabbed, in one day before dark at Charlemagne's demand. Yet the driving of the Arnulfing had it finished, with plates of gold and silver and notable paintings on the walls, in four years, instead of four generations. Folk came from the Frisian marshes and the shrines of the Province to wonder at it.

No one in Frankland had skill to cast or carve a statue. Yet between the Mary Church and the palace shone the bright brazen statue of Theodoric, the good Goth, on his horse, as if copied from life.

From Aix the missionaries went forth, beyond the Elbe and the neighboring Slavs to the wild Sorbs (Serbs) and Croatians.

Far off in southern Italy young Grimwald, the Beneventan, had married a Byzantine princess and declared himself at last to be "as I have always been, a free man." To remedy that, Charlemagne sent the brilliant Angilbert.

In the west the Pyrenees were lost to the Moslems. To courageous William of Toulouse the king sent stark liegemen who aided him to win back, patiently, month by month, the frontier towns and mountain passes.

Far in the east the pagan Avars fought against Arno's missions. Eric of Friuli went up to subdue them, with the baptized *tudun*. The pagan chieftains died, or migrated to the steppes.

Thus in all the communities of the west, Charlemagne had become a force. His *missi* carried the master's urging as far as the Istrian churches on the Dalmatian shore. "Charles' men" gathered in the churches with new hope.

But what was Charlemagne?

Paladins who labored beside him hardly asked that question. They had time and thought to do no more than carry out the lord king's will. Arno, at grips with Avarland, did not pause to ask it.

The man who asked it of himself, in the seclusion of St. Martin's cloister, was Alcuin. For Alcuin, never free from illness, felt the end of his life coming near. Tours lay beyond the Frankish homelands, close to the ancient southern Gaul, where memories of the Empire remained. Moreover Alcuin's tireless mind kept in touch by letter with changing personalities and events throughout the dominion that had as yet no identity. He remained Charlemagne's unofficial minister if no longer his mentor.

Although he kept his sense of humor, the Briton was changing his viewpoint as the time of his atonement for life's sins drew near. No man had quoted Virgil's verses more readily than he, but now he censored the reading of such "pagan poetry." It amused him to think how the new ban on pantomimes at court would disappoint Angilbert, who enjoyed theatricals. Yet the theater was, as Augustine related, an invention of the Devil.

It troubled Alcuin that Charlemagne would take no heed of the needs of the Anglo-Saxon kings. "A faithless folk," the Frank exclaimed when those in Northumbria killed their ruler. Moreover, increasingly, Charlemagne devoted himself to strengthening the churches of his homelands. He spoke of himself now simply as king of the Franks. No longer as king of the Lombards or Patrician of Rome. Of course in the public eye Pepin was king of the Lombards; yet his father ruled through the *missi dominici*. What would befall the western nations if Charlemagne should die? What, above all, would become of the vicar of St. Peter in Rome?

Between his constant letters, resting his aching head in the quiet of the night, Alcuin pondered this riddle: Charlemagne had become greater in power than any king in the west, yet had no title to that power; his personality had outgrown the rude Frankish rule. *What was he?*

An emperor—no doubt about it. Why, if Britain and the other island of Sicily were added to his dominion, he would rule over more lands than any Roman emperor of the west. True, Spain remained beyond his Christian rule, but that pagan land might still be subdued. Augustus Caesar had been lord of less at his coronation.

Alcuin thought in this fashion of the *Imperium* of ancient Rome because no other empire had been known in the west. Moreover in the east just then a woman, Irene, clung to the throne of the shadowy successors of the Caesars, the eastern emperors of Constantinople. Irene had sinned, in blinding her own son Constantine, to keep power in her hands as wearer of the purple——

Yet Alcuin knew that his king David had no such dream of empire. The barbaric Frank believed himself to be anointed king, as David was, by the will of God; he believed Augustine, who foretold how the mystic city of God would follow after the fall of the earthly Rome. And what Charlemagne believed could not easily—if at all—be contravened.

Realizing that his riddle must be answered, Alcuin could not think of an answer. He put it, in writing, to a very few trusted friends.

The one man he could not invoke in his quest for an answer was Charlemagne.

One task defied Charlemagne. He had ordered a canal to be dug through the high Bavarian valley that separated the headwaters of the Danube from the Rhine, and the work went badly.

"He set his hand to every duty," said the Dwarfling, Einhard, "wherever he might be." So he embarked upon the riverway, sailing up the Altmühl stream as far as skiffs could fare to the obstinate valley. It was the *Brachmanoth* then, the Ground-breaking Month (June) and he took this to be a good omen.

They rode on through floods from the snowfields; they hunted boar through the thickets and feasted under pavilions. Careful Meginfried carried the court documents, and grim Audulf, the Seneschal, saw that food was carted in, to eke out the boar's flesh. Liutgard, the fragile young queen, made light of the rains, saying that the sun blessed all who came to the mountains. The daughters added their voices to the merriment, when their father rode up to find and drive out the evil that hindered the digging in the valley.

Fastrada's babies were left at Franks' City (Frankfurt) but the elfin child, Rothaid, followed slim young Delia about, trying to do what the older girls did.

There were others. Bertha, a mature woman of more than twenty, had her two babies, by Angilbert. Rotrud, although no more wedded than her sister, carried a child with her.

Not by word or look did their father show dislike of the bastard grandchildren. With affection he watched his daughters nurse them at breast. Lustily did the grandchildren wail when they hungered. At suppertime, his daughters robed themselves in blue satin, pouring the wine for him. By God's favor, his family was increasing.

The Dwarfling said of the girls: "So greatly he enjoyed their company, he could not bear to part with them."

At high noon was held the feast of Brachmanoth; the older girls put wreaths on their shoulders and arms, carrying to their father trays of strawberries, pears, cherries, and early

213

grapes. Little Rothaid was given nothing to bring. She had a wreath in her corner, and there she pretended to dance when the harps and cymbals made music.

In the merriment only one man noticed Rothaid dancing with furtive steps alone. He was the eloquent, sunburned priest of the Spanish mountains, Theodulf the great poet. He had come out of ravaged Narbona, a fugitive with a girl child, and nothing else to his name—the Goth he called himself. But in anger he was grimmer than the saintly Sturm, in drinking swifter than the stout Thuringian grafs. Alcuin nicknamed him the Pontiff of the Vine. Charlemagne gave him refuge, duty, and poems to make.

This headstrong priest out of Spain chanted his poems; so had the Psalmist given forth the Song of Songs; so did the pilgrims thronging the roads give praise for their joy. Only Ercambald, the secretary of Charlemagne, and dry little Dwarfling scribbled their histories in painful prose on parchment. Theodulf let out his voice over the court, after feasting on good meat and stout wine—and woe to the seigneur who was too drunk to listen. For the Goth directed the point of his song at the drowser, until all laughed and the fellow, waking, staggered from the hall.

Theodulf had caught the mockery of the Arab poets of Córdoba, he had sensed the wit of Ovid. Listen to the birds, he cried at the lords of Frankland. Hear how the crows drown melody with their cawing racket; notice how the magpie feels conceit because he imitates a human voice; watch how the strutting peacock screams when it tries to talk! Listen to them, and hear yourselves.

To those too well satisfied because they had made a pilgrimage to atone for sins, he observed, "You will not arrive at heaven by walking on your feet."

This stormy Goth, beholding Rothaid dancing alone, realized how children must bear grief in silence, and how the Frankish king who gave generously in mercy could be cruel if he witheld his mercy. Dominating those around him, he healed or hurt by happenchance. Yet his nature called on him to dominate. Was he fit to rule so great a multitude?

The Goth himself would not be put upon. His brethren had been the outcast folk, his refectory the roadside, his hymnals the wailing of the hopeless. More than the others around Charlemagne—more even than quick-witted Angilbert—the Goth had imagination.

Under the pavilion of the king, Fredugis, a Celt disciple of Alcuin, lectured the students upon magical numbers and the meaning of eclipses of the sun and moon. The girls were all there, quiet if not listening. Small Rothaid came after them, lying where a rope raised the pavilion's edge. The Scottish master, beholding her, waved her away.

Then the Goth roared with anger. "Scot or sot! Forbid not the children to come to instruction!"

"The child troubles me, and I can but weary her with my instruction."

"Then take care to please her. Do you lecture for the pleasure of hearing yourself, or letting others understand you?"

The scholar from Britain did not know how to answer, but after that he did not send children away. When they bade the Goth be a friend to Fredugis, he retorted "I will be friends with a Scot when a dog will nurse a rabbit."

Now in spite of Charlemagne's exhorting, the ditch of the canal in that valley, two thousand paces long and one hundred paces wide, could not be deepened. Water seeped in, to turn the ditch into a quagmire. The banks of the cut slid down. Men were trapped in the mud of this place they called the Ried.

Thousands of picks and spades labored to clear it; the king commanded dams to be put up, and channels cut. Yet each night the quagmire resumed its hold on the valley bed. Moreover during darkness inhuman moaning and gasping resounded from the accursed earth; a stench came out of it.

Kerold's messmates maintained that foul fiends had imbedded themselves there in the Ried to strive against the Christian king.

Whereupon Kerold himself cried shame on such gab. "Do you, who are fit only to kill flies, say that you have seen fiends striving here? Now I will testify to the thing I have seen. It was no fiend but the Devil himself that fought with our most glorious king here at the edge of the evil swamp in the hour of deepest darkness. Our king was armed only with his sword, because he had left his knife and spear in the tent. Well, drawing his sword of the finest iron, he raised the hilt with its cross and the Devil began to shriek and moan, as you have heard. Then our most believing king struck the blade of his sword into the Archfiend's midriff, while calling upon the valiant archangel Michael. Now it is the remains of the Devil himself that you smell and hear slipping and writhing about in this bog."

It seemed to the messmates that Kerold, in this instance, spoke the truth. For the rank bog defeated the efforts of all other men.

Rains brought floods that swept away the restraining dams. Charlemagne realized that by his coming he had accomplished no good. In a fit of black anger he walked out to the hill where the dam had been. At such a moment no one of the court ventured to follow him. Only the seven-year-old Rothaid followed, for reasons of her own. And the Goth went after her because he knew the king wished to be alone with his anger.

The Goth saw them out in the wind-swept rain, Charlemagne resting on a boulder, his head in his hands, and the child drawing near him. The king had no thought for her until she picked at her skirt and began to dance some steps without any music back and forth before him. The Goth came no nearer.

Noticing her, Charlemagne pulled her up to his knee and drew the edge of his mantle over her, to shield the child from the wet. In so doing, he saw the wayward Goth.

"Theodulf," he said, "now I am shamed. In this evil hour little Rothaid brings me the comfort of her loving dancing."

When the king returned to his tent he gave command to journey back to the river the next day because the rains put an end to work on the canal.

The valley of the Ried was never excavated, and after years the canal was abandoned. The annalist at Salzburg wrote: "It was useless work. No forethought or wisdom can prevail against the will of the Lord."

Theodulf, however, was heard to say, "Blessed be the Lord, who bestowed on me, unworthy as I am, such a seigneur as Charles." And Charlemagne gave to this outspoken man the bishopric of Orléans. There Theodulf amazed the people by bringing schools "for singing and writing" to the villages.

A greater thing than the Ried canal defeated Charlemagne. He tried, during that time of stress, to confine his responsibility to his ancestral Frankland, centered in Aix. He found he could not do it. Too many people appealed to him now. He might have refused their appeals but it was not in his nature to do that.

To carry out this new duty of protector-at-large, he was obliged to journey forth again from Aix. To restore order within Saxonland he moved with his court to the Weser region, rescinding the harshest penalties of his hated Capitulary to the Saxons, and watching over the transplanting of the villages; thence he was drawn to the settlements among the trans-Elbe Slavs—to Alcuin's great anxiety.

For this space, 797–98, the annals reveal how missions came from afar to the perambulating court of the king. An Arab lord of Barcelona brought him the keys of that seaport. (For William of Toulouse was opening up and fortifying the eastern passes of the Pyrenees.) This Arab Abdullah, exiled son of the great Saracen Abd al Rahman, sought the friendship of the Frank, and related to Charlemagne the wonders of Baghdad, where brazen lions roared like organs. And Charlemagne dispatched envoys to Baghdad to ask for the gift of an elephant.

From the western Pyrenees, Alfonse, king of the Asturians and the Gascons, sent tribute, with captives and trophies from Moslem Lisbon. The very Christians who had first withstood the Franks held themselves to be subjects of Charlemagne, the victorious Christian king. So did the Avar princes.

From Byzantine Sicily, the Patrician saluted the monarch of Frankland by letter. More—Michael, Metropolitan of Constantinople, brought greeting from Empress Irene, announcing her accession to the throne of the Caesars (but not the blinding and imprisonment of her son Constantine).

Monasteries begged for support. Charlemagne bade the hooded folk work the fields, to bring in greater harvests. These cloisters were arteries of new life; yet the monks, retiring from the storms of the age, escaped responsibility for others. "Will you shut yourself up in a safe prison," he demanded of no less a priest than Arno, "or go forth to convert Siegfried, king of the Danes?"

He began to resent the absence of Alcuin, Angilbert, and Adalhard in their abbeys.

From the outpost of the east, crumbling Aquileia, came an old pupil of the Academy, Paulin, to whom Liutgard had sent the gold armlets. ("His name," said Alcuin, "is traced not on tablets of wax but in our hearts.") Paulin was sick for grieving over the ruins of Aquileia, which had been one of the last splendors of the world empire, before Attila's Huns demolished it. "A city of princes," Paulin cried, "has become a poor hut; briars overgrow its broken churches; even its dead have no rest—for robbers wrench the marbles from its tombs."

What aid could Charlemagne give this ghost city? He loved and admired Paulin, the priest of Eric. "What people dwell there?" he asked.

"The survivors of old days sought refuge out on the isles of the sea, at Grado and the Venetian lagoons. They are gone. Now starvelings and beach beggars come to my altar."

"Build hostels. Take in the wayfarers to the east."

Charlemagne sought to make each diocese take in travelers as guests. His drifting population needed doors to be opened and land to be offered. To Paulin, with silver, he gave a title revered in the east. Patriarch of Aquileia—priest of the ghost city.

From Toulouse came his son Louis, too poor to provide presents to the bride he brought with him. There in prosperous Provence and fertile Gascony the tithe gatherers were thieving and the circuit judges sold their verdicts for a price. Louis, who contemplated life so earnestly, could not cure this bribery of officials. And Charlemagne could not go to Aquitaine.

In such cases he called upon shrewd and righteous servants to take his place. Now he summoned Theodulf the Goth, to journey through his old homeland as *missus dominicus*, with power to judge officials. "Accept no gifts. Listen to everyone. And report what you find to me."

By way of report Theodulf sent a scathing poem, *To the Judges!* He told unsparingly what he had found in the tracks of the judges who had gone before him. Everywhere the folk met him with bribes before he could hear their suits.

"One man brings me oriental gems, to make over to him his neighbor's land. Another has gold coins with Arabic inscriptions, as the price to me of a house he wants.

"A servant of a third comes, describing a marvelous vase of the purest silver and greatest weight, all ornamented with Hercules in fury—so clear you might see his iron club crushing in the smoking face of his foe. There Hercules also drives the oxen out of their cave, and you see plainly how they dread being pulled by their tails. This beautiful vase he offers me for the mere changing of the papers of a large number of persons."

The Goth accepted only apples or a succulent chicken tendered him by village folk. His verses mocked at the circuit judges—rising at early dawn to take bribes, but slumbering until noon when duty called them—rising at noon from their benches to stuff themselves with food so they slept through the afternoon cases—hearing influential pleaders with keen ears, and becoming deaf when poor folk argued.

Where Theodulf went, new respect came to the *missi dominici*. A few devoted followers made the force of Charlemagne's personality felt in ever widening territories.

At St. Denis, the grateful Fardulf was building a hostel palace "for the coming of the king." At Salzburg, Arno was bringing his preachers to behave as apostles and not as tax collectors. At Tours, Alcuin labored through the nights collecting and comparing manuscripts of Jerome's Vulgate writing of the Bible, so that a new and clear great Bible might be put in the hands of the king. At ghostly Aquileia, Paulin made citizens out of wayfarers.

Yet as they labored, Alcuin's riddle came into the other, searching minds. Perhaps Alcuin's letters pointed it out to them. What was Charlemagne, who had become more than a king?

They found the answer quickly enough. He was head of the new *imperium Christianorum*—the Christian empire.

It began, like so many other happenings, in the unknown east. From that east had come the forces which gave strength to the king of the Franks. The Scriptures themselves emerged from the tongues of nearer Asia, with the preaching of Paul of Tarsus. The monasticism of Benedict of Nursia came from the hermits of the Egyptian desert—western law had been shaped by the Code of Justinian. In the east, in Constantine's city, was guarded the heritage of Rome, the sciences and arts of the lost past.

On the other hand from the seas and coasts of the west nothing had come, because nothing had as yet been created there, among the forest dwellers and sea-raiding peoples. Even the fairest souls of the west, Bede and Columban and their brethren, had gained the blessing of learning roundabout by the sea-trade route, from Constantinople to the Irish coast. The very bribes offered Theodulf, and the rarities of the Avar treasure, had been fashioned by eastern hands.

The great upheavals of human beings took place, within this eastern hinterland, and each one, like a tidal wave, sent its swell into the western lands, to end in ripples at the unbroken forests.

Nearly two centuries before a rebel had arisen against the wealthy, stagnating empires of Byzantium and Sasanian Persia, when Muhammad had brought a new faith into the deserts beyond the Holy Land. The tidal wave of conversion to Islam as well as the swords of conquest had swept the coast of Africa, sending crosscurrents through the Middle Sea, and had washed through the passes of the Pyrenees, where William was still waging the war of believer against unbeliever. Yet in the east, Muhammad's faith had been that of a puritan who would worship only God alone; the fire of his spiritual conviction—demanding prayer without clergy, worship without churches, and faith without qualification—had caught among the sympathetic eastern Christian sects, which revolted in their turn from the hierarchy of Constantinople. There were puritans in the Christian deserts. And in the dry plains of Anatolia they rose to break the images of the churches, to tear off robes, and destroy paintings that seemed to them to mock at their personal faith.

This conflict between image breakers, iconoclasts, and image lovers, iconodules, raged for generations. The empress Irene, probably from conviction more than policy, restored the sacred images to shrines.

It was no idle question of ritual that inflamed this controversy. It was broad as the world, and particular as the soul of every believer. Who could answer such a question? If you made your prayer before a statue of the Virgin Mother, were you not praying to a graven image, instead of to God?

In growing bitterness, the iconoclasts and iconodules imprisoned, blinded, and slew their antagonists. Until in the east at Nicaea (787), a Seventh World Council of the Church gave its answer (under Irene's authority) to the question. "Emblems . . . shall be visible, lawfully, on vestments, vessels, walls, and roads, to recall to men's minds what they represent."

Such images, the Council declared, should be respected and *venerated*, even honored by candles and incense, but must not be *worshiped* in themselves. The worship of men must go to God alone.

The wave of controversy swept west to Rome. There Hadrian gave his approval to the answer of the Council, and blessed Irene for restoring the images to churches. Although there was less of ritual and panoply at St. Peter's than in the Eastern Orthodox churches, Hadrian and his Catholics held fast to their images of the saints and the crosses of wayside shrines.

From Rome the wave of controversy reached the court of Frankland. There the churches were rather rude affairs, lacking statues because no artisans could make statues. But they had crude wall paintings and precious relics like the mantle of St. Martin. So the questioning struck home to Charlemagne. Was he not right in depicting the splendor of heaven on the walls? Was there no virtue of healing in the bones or belongings of saints?

Yes, he said with emphasis, and added, "Images must not be destroyed."

That would have settled the question in the Frankish churches if it had not been for one of those misadventures which seem impossible today but were all too easy in his age of haphazard communication. Somebody in Rome or Frankfurt mistook a word in translation. The word *revere* was written down for Charlemagne and his ecclesiastics as *worship*. Accordingly, it seemed to them that the Council of Nicaea and Hadrian himself ordered the worship of all emblems. This roused Charlemagne to instant anger. It seemed to be a return to paganism. Could a wooden wayside cross be like to God Almighty? "Images should not be destroyed," he stormed, "but they must not be worshiped!"

Theodulf agreed, and Alcuin, returning then from England, had to admit that the Council of the east and the Pope were wrong. Charlemagne's anger, however, had far-reaching consequences. He looked on the Byzantines as tricksters in religion, and on Hadrian as debasing himself to them; he summoned a council of his own at Frankfurt (794) to debate this burning question of images and God. From the council he demanded a clear answer, and he got what he asked for. At Frankfurt his clerics scorned and condemned the adoration of images of saints. Only the blessed Trinity might be adored.

More than that, the king and his scholars wrote down their belief in the famous *Carolingian Books*. And then and there Charlemagne—owing to the wrong translation of a word—laid down his own mandate of responsibility. "Having received from the Lord, in the bosom of the Church, the government of our kingdom . . ."

By that the Frank meant exactly what he said. As head of the Church he governed his kingdom. Before anything else came this responsibility as priest of the Lord. And in the circumstances of those years it must have seemed to his clergy that both Rome and Constantinople had fallen into error. Charlemagne felt his faith to be challenged. Like Martin Luther in another reformation, he might have said, "Here I stand; I can do no otherwise."

Like Luther, he turned to the Scriptures for verification. The edicts of the *Books* may have been shaped by Alcuin and the others, but they sound very much like Charlemagne, ". . . bishops shall understand the prayers they utter at Mass . . . they shall understand the Lord's Prayer and teach its meaning . . . likewise they shall read out no false writings or lying letters . . . or they will lead the people into error . . . nor shall they allow priests to teach to the people things of their own imagining, not in the Scriptures."

223

This exhortation to his clergy in turn brought the stubborn Arnulfing face to face with the current heresy in Spain. There the Christians in the northern mountains had been touched by the thought of Moslem and Jewish scholars. They had developed some independent ideas. One of them, Felix, bishop of Urgel, challenged the concept of the Trinity, maintaining that Jesus the man had been no more than the adopted Son of God.

An honest man, Felix preached his belief in Adoptionism zealously, and it was spreading through the churches of the Pyrenees. In Charlemagne's mind Jesus had shared the divinity of the Father. Could an ordinary man, however adopted, bring salvation to all human beings?

He called upon Alcuin and Theodulf to deny the heresy and convince Felix of his mistake. He sent Angilbert hurriedly to Rome to consult with the new Pope.

So it happened, as the century drew toward its end, that Charlemagne felt himself to be the chief defender of the Church "internally" while Hadrian's successor remained an unknown factor. At the same time Alcuin wrestled with these problems of belief, and the inflexible will of his king.

"I flew to my beloved nest," he said, seeking seclusion at St. Martin's. There by his river, dissatisfied with his work as abbot, he longed to relieve himself of almost impossible responsibility, to enter the peace of monastic life. Could he find any solution to the problem of Charlemagne's personality and growing domination?

Alcuin's task of editing the new text of the Bible entire seemed beyond his strength, and he wrote Charlemagne that his mind failed him. Someday, he implored, a second Jerome or an inspired fellowship of scholars would accomplish it but he could not.

"Do not wait for an age of perfect minds," Charlemagne answered. "It will never come."

He wanted the new Bible finished, clear to the last word, and put into his hands. So Alcuin labored on, poring through the texts of the Fathers, to refute Felix, and exploring the early Greek fragments of Scriptures, until the pain in his head made him stretch out on his cot.

Then came the undreamed-of tidings from Rome.

In blunt words the annals of 799 relate how "The Romans seized Leo the Pope, putting out his eyes and cutting off his tongue. Carried into prison, he escaped at night over the wall, to the envoys of the lord king, that is to say Wirund the Abbot and Winigis, duke of Spoleto, who were then at the basilica of St. Peter."

So began the year of decision.

For a man who had vowed to defend his people outwardly while strengthening their faith inwardly this year brought a succession of crises. In Spain, where Charlemagne wanted to root out the dangerous Adoptionism, defeat came unexpectedly on the sea, where Arab raiders swept over the islands (Balearics). A wave of restlessness touched his coast elsewhere, stirring the Bretons and the trans-Elbe Slavs. Two of his *missi* were killed.

Worse tidings came from the eastern March. Arno had left, to hasten to Rome. "Two of the chief men of the Franks fell," Einhard relates. "In a town on the coast [near Fiume] Eric, duke of Friuli was struck down by treachery. And Gerold, governor of Bavaria, met his death while riding up and down before his men, gathered against the Huns."

For his brother-in-law Gerold, Charlemagne grieved. But he felt keenly the loss of the matchless Eric, who had mastered the Avars. Eric had always carried with him a small writing of the devout Paulin, a *Book of Exhortation* for a Christian at war. All his wealth Eric had given away in alms; he took no thought for his own safety. "These brave men," Charlemagne said of them, "pushed forward and guarded the borders of the Christian domain."

Who was to take their place? Charlemagne must journey again himself to the eastern March. Yet at Paderborn in his encampment he watched the roads where Saxon nobles were being led out to new homes in Frankland while Frankish settlers migrated to Saxon towns. Across the Elbe his son Charles had journeyed to take the submission of the Slavs. How could he depart from Saxonland?

To Paderborn came a Byzantine envoy with a strange message from Constantinople, by way of Michael, *strategos* of Sicily. The empress Irene sent gifts and greeting to the king of the Franks with the explanation that she had imprisoned her son Constantine for his crimes, so that now she ruled alone and desired the friendship of the Frankish king. What kind of woman would put her son in chains? And how could a woman keep this last throne of the Caesars?

While he waited at Paderborn, his mind was drawn south and east. Beyond the other needs, there was the appeal of the wounded Leo, apostolic lord of Rome, journeying to seek him in the Saxon forests . . . forty-five years before, the Frank had gone out into the winter's storm to meet Stephen, who sought the aid of his father, but he could not leave his camp to meet the unknown Leo. In his stead, Pepin went out a way.

Before his pavilions within the wooden frontier town Charlemagne greeted the injured Leo. Arno and stark liegemen of Frankland escorted the fugitive apostolic lord. Leo had journeyed far to meet the master of Europe. A pavilion awaited him by Charlemagne's. There the two talked alone, while the armed host around them buzzed with suspense and gossip.

Obviously Leo's eyes had not been squeezed out of his head and he could articulate words with his wounded tongue. The prelates of his train claimed that a miracle had healed him. . . . All agreed that a feud had broken out in unruly Rome; Leo lacked the support of noble families, and when he mounted his horse to ride from the Lateran, he had been attacked by a band armed with swords and clubs. Since the watching crowd scattered in fear, few agreed on what happened after that. They shook their heads, saying that Leo was not a Hadrian.

Letters from his enemies claimed that he had been guilty of criminal immorality and perjury. Yet it seemed as if his greatest offense had been to antagonize the strong faction that sought to rule Rome.

Because Charlemagne kept his own counsel, after hearing Leo, the liegemen could not know his mind. Certainly he respected Leo as the apostolic lord, because he asked the other to consecrate the altar of a new church. Still, he declared that Leo must return to Rome, under his safeguard, to face the charges of the accusers. Charlemagne would follow, to be judge at the hearing.

So it may have been that Leo accompanied the Frankish spearmen out of the forest roads with an uncertain mind. It would be an ordeal to face his enemies in his own city, after fleeing from them bleeding and half blinded.

Arno accompanied him, as before, but Alcuin was too weak to ride to Saxonland, and Theodulf the Goth was still on the Spanish front, where Frankish ships were retaking Majorca, and the keys of Huesca were being sent to the king by William.

In his retreat at Tours, however, Alcuin kept informed of events through Arno. Only less than his devotion to Charlemagne was his deep loyalty to St. Peter's. It seemed clear to him, pondering over his books, that the will of the Lord had led the injured Pope to the greathearted Charlemagne. Alcuin could not judge this case impartially. He raged against the rioting "sons of discord" in Rome, where "of old our faith shone forth with greatest light. Men, blinded in heart, have blinded their own Pastor!"

Eagerly he approved his king's decision to judge the crime in Rome. Then his brooding focused upon Charlemagne. Who else could remedy the sorry state of the Christian lands and restore to Rome the great light of old? This thought he put into a remarkable letter to Charlemagne.

"Up to now there have been three persons highest of all in the world. First is the Apostolic Eminence who rules by vicar's power the seat of St. Peter, prince of apostles. And what has been done to that ruler only now Your Courtesy has informed me. Second is the imperial dignity and secular power of the Second Rome [Constantinople]. And how impiously its governor has been overthrown by his own people is told everywhere! Third is the royal dignity in which the providence of the Lord has made you ruler of the Christian people—you, exalted in power above the aforesaid dignitaries, in wisdom above them, and more glorious in your kingship. Do you not see how the fate of the churches of Christ depends upon you alone? Upon you it falls to avenge crime, to guide wanderers, to comfort mourners, to raise up the good."

By sincere exhortation and subtle reiteration the unoffical minister of Frankland called upon his king and friend to rule the Christian west as an emperor. But he did not use that word.

Charlemagne gave no sign of indulging in such rationalization. He tried to coax Alcuin to Saxony, where natives and Franks were being transplanted. Alcuin would not be coaxed from "the abode of peace to a place of contention." Then the king wanted his adviser to accompany him to glorious Rome from "the smoke of the roofs of Tours, so troublesome to your eyes." Alcuin retorted that the smoke of Tours was not as hard on the eyes as the knives of conspirators in Rome.

One thing, however, Charlemagne would not be denied. He needed Alcuin's learning to refute the heresy of Spain before a council. So he decided to go and fetch his simple-minded champion, and Theodulf as well.

When the winter storms stopped traffic on the roads, Charlemagne was sheltered at Aix. His stubborn mind wasted no thought, apparently, on policy or dignity; there were too many needs to be met. He plunged into the decoration of his small cathedral and the walling of the great outdoor baths fed by the warm springs. "He used to invite his nobles and friends and even his bodyguards to bathe with him," Einhard relates. "Sometimes he had a hundred persons in the bath with him."

Whether swimming, feasting or dressing at dawn, he arranged for the coming year, which was 800 of salvation. (The new year began on Christmas Day.) And word went out from his hall at Aix that Charlemagne would journey again around the borders of his kingdom.

The horsemen of his *turmae* calculated that would be a long ride. "Will our most peace-loving king turn his reins at the swift Loire?" they argued. "Not he. Over the pagans in Spain he will ride to Africa, the third part of the world, where the elephants are. He will fare on to the Holy Land, where stands the Sepulcher."

Had he not sent a monk, Zacharias, with gifts to the churches of Jerusalem? Was not an elephant on the road to him somewhere, sent by the mighty kalif of Babylon, or Baghdad? Echoes of this popular speculation reached Alcuin, whose heart was confined to Rome. After the deaths of Eric and Gerold, he feared to have Charlemagne venture along the borders again. "Be content to hold what you have. In pursuing the lesser gain, you may lose the greater."

Another voice urged the king not to journey forth. His young wife, wearied by the ordeal of Saxonland, longed to stay with the court at the new palace of Aix, where all the women had the luxury of sleeping chambers warmed by embroidered hangings against the night cold. "Do not go upon the roads again," Liutgard begged in her weariness.

Early in *Lentzinmanoth* (Spring-festival Month—March) Charlemagne set out.

Where the frontier needed him, he went at pace. Down the Meuse to the coast he sailed. At his villas or noted shrines, he stopped the night with Liutgard. From the restless Lowlands, he ranged along the Channel coast, starting fortifications at the river mouths, where raiding fleets came inland. By May he was across the Seine, inspecting pacified Brittany. As the month ended he reached the valley of the Loire, and joined Alcuin at St. Martin's shrine.

"He came there to pray," the annals record, "but remained some days on account of the failing health of the lady Liutgard his wife, who died at that place the fourth of June. There at St. Martin's of Tours he buried her."

The ailing Alcuin felt deeply the death of the simple girl who had tried to carry out the duty of a queen. At the altar over the tomb of the "good soldier" Martin, he prayed, "Lord Jesus, gentle and merciful, have mercy upon her whom thou hast taken away from us . . . Ah, may this daughter so dear to us be dear unto God, I pray."

Charlemagne would not delay. Taking Alcuin with him, joined by Louis, up from Toulouse, he hastened north, gathering in Theodulf at Orléans, visiting the family tombs at St. Denis, where Fardulf waited. A month after Liutgard's burial, he was back at Aix, preparing for the religious council.

In the bay of the great hall he sat enthroned, wearing the embroidered cloak, girdled with the jeweled sword, crowned with the slender jeweled diadem. Flanked by his lords, lay and ecclesiastical, he listened six days to the great debate between Felix of Urgel and Alcuin of Tours, venerable men, learned in the sweet wisdom of the Fathers.

It was an ordeal by battle of minds. In that early age heresy had not been recorded as a crime. A new belief might, indeed, develop into a truth. Had not Paul himself broken the canons of his time? But the truth must be demonstrated beyond doubt. Charlemagne felt the responsibility of the test heavy upon him. Felix, a bishop, was a man of good life; but, did he preach the truth? Was Christ Jesus by any conceivable possibility adopted as Son, and neither true Son of God nor even true God—only by name?

Felix himself declared that he had permission "of our glorious king Charles . . . to put before him my opinions. By no violence was I brought there, but for judgment, and confirmation of my belief, if it were not rejected."

It was rejected by Charlemagne, at the end of the week's argument. Felix yielded to Alcuin, making new confession of faith and beseeching pardon for stirring strife within the Church. The ordeal had wearied Alcuin.

No sooner had Charlemagne arranged for the Spanish bishop to be taken to a monastery, and for new preachers to go down to the Spanish March, than he was off to Mainz to order the control of Saxonland for the summer.

Alcuin gave him a parting wish. "Rome, the capital of the world awaits you, its overlord ... come back quickly, David, my well-loved. All Frankland makes ready, joyously, to welcome you with the laurels of victory."

Then Alcuin hurried back to Tours to await tidings from Rome with feverish anxiety. At the end of August Charlemagne was off up the Rhine, with some of his daughters and his son Charles. Threading the familiar passes of the Alps, he turned, not to Rome but to Ravenna. There in Theodoric's palace he heard reports of Eric's old charge, the eastern frontier. Pepin came up from the Beneventan border. South Charlemagne rode, by the sea, to the port of Ancona.

At the end of November he came in sight of the red-brown roofs of Rome and the pine canopies of its hills. Again, as he had done twenty-six years before, he called for his seigneurs to robe themselves in splendor, and with music playing he went on to meet the Pope.

Leo came out a dozen miles to welcome him and to feast with him for a night. The next day Charlemagne rode around the wall of Rome, through the lines of banners. Heavy, and slow of foot, gray of hair, he climbed the steps to St. Peter's. This time he did not go down on his knees.

The mystery of what happened there, at the shrine on Christmas day, has never been cleared away. Yet it has been debated for more than eleven centuries.

Before it came the vindication of the Pope. In the Triclinium hall of the Lateran palace the high clergy of Rome and Frankland assembled to hear Leo and the pleas of the conspirators who attacked him. This time Charlemagne sat as a judge in robes beside the accused vicar of St. Peter.

Although no army followed him—the elite horsemen of the Franks were off in malarial Beneventom with Pepin, to enforce the will of the king—his presence kept quiet the turbulent streets of Rome. The city itself had grown handsomer, with Hadrian's new buildings and Charlemagne's gifts.

In the hall of the assembly a new mosaic decoration must have caught the Arnulfing's eye. Leo had ordered it put in the wall. It showed St. Peter, large in size as such an eminent personage should be, holding out in his right hand a pallium to the smaller, kneeling Leo, and offering in his left hand a standard sprinkled with roses to "Charles the king." So this mosaic Charlemagne, stalwart and soldier-like, with wide Frankish mustache, appeared as the equal of the Pope and as standard-bearer of the Church. (Much and badly restored, this mosaic group stands now at the side of the Sacred Stair.)

Apparently Charlemagne took no part in the vindication of Leo, which must have been discussed outside the hall. At St. Peter's he heard the solemn declaration of the man beside him, holding up the Four Gospels in his hands ". . . wherefore I, Leo, pontif of the Holy Roman Church, being judged by no man and constrained by none, of my own free will do purge myself in your sight . . ."

With no other voice raised in argument, Leo took the oath of self-vindication. Those who accused him, leaders of the Roman faction, were heard and condemned to death by the bishops, and spared by Charlemagne, at Leo's request, to go into exile in Frankland.

By then it was mid-December. Still the clerics sat in consultation, off the record. Theodulf, Arno—now consecrated as archbishop—and a disciple of Alcuin formed a tight group, urging Alcuin's reiterated thought, that Charlemagne's dominion had grown into an empire, a new empire, *the Christian empire.* Was he not its sole protector? Then what should be his rightful title?

In the annals of one monastery, Lorsch, this was written in the words: "The title of emperor being vacant, Charles the king would be summoned to it by the will of the Christian people."

Had not Charlemagne sought to unite the Christian people? Did not the venerable abbot of Tours exhort them to lift up their eyes to this empire without visible frontiers, the veritable appearance on earth of the city of God, predicted by the divine Augustine?

What if the Roman politicians smiled at it? What matter if Leo himself greeted mention of it with silence?

The three friends of Alcuin sat with Angilbert, who had passed long years at Charlemagne's side. What was Angilbert's thought?

"Now he surpasses all other kings, together, in power. As for himself, he is just, honest, and restrained."

On the second day before Christmas these four friends of Charlemagne sat in discussion with the pensive Leo. No secretary wrote down their talk. Unquestionably Leo felt gratitude for the succor of the king; he still bore the scars of the conspirators' knives; he had taken, at St. Peter's altar, the oath of self-vindication, which only Pelagius in Justinian's time had taken before him.

Theodulf and Arno were men of stark words; they had followed their missions on the roads of the Christian lands; they had gone out to the strife beyond the borders. In their minds they carried Alcuin's words: that Charlemagne surpassed all other kings; that he was bringing peace to the Christian lands. Theodulf's imagination pictured it as peace not in their time but for the children.

Leo heard them. Upon him, as upon Hadrian, lay the responsibility of the Church; he was the sole champion of St. Peter's and Rome. . . .

Up from Ostia came unexpected news. Zacharias, the monk, landed there with the envoy of the patriarch of Jerusalem. He, who had carried the gifts of Charlemagne, bore back the keys of the church of the Sepulcher and Calvary, and the standard of Jerusalem to the king of Frankland. The Roman clergy and the Frankish seigneurs rejoiced at this good omen. They sent horses speeding down to hurry the messengers from the Holy Land to the nearest gate.

On the eve of Christmas Zacharias brought the keys and the standard to Charlemagne. It was like a blessing, to be given these symbols of Christ's city on Christmas eve. . . .

Early Christmas morning, Charlemagne, king of the Franks, entered the portico of St. Peter's. Advancing between the purple hangings of the nave pillars, he stepped up to the triumphal arch, where a thousand candles glowed. At Leo's urgent request he wore—for the second time in his life—the tunic, chlamys and light slippers of a Roman Patrician.

From the bell tower above echoed the summons of the four-centuries-old church. Around the soaring illumination of the arch candles pressed the clergy of St. Peter's and Rome, the bishops of Frankland, the lords of the nations, and the nobles of Rome. Behind Charlemagne waited Pepin, who had been summoned to the city for this day. Near the altar waited the daughters. At the portico stood the liegemen bearing the king's Christmas offerings of a silver table, and a paten and chalices of gold—the weight of a heavy man, of the king himself, in precious metal.

The bell's echo ceased as Charlemagne knelt to pray before the porphyry columns and the statues of the saints and angels placed by the dead Hadrian above the crypt that made a tomb for St. Peter.

In this first prayer of the new year there were memories of twenty-nine years gathered about the giant king, of Hildegard's children, and the dead Liutgard, of his sworn promise to Hadrian that he had kept only after his fashion——

As he rose from his prayer, Leo stepped to his side and

234

placed a crown on his head. The glow of the candles flickered in tiny light from jewels in the crown.

Voices shouted in chorus, "To Charles, Augustus, crowned by God, great and peace-giving Roman emperor—long life and victory!"

Twice the clergy and nobles of Rome repeated the shout, and the Franks joined in. Charlemagne, listening, did not move. Then Leo with the altar attendants was holding out a mantle of imperial purple, putting it over his shoulders, and kneeling briefly to bow before him as a Caesar, an Augustus and emperor of Rome. Then Leo was moving toward the altar, and silence came with the invocation to Mass. . . . In the prayer at the end after his name came the word *Imperator*.

When the last of his gifts had been lifted toward the altar, Charlemagne left the nave and strode in silence to the court-yard steps. Faces pressed around him and the sound of a *Te Deum* did not cease.

To Einhard, the Dwarfling, Charlemagne exclaimed, "If I had known what Leo meant to do I would never have set foot in this church, even on this holy day!"

So Einhard wrote it down in his life of Charlemagne, and so it is read today, to add to the mystery of the coronation of Charlemagne. If the giant king did not anticipate such a crowning, what did he expect? And what, in reality, did the Pope intend to do?

The wisest scholars have been unable to solve the mystery for us, because they have such fragmentary evidence to work with. They believe that Alcuin expected the title of emperor to be bestowed on his friend, at Rome. But no one has been able to decide what the giant Arnulfing expected.

They could hardly, as it were, slip the emblem of world empire on the head of a man unaware of it—least of all on the head of a barbarian Frank who disliked Roman titles and did not really understand, in spite of his earnest self-education, what an Augustus Caesar was. Not when that man had spent

235

the last year in attending to a multitude of other tasks all over Europe and had come to Rome to hold a judgment upon its apostolic lord, and then had entered St. Peter's to pray and make his offerings on Christmas Day. So the younger historians point out, and you can read their amusement between the lines.

No, Charlemagne expected something there at the altar, but nobody knows what it was. Remember that when the council remained sitting in the Lateran, after Leo's exculpation, it seems to have been led by Arno into discussing that particular matter. The chronicler of Lorsch usually had his facts right. Because Charlemagne was adverse to the word *empire* Alcuin's bloc seems to have spoken of "the whole Christian folk," which fitted with his own concept of his people. Perhaps the council expressed its wish that he be proclaimed as more than king of the Franks and Lombards—as king or *Imperator* of the western Christian people. But certainly he did not expect what the Pope did at the altar.

Beyond the argumentation, we have a clear impression of the desire of all these men, of the yearning of Alcuin to honor his friend and protect the churches, of the "imperialistic" clergy to hope for something whole and stronger to come through Charlemagne, and of Leo himself to create a new and unchallenged authority to support him after his unhappy ordeal.

What Leo did, apparently, was to trick Charlemagne and the bishops of Frankland. He proclaimed the Arnulfing ruler "by the will of God" not of a nebulous Frankland or a borderless Christian folk but of his own existing city of Rome—and of a vanished world dominion that had included Britain and Constantinople, as well as the Holy Land, Spain, and Africa, now held by the kalifates. It was a bold move. By bestowing the crown with his own hand, did he not set a precedent that future emperors should be proclaimed by future Popes?

Out of his act grew endless questioning—of the continuity of the Roman Empire, of the two swords of the world, of the

236

powers of Popes and emperors, the Holy Roman Empire itself, of the nature of the medieval Christian dominion. This questioning, turning too often into strife, endured until Napoleon sought the crown of empire, and even after that.

What Charlemagne did, at the moment, was to back out of his coronation.

When he reached his chambers in the bishop's house near St. Peter's he took off the Roman regalia and never put on the purple, embroidered garments again. When he left Rome after Easter that year, he did not return. Nor did he make any change in the officers of his court, or the titles and duties of his sons. Pepin, who had been at the Christmas coronation, was sent back to the heat of southern Italy, where the good Chamberlain, Meginfried, died of malaria.

It took Charlemagne, in the role of a second Constantine and everlasting Augustus, quite a while to think the thing out. What Arno and Theodulf advised, we do not know. He had to worry it out for himself.

Beyond his household guards—still in helmets and weather-stained cloaks—the volatile Roman populace paraded, bringing up banners and shouting their devotion to their new emperor.

For he had accepted the crown. In the chanted liturgy, transfixed by the altar, he had been passive as one of the purple-draped pillars. How joyously his daughter had greeted him in the court!

To his practical mind, in receiving the crown he had gained nothing else. Not an inch of land or a single human being had been added to what he possessed before. Beyond the Aurelian wall of the city Nero's circus gaped, grass-grown, and Trajan's victory column reared over beggars' huts.

He had been given their *Imperium*. Yet the assemblies of Frankland had no voice in this exaltation of their king to emperor. Nor had the only remnant of the Empire, the city of Constantinople, chosen him, an untaught barbarian, by vote of its patriarch, senate, army, and people. What would the enigmatic Irene say to his coronation in the west?

In spite of himself, he meditated about Irene. Some called her a she-devil, others vowed she had magical beauty. Now that he had the name of emperor, he might wed an empress——

Then, feeling the rough wool of his shirt against his skin and rubbing his hard fingers through the stiff mesh of his clipped hair, he smiled as if he had heard a good gab. It was rubbish, it was worms out of a dunghill to argue, like these political philosophers, that because Irene was a woman they needed a man as emperor in Constantinople to fill out the throne. Constantinople chose its own rulers, and it was certain the city would never summon him, a Frank from Rome, to the throne——

He might have the title of a Constantine, yet he possessed no city, no fleet, no code of law, no legions except for the dubious armed host that followed him.

When he reasoned as far as this, Charlemagne stretched out his aching arms and laughed at himself. For the Lord God had chosen the foolish things of this world!

Soon enough, a letter of thanksgiving from Alcuin reached him. "Blessed be the Lord God who hath led you forth with triumph, for the salvation of his servants!"

The messenger who carried the letter declared that at Tours Alcuin was stopping all visitors, demanding of them when the emperor would come back, and how soon would he arrive in his homeland?

As soon as the Easter festival ended, Charlemagne left Rome. But before he parted from Leo he gained an agreement that henceforth the consent of the ruler of Frankland would be required in the consecration of a new Pope.

Heedless of an earthquake that desolated some Italian towns, Charlemagne rode on, as before. Repairing damages where he could, listening to the petitions of the country people where the name of emperor had not been heard for three hundred years—not since the day of Justinian, who had attempted to revive the empire in the west and had failed— he made his rounds. From Spoleto he followed the coast north to Ravenna, lingering a few days in the palace of Theodoric, stripped of its columns. Then in Pavia he swam in the bath of the Lombard kings, and sat in state to receive envoys from Harun, kalif of Baghdad, who had brought no elephant with them.

Toward the mountains he rode, with the keys of the Sepulcher. Before him went the standard of Jerusalem, after him followed the cavalcade of his daughters, their Valkyrie voices echoing in song.

Up the ravine he led his following, to the melting snow of the rock walls of the Mount of Jove, on to the gleam of lakes, past the abandoned mud of his canal, into the forests of his homeland. It was his last passage of the Alps.

Merrily he led them to hunt on the journey. In his massive, troubled head a conviction was growing. One thing he knew for a certainty. Although he was no Roman emperor, the responsibility of empire had been laid on him. His people were, now, the whole Christian folk.

Down the swift Rhine they sped in boats. Beyond the Moselle's mouth, they turned aside to Aix. Although he had no imperial city, he would build one there, at Aix.

Chapter IX

CHARLEMAGNE'S CITY

"THREE SILVER TABLES are in the treasury," observes Einhard the Dwarfling. "On the square one appears the picture of the city of Constantinople; on the round one, a plan of the city of Rome; on the third, which far excels the others in beauty, there is a plan of the whole universe made with three circles."

Charlemagne, then, had obtained his map of the world. But why the cities, so carefully incised on the tops of silver tables? The tables, of course, may have seemed to him more serviceable than wall paintings, like the one in the Lateran. But the cities served a definite purpose; they offered to his eyes the veritable likeness of the first Rome, and the second Rome (Constantinople), which he had not visited but might still behold. And his own city of Aix might become a third Rome.

Now however skillful the drawing of these city plans—and Einhard thought they were wonderful, and quite worthy of his hero king—they did not reveal to the giant barbarian what had *created* those two Romes. The first had grown up by accident on the hills above the muddy Tiber, because the Roman Caesars had controlled the outer sea, with its trade. They called it "Our Sea." And in fact their empire had never progressed very far inland from this Middle Sea (Mediterranean) that sustained it.

240

Charlemagne's City

Then Constantine the Great had moved the seat of his Empire to the east, to "Constantine's City" to the junction of the inland seas and the trade routes of three continents. Its unique situation had sustained it against economic stress and barbarian invasions for almost three centuries. That in spite of the many Caesars who had been mad, neurotic, or downright incapable.

At Aix, Charlemagne was far from the power-giving sea, and moreover kept from its trade by Arab fleets as well as by the Byzantine navy. Around Aix there was no possibility of reviving the Roman *Imperium*—not among the shaggy forest folk navigating rivers in their coracles. Yet Charlemagne after being crowned Roman emperor had forsaken Rome and Ravenna—and even the central site of Pavia. He was determined to make Aix his capital city, and so far he had not failed to accomplish what he set his mind on.

One glance at his imperial city-to-be would have discouraged most men. True, the little river Würm wound pleasantly beneath the elms of the green valley. Its sailing skiffs brought fish to the market on the bank. His palace of gray stone topped a gentle hill, and its pillars of purple porphyry and green marble recalled Ravenna faintly. His octagonal basilica, however, did not much resemble St. Vitale in spite of the labor bestowed on it. During his absence the workmen had run out of mosaics and had filled in the walls with colorful stone chips. Moreover his marble seat in the pillared gallery had been hewn so small that he could barely squeeze his hips into it. In fact the Mary Church itself was really no larger than a chapel. Already pilgrims spoke of Aix, the Chapel.

At St. Peter's he had observed how ornaments gave splendor to a house of the Lord, particularly if brightly lighted. "He adorned the beautiful basilica at Aix the Chapel," Einhard explains zealously, "with gold and silver lamps, and with rails and doors of solid brass. And he gave to it a great number of vessels of gold and silver, with so many fine robes that even the doorkeepers need not perform duties in their workaday clothes. He took great pains to improve the singing, for he was skilled in that, although he never sang in public except in a low tone and in chorus with others."

Bright furnishings and robes, however, could not remedy the peculiarity of the nine-year-old capital of an empire-to-be. Since the officers of the court journeyed with Charlemagne, and their families and servitors accompanied them, whenever the king left Aix it became a deserted town. On the other hand when Charlemagne returned, the place swarmed like a hive, with humans who set up stalls in the market, and huts around the houses of the seigneurs. Visitors pitched their pavilions down the hillside so that guards had to be posted to keep them out of the consecrated ground of the cathedral and Jewish cemeteries.

Such a thronging of noble people in turn drew merchants from Spain, woodcarvers from the Silver City, jugglers from the taverns, and all the hundreds from everywhere who had pleas to make to the new emperor. The home-abiding Franks accepted Charlemagne's exaltation without blinking; not understanding what it meant, otherwise, they drank hail to it and sang his praise. When he was careful to have all freemen more than twelve years of age take a fresh loyalty oath "also to him as Caesar" they swore willingly enough. Was not the son of Pepin the Arnulfing worthy to be *Imperator* and Caesar also? They only wished they could raise him anew on their shields, in good Germanic fashion.

He cured this seasonal peculiarity of Aix by making it his permanent home. After that, the huts became solid stone dwellings, and wealthy seigneurs turned the neighboring farms into villas. The antiquated Roman barracks were converted into hostels for pilgrims.

Almost at once tidings from Italy cheered the citizens of the new Aix. The fabulous beast, the *elefans,* was coming out of the east to Charlemagne! Ercambald the secretary had gone to Italy to arrange for a ship large enough to transport the giant elephant over to Christian soil. Einhard the writer udded that the name of the elephant was Abul Abbas, and that he had been sent to Charlemagne by Aaron or Harun, king of Persia, or at any rate king of all the east except India.

But why, they asked Einhard the Dwarfling, was only one elephant sent?

"Aaron sent the only one he had," Einhard explained wisely.

Like the coming of the organ, the advent of Abul Abbas was noted by the monk who kept the annals. "In October Isaac, a Jewish merchant, crossed from Africa with the *elefant* to a port of Liguria; and because it could not get over the Alps in the storms, they spent the winter in Vercellae."

It seems that Charlemagne kept himself informed of the progress of Abul Abbas, who had had to detour on foot around hostile Byzantine territory. By now the ruler of Frankland had puzzled out a satisfactory title, to replace the detested *Augustus, Emperor of the Romans.* He was, he announced, "governing the Roman Empire in the west." That was true enough, and easily understood.

With the new coins, however, he had more trouble. Like a seal, a royal coin needed to bear an exact title. Eventually he decided upon the name, *Carolus Imperator.* He was indeed Charles and emperor. One coin struck in Rome had the inscription *Renovator of the Roman Empire.* He had another struck at Aix with *Christian Religion* on it.

In this way, by the slogans on the money, the politicians at Rome proclaimed that he would rebuild the Roman Empire, he claimed that he would protect the Christian religion.

Just then—in 802—the city of Constantinople cast its ridicule on the new Caesar.

Charlemagne had expected it. Although he lacked imagination, he had no trouble picturing to himself how the court at Constantinople would hear the news of his coronation as Roman emperor. They would be angered, those Byzantines. Just as he himself would be angered if a Thuringian graf stepped

243

up to claim a seat on his throne. But how would they react? More than their anger, Charlemagne dreaded their ridicule. He knew his own awkwardness too well to tolerate any mockery.

Yet when the Byzantine envoys arrived, they were affable. Slender, in their stiff embroidered robes, they bowed low to him and named him in eloquent Greek great king, most Christian monarch, and victorious lord of the west. They did not use the title *Basileus* that meant emperor to them. No, they did not greet him as Irene's equal.

Instead, they offered the friendship and good will of the empress. More than that, in veiled words they suggested that the saintly Irene—adored by her people, to whom she had restored the sacred images—might be inclined to marry him. Such marriage could unite the west and east of the surviving Roman world.

Charlemagne had not taken a wife since Liutgard's death. There was only a comely woman from Frankfurt who came to his sleeping chamber. Did Irene, in truth, offer to join their thrones in this way?

She was a Greek. His envoys said she rode through her streets in a chariot gleaming with gold, drawn by white mules; she sat on a throne high above other mortals, half hidden in swirling incense. . . . She had refused to wed her son to Rotrud . . . But she might have need of Frankish swords to guard her frontiers against pagan Slavs and Bulgars.

Once on the Adriatic shore he had seen a Byzantine warship pass, with red oars flashing and banners streaming. A Norse dragon ship could be carried on the prow of the monster dromond. Irene had power on the sea, and Charlemagne had begun to ponder that sea, clearly marked in the middle of his world map.

Charlemagne remembered how valiant men had died because Fastrada longed, as queen, to have power over them. Pilgrims from the Holy Land said that the sun itself had been

244

darkened by an eclipse when Irene blinded her son. Were her words like the drip of honey, sweetening the hard bread of truth?

Still they pleased Charlemagne because they did not ridicule him. If she had forbidden her *missi* to call him *Basileus*, at least she, as Augusta, had spoken of marriage that would make him in reality an Augustus. Or had they?

Carefully the Frank pondered her message, and made answer to the envoys. "In the measure that she offers it, I who govern the empire in the west, return friendship and good will to the empress of the Romans."

Then he waited with curiosity for Irene's response.

It did not come from her. At the end of the year his own envoys came back with the tidings from Constantinople—of Irene exiled to an island by revolt of her nobles and army. She had been overthrown for deposing her own son, for giving supreme power to her galaxy of eunuchs, and for contemplating alliance with a barbarian Frank.

In Constantinople reigned Nicephorus as *Basileus*, chosen by God. The army and iconoclasts supported him. On her island the proud Irene occupied herself with a spinning wheel.

At Monte Cassino, Charlemagne had seen the ample library where Paul the Deacon labored at his history of the Lombards. Inspecting its shelves of precious volumes, laid carefully one upon the other, he had been filled with envy. Now his new palace held the library of Charlemagne.

It overlooked the covered way leading to the Mary Church. When he stood at one of its reading desks, the golden cupola reflected the sun's gleam into his eyes. Around the walls lay the archives brought in by Ercambald and Einhard, the small grammar of Alcuin, with copies of the Fathers' writings, notably a *City of God* bound in silver set with precious stones. Upon a Bede the Venerable, snug in enamel-work laid upon polished wood, rested St. John Chrysostom within soft velvet embroidered with gold thread by the girls. Virgil lay there with Suetonius, historian of the Caesars. Apart from the others reposed the great Lectionary, twenty years old, inscribed in large letters for easy reading on purple parchment, with small paintings of the four Evangelists. St. Mark in this fine book was shown being helped by his symbolic lion, with wings.

Charlemagne kept by his bedside the slim book he had asked Alcuin to write for him. He wanted it to be short and practical—to have the right prayers, hymns, and sayings for the proper days of the calendar, in brief. This breviary accompanied him on his journeys. (It was the first breviary to be made.)

Yet however devotedly the abbot of Tours labored to prepare books for his friend, it was an arduous task to persuade him to lend a volume from the library of Tours.

"You hold out your hand so eagerly to receive a book," Alcuin chided, "but when I ask for it back again, you will hold it behind your back."

For years Charlemagne had made a practice of copying out the volumes in the scriptorium of the Palace School, and Alcuin had done the same by the skilled hands of the monks at Tours. If every monastery had its library filled, there would be no need to borrow, one from the other, and perhaps lose a work of Cicero or Tacitus of which no other copy existed. In this way, many rare works in the beautiful Celtish script of Britain found their way to Frankland, while Charlemagne always carried home a trove of rare writings from Lombardy and St. Peter's library. It was hard to refuse him, as Alcuin discovered, when he begged for a book.

Probably neither king nor schoolmaster realized how quickly they were setting up in Frankland a sort of survival center of classical writers and the Fathers. Rare volumes that had been locked up at St. Gall or Lindisfarne were circulating in Charlemagne's schools. And now most of the Lindisfarne library had been burned in the raid of the Northmen.

Alcuin liked to surprise his friend with a newly found or fine book. Coming to Aix himself in the mild summer months, he approached the expectant Charlemagne bending under the weight of a bulky object wrapped in embroidery. On the arm of the king's chair he laid his great Bible, the corrected text of St. Jerome, freed from the mistakes of slovenly copyists.

"Now my David," he remarked, "you can no longer say that your people pray badly because they use the wrong words."

The top cover of the new Bible bore, set in silver, an ivory plaque on which the Crucifixion had been carved, with angels above and mourners below, and the four Evangelists seated at work writing in the corners, helped by their symbols. It was satisfying in every detail.

"Nor can you say now," Alcuin added, "that your priests read badly because the words are badly written."

Eagerly his friend turned the smooth vellum pages. The first letter of each part caught the eye, being illuminated in bright colors; the words were clearly separated, and each letter stood unmistakably for what it was. At once Charlemagne ordered a master copy to be made of the Bible, in his library; from the master copy, twenty volumes were to be issued to the dioceses of the empire.

In the library he ventured to ask a question of his teacher. He did not blurt it out, as in the time when they had sat together at the schooling. Turning to Augustine's book, he pointed out a line over which he had puzzled for hours. "To Constantine," it read, "was given the honor of founding a city, to be a companion to the Roman Empire, like a daughter to Rome itself."

"Do you think," he asked with hesitation, "that another city could be founded, another such companion to—to Rome?"

Alcuin looked at his friend, not at the inscribed words, which he had read at a glance. In the emperor's mind—for Alcuin thought of his friend now as the emperor—was the question: could his city of Aix become another Rome?

Outside the embrasure, rude thatched roofs huddled about the solitary dome of the Mary Church. The town had no walls except the gentle rise of the hills against the sky. Rome had walled in its river and hills overlaid with palaces and temples.

"If there can be no third Rome," he said, "there can be a new city of God."

He was more than seventy years of age, weakened by fever and stiff with arthritis. In spite of his devotion to the emperor, many things disturbed him in the new palace with the gilt eagle over the portico. Strangers crowded the great hall, more than forty paces long. Women with unfamiliar faces bustled their children about the living quarters, yet they wore royal linen and gave commands in shrill voices. He hardly knew Rotrud, his pupil of twenty years before.

At the School, where his disciples taught, he cautioned one of them, Fredugis, with acerbity, "Do not let these crowned doves who fly around the chambers of the palace come pecking at your window!"

When he discovered that Charlemagne wanted to change the new year's day from Christmas to the ending of winter's darkness, Alcuin cried out, "I left this a Latin school, and I find it an Egyptian, making a calendar by darkness!"

In the library itself he noticed Einhard, now mature in years, poring over Suetonius' intimate lives of the twelve Caesars. "The Excellency, our glorious emperor," the Dwarfling explained, "so much resembles Augustus Caesar, the first of the Roman emperors."

"He resembles himself!"

To Adalhard, reading aloud the measured lines of pagan Virgil, he exclaimed, "Why do you yield yourself to such Devil's enchantment?"

Yet limping along the shelves, touching the precious covers of the books he had made, he bent his head as if listening. "Ah, they make so many melodies for us," he excused himself. "In silence, they sing to us."

Charlemagne's City

Because of the books, Charlemagne would not release Alcuin to leave the world, as he wished, for the retreat of the Benedictines at Fulda. There was so much still to be revised as only Alcuin could do it.

When the aged man wrote out for him an ode to Michael, archangel of the flaming sword, Charlemagne puzzled over the last line. "Your scholar has picked out this melody for his emperor."

By then the School had trained a generation to exert their minds—for all Alcuin's grumbling. Its pupils filled the monasteries in far lands. At Tours Alcuin could not refrain from urging pilgrims and students from Ireland and Britain to seek the emperor, who would nourish and protect them. Let them tell their hopes to the tireless shepherd of the Christian folk.

So many islanders found their way to St. Martin's that the monks gibed at "these Britons swarming like bees into a hive."

An Irishman was master of the Palace School. Inevitably strife broke out between the canny islanders and the tough-minded natives. Charlemagne's melting pot of minds had been simmering for years and now it boiled over. Theodulf, who admitted that he would see eye to eye with a Scot "when a wolf will kiss a mule" started it.

A young cleric, judged guilty of crime in Theodulf's city of Orléans, fled to sanctuary at St. Martin's altar in Alcuin's city of Tours. The clergy of Tours would not yield him up. When Theodulf sent armed officials to extract him from the church, the people of Tours rang their bells and turned out to battle in the streets, until Alcuin and his monks rescued Theodulf's officers, while refusing to give up the fugitive. Quickly enough Alcuin wrote Charlemagne his side of the case: that the escaped cleric had a right to sanctuary, and to appeal to the emperor.

Charlemagne did not see it that way. "A letter from Theodulf," he responded, "came to me the day before yours . . . you are in contempt of an order of my domain . . . it does no good to tell me of St. Paul's appeal to Caesar. St. Paul was not guilty like this clerk. Let him be returned to Theodulf. We are surprised that it seemed right to you to go against our will."

In so many words the monarch of Christian Frankland denied the right of sanctuary where it conflicted with an order of his government. He was angry enough, because he lashed out at Alcuin for bringing discord "between two wise men, doctors of the Church." And he gave his aging master a nasty blow by calling the brethren of St. Martin's "ministers of the Devil," whose manner of life he himself had hoped to change by sending them Alcuin as abbot—only to find Alcuin prompting them to greater evil.

Into this diatribe crept Charlemagne's growing prejudice against the monastic system that removed young men from his service, to allow them—or so he thought, at times—to lead pampered lives.

Now the lay brethren of St. Martin's had worried Alcuin enough by their habit of seeking wine and women beyond the walls. He yielded at once to Charlemagne's authority, but he would not accept this censure of his monks, and his church. He retorted that he knew the brethren of St. Martin's better than those who accused them. The men of Orléans who tried to break into the church were the most guilty. And: "I have served so long in vain . . . if I should sin by disloyalty in my old age . . . all the gold in Francia could not bring me to raise such a perilous tumult within the Church."

Inexorably Charlemagne sent his *missi* to root out the guilty in Tours. Unflinchingly, Alcuin smuggled certain young monks of his to sanctuary far off, with Arno at Salzburg, from "the blazing wrath of Theodulf."

Such a clash of strong minds over the question of authority and human rights was a sign of reviving mental life.

Charlemagne's City

In this melting pot of peoples that had been Frankland, the revival was beginning. No minstrels wandered the roads as yet, where pilgrims sought new shrines; no portrait painters or sculptors created masterwork for princes. Clumsy hands carved wood with designs copied from Byzantine ivories; goldsmiths shaped small vessels like those of the Avar treasure; women at their looms copied the pictures of Charlemagne's Four Gospels. In the monastery of Reims the monks began to draw lifelike figures with new zest.

Crudely, but with unquenchable vitality, the western spirit began to express itself in the movement toward better life that we know as the Carolingian renaissance, which means simply the rebirth under Charles. It found its own way of writing in the Carolingian script.

The printed letters we read today we take for granted. Yet fifteen centuries ago, after the ending of the *bonae litterae* of the Romans, there existed only a Babel-like variety of writings copied at first awkwardly from the Greek and Roman, and then from each other. By the time of the Merovingian Franks, writing had debased, with thinking, to its lowest level.

During this darkness of the Middle Ages, handwriting survived only in the monastic centers and—very rudely—in the few court secretariats. Being widely scattered, these survival centers tended to form scripts of their own. There was no longer a model to work from, and the scribes, laboring with pen or marker in badly lighted chambers upon scraped lambskin sheets, naturally produced what was easiest for them rather than what was easiest to read. A scribe could usually read his own writing, but few others managed to do so.

Of course most of them had seen the large, square Latin capitals carved on walls or tombstones—a sort of tombstone language. But it required labor to trace out an entire book in capitals, besides using up too much of the precious parchment. The angular capitals did well enough for a page heading; for the page itself the scribes used their own cursive writing. Even the Papal chancellery developed a wavering script that had to be deciphered by the initiated. Something of the fine ancient Roman hand survived in Ireland, and became the graceful insular lettering of Lindisfarne.

Meanwhile the few Spanish monasteries clung to a neat but entirely different Visigothic hand, while the Beneventan monasteries around Monte Cassino developed a small lettering, all run together, that did well enough for Beneventans. The trouble was that the letters themselves tended to take different shapes in different places, while the Irish evolved some entirely their own, which went with missionaries like Gall and Columban to the depths of Frankland.

There one monastery, Corbie, where Adalhard studied, evolved something like a common denominator of writing, partly from ancient Roman, partly from Celtish influence. (All this while the writing of Constantinople remained legible enough, but it remained Greek, which was hardly ever read in the west.) Patiently, in copying out their books, the scribes at Corbie hit upon a writing known as minuscule, having two vital advantages. It was small enough to pen easily, while keeping the clear form of the larger (majuscule) letters. It looked well and everyone could read it after a trial or two.

This rude Corbie minuscule found favor in Tours, where the scribes improved it to make *every* letter distinct and separated a little from the others. This Tours script entered the Palace School of the Franks. It appeared in gold on the first purple page of the great Lectionary or reading Bible of Charlemagne by the time that Alcuin took charge of the School. Alcuin by no means invented this writing, as is sometimes said, but he favored it, as did Charlemagne, because he could read it easily.

The two of them prepared a Psalter for Hadrian, written in gold in the fine new hand.

As they increased the output of copied books, the Corbie-Tours-Aix script spread to the borders of Frankland. Both men realized the advantage of having a uniform script in all centers of reading, and Charlemagne made it mandatory.

It was no easy task to train hundreds of men to write the same script. "I don't get very far," Alcuin admitted to his friend, "owing to the lack of culture here." To write well, a scribe had to read easily. More, he had to punctuate like the others. As a reminder of that Alcuin put a placard in his scriptorium: "Make your meaning clear by punctuation, or the reader in church will read wrongly to his brethren." That sounds very much like Charlemagne.

The inflexible determination of the king emperor and Alcuin's genius for editing accomplished the task. In Psalm book, Mass book, Lawbook, and all the others, volumes in the new script went from Tours and Aix to the farthest towns. The common denominator of writing had been found, and the incoherence of the darker ages ended.

More than that, by copying out in multiple so much of classic and early Christian literature, texts were preserved that would have been lost to scholars of the later Renaissance, and to us.

The script is known today as the Carolingian minuscule. It endured, in spite of the intrusion of ornate Gothic, in later centuries. When the humanists of the great Renaissance sought for a better writing, they revived the Carolingian minuscule, especially in Italy. It became known then as the Roman. When the earliest printers looked for a model for their type among the manuscripts, they attempted to use Gothic and then turned to the Carolingian-Roman. So it survives in the pages you read today.

No triumph in ancient Rome caused more stir than the arrival of the elephant, Abul Abbas, at Aix. The fabulous monster from Babylon swayed up the muddy market street and pulled the fresh grass from housetops with the incredible arm that served him for a nose. He bellowed with a trumpet blast and the horses in the alleys ran wild over the sheep huddled by the meat sellers.

Charlemagne was satisfied because Abul Abbas pulled apart the stable they gave him; he uprooted young trees, and still ate grapes from the king's hand. Isaac, the merchant who had journeyed for two years with the elephant and the dark-faced keeper, said that Abul Abbas might live for fifty years more if he became content in Frankland. Certainly in the hot summer days Abul Abbas appeared content, eating up a field of grain for a meal and lying down in the river for a bath. Every day the king would stop in his rounds to watch his uncanny visitor, the gift of a kalif.

At least Einhard insisted that Aaron had sent Abul Abbas out of his great love and admiration for Charlemagne. But the gossip of the beer tables had it that Isaac bought the elephant himself as a bit of business.

"Aaron holds our glorious king dearer than all other monarchs of the earth!" The Dwarfling defended his hero.

"By what token say you so?" The beer drinkers remained skeptical, because the Franks sent to Baghdad as envoys had died, or otherwise disappeared, and only Isaac and Abul Abbas had returned.

"By token of the rich presents we have from the Persians."

"What presents?"

"The perfumes and all kinds of stuffs."

The gossips still held that the small secretary was gabbing. Yet in the king's treasury appeared a marvelous golden tray of Khusrau, surely the gift of Harun ("Aaron") the kalif. Here was also a huge pavilion that amazed Saxon hostages who tried shooting their arrows over it. Its cords were dyed with strange colors. After the appearance of Abul Abbas any rich treasure from the east was called the gift of Harun. The clock, for instance.

This bronze water clock pleased Charlemagne, who found it more exact than marked tallow candles or sandglasses.

Within it the dripping of water measured off each of twelve hours, releasing a bronze ball that struck a bell which chimed at the start of each hour. It helped him follow the movement of the star clusters at night.

By now he kept speakers at his side. They interpreted to him what Gascons, Greeks, or Avars said. Exiles like Egbert of Britain sought sanctuary at Aix. Something unheard of was happening. Out from the embryo city on the Würm the king's peace was extending beyond the borders. Saxon hostages settled in the green valley. Prince Charles made his last march to the Baltic. Without speeches in council and taking of oaths, the war of thirty-two years with the Saxon folk ended. Beyond the Rhine, Frankish settlers built towns that stood without ravaging or burning. Charlemagne's brutal transplanting of peoples had quenched armed strife, but the newer generation growing up without feuds or religious hatred really sealed the peace. The king's ban on weapon carrying may have helped. His parish schools, merging children together, broke down clan antagonism. He had the Goth to thank for that.

Moreover this new generation—Einhard's generation—had known no other ruler. Its loyalty went to the giant Frank. Alcuin might speak exultantly of the new Christian empire, but the folk of the farming mesnies were united only by the belief that Charlemagne ruled them all alike.

"He had their rude songs of the deeds and wars of old-time kings written down with care," Einhard relates, "to preserve for future generations."

Perhaps in trying to preserve the old Teutonic myths, Charlemagne made atonement for the felling of Irminsul thirty-two years before. But the songs he had copied out were lost in the new darkness that came after him.

In his own habits—except that he insisted upon the obedience due him as emperor, no longer king of the Franks—Charlemagne changed not at all. He still played a game with a strange ambassador, a Byzantine for choice, by having the man led from paladin to paladin through the corridors of Aix, until the uninitiated stranger found himself bowing down to Chamberlain and Constable before being confronted by the real king shining in cloth of gold on the throne where the sun blazed behind him. Otherwise he kept to his old blue mantle, apple-wood walking stick, and headlong boar hunting. He objected to the gay apparel his nobles brought back from foreign parts. Alcuin warned his friend the archbishop of Canterbury, "If you visit our lord king, take care that your people do not appear before him in gold and silk." The waggish monk of St. Gall had a tale to tell about that, in later years.

"One rainy day Charles was wearing a sheepskin, cheap enough, while the others of his retinue strutted about in robes of pheasant skins and peacock plumes, and silk with purple ribbons, some of them wrapped in ermine robes. It was a holiday and they had just come back from Pavia, where the Venetians dump all the wealth of the east. 'We must not be slothful because we are at leisure,' said he. 'Now let us all go hunting and kill something, and let us go in these clothes we are wearing.'

"So they went scouring the thickets, tearing their way through tree branches, thorns, and briars. They were fouled by blood and skins of wild beasts, and in this state they returned home.

"They all searched for fires to warm themselves, when the most crafty Charles said, 'Everyone must go to bed in his garments to dry them.'

"The next day he commanded them to appear in the same garments, which no longer made a splendid show, being creased and shrunken and rent. Then Charles, full of guile, said to his Chamberlain, 'Give my sheepskin a rub and bring it here.' It came in clean, white, and whole, and the Great Charles took it again, speaking as follows: 'Which is more valuable and useful, this garment bought for a piece of silver, or yours bought for pounds of silver?'"

As Alcuin found his rest outside the shrine of St. Martin, where the trees of the orchard rose like the pillars of a cathedral and the birds sang with angelic voices, so Charlemagne sought relief by his river, where his daughters in regal robes ornamented his table under the elms with flowers, and sang with their children. Until the year of the Saxon peace, 804, Alcuin, who had longed to take a monk's vows and escape from the world's labor, struggled to revise a *Rule* of St. Benedict, to be copied for all the monasteries; Charlemagne dictated his capitulary, requiring *reading of the canon and rule of St. Benedict,* among his other edicts. Before Alcuin died he wrote to Adalhard, now abbot of Corbie, "I have laid away the sword belt of my labor as soldier."

No armed paladin had been so steadfast a champion of Charlemagne as this master of the schools. His passing broke down something of the remarkable continuity of thought in Frankland. The nicknames of the Academy are heard no more.

William of Toulouse, perhaps the strongest mainstay of the the king, left the enclave of the older generation in a fashion of his own. The hero of the Spanish March laid aside sword and saddle to enter a mountain monastery that he had supported during his campaigning. They say that he took up the duty of carrying water, mounted on a donkey, out to the brethren at work in the fields. Angilbert likewise confined himself more to his abbey.

What Charlemagne could have accomplished without this remarkable group who plowed their lives into the fruition of his, no one can say. He had learned much from all of them; they had been faithful to him. Now, at sixty-two, he had no Alcuin to guide his mind, and no Eric to guard his back. Under his urging, those priests and paladins accomplished greater tasks than they had imagined could be done. Could others serve him so?

Charlemagne considered this matter, and called upon all he nourished to render a mightier service. "Now there is a

257

greater duty to be met," he told them, "for, with strength
of body and mind, service must be rendered to God."

Einhard, his shadow, noticed this change in him. "After he
had received the name of emperor——"

The year of Alcuin's death and the Saxon peace, 804, was
the year of hope at Aix. In the south the Spanish March stood
firm with the towns and towers William had erected; in the
north the lawless Godfried, king of the Danes, sought to
meet with Charlemagne in council; from Aix the emperor was
sending money over the seas to Christian poor in Africa and
Syria, to Carthage and Jerusalem. From Rome, Leo was
journeying to Charlemagne not in fear and need but joyfully
to discuss whether or not a miracle had taken place at
Mantua.

For these few months the lands are nourished, the people
have taken the sacramental oath to render service to the
Lord. They have a dawn-of-day expectancy of mercies to
come to them. By the palace stair, the bronze clock chimes
the hours in new fashion. They were to be few, these hours of
a lost community——

Leo himself enters the frontier with relief. In the high
Alps Audulf, now Count of the East March, escorts him down
to the monastery at St. Maurice, where Charles, the king's
son, waits with his liegemen to honor the visitors from Rome.
They ride easily past pilgrim bands, past the trains of oxcarts
hauling the goods of Pavia and the Venetian isles to Aix, for
the road tax on merchants has been lifted. The riders escort-
ing them wear Lombard cloaks, clasped with Moorish silver;
although born Thuringians or East Franks, they hold themselves to be the emperor's men.

By the octave of good St. Martin, Leo is at Reims, where
Charlemagne waits with paladins and huntsmen, in the
square of the great church of St. Remi. From the portal
comes the melody of an organ; its wall shows Moses leading
his people unharmed up from the Red Sea, while waves en-

gulf the armed riders of a Pharaoh who looks like a Hun. . . .

The people speak of harvests gathered in, and seed laid by for planting in Ground-break Month. At the long valley of Aix, where the gold dome shines, the people wait with the banners of the churches, much like Rome. But the way to the palace portico leads past sheep pens and cow stables; the statue guarding the steps is a fine bronze bear.

Where the throng waits to catch sight of Leo, tumblers disport themselves, forking their legs agilely and tossing knives about their heads for pence. When Charlemagne dismounts, with grooms at his stirrup and the soldier-like Chamberlain waiting at the step to take his riding cloak, no trumpets sound. An old man pushes forward boldly, striking a harp with gnarled fingers, chanting greeting to a king returning to his hall. And Charlemagne gives the singer a gold ring from his arm.

Watching this, Theodulf, bishop of Orléans, exclaims, "He is the glory of the poets!"

For the feast after the journey the hall is hung with cloth of Arras, purple silk covers the benches of the guests, silver candelabra light the long tables, adorned with autumn flowers and berries. The Seneschal in court robes ushers in the bearers of the great trays, displayed to the guests. The cup bearer follows with his bearers of wines. By the paladins gleaming in scarlet and gold, children squeeze into the benches eager for the feast to begin. Their whispering rises like a small wind gust in a thicket, until silence comes with Leo's blessing.

At a sign from Charlemagne the palace chaplain prays for mercy to be received by the Christian folk. In spite of the splendor of garments and precious metal, the assembly seems at that moment to be no more than a large family gathered joyously to feast on the last of the Twelve Days of Christmas which begin a new year for them. And through their merriment, the chiming of the bronze clock marks the hours. . . .

The great hope of this beginning of the Christian nation was dimmed by the misfortunes of the next five years.

First, Godfried the Dane king failed to appear at the peace council. Instead, his seafarers began raiding. The annalists of Aix call the seafarers impartially Danes or Normans or Northmen. Out of bleak Scandia, the Baltic islands, and the Dane March they came during the summer sailing season in swift long ships that carried horses as wall as warriors. These earliest Vikings (men of the fjords) drove their shallow vessels far up the rivers and landed to mount their horses, riding to a town, stripping and burning it as they had done at Lindisfarne. They entrenched their camps at night. They were bold fighters who sacrificed to the old gods, and sought out churches for the valuable altar vessels. If an armed host advanced against them, the Northmen took to their horses again and rode back to their dragon ships, where no pursuit could follow.

Having failed to reach a sworn peace with them, Charlemagne tried to arrange a defense for his sea borders. (In his journey of 800 he had warned the coastal folk and started watchtowers building.) But his Lowland and Channel dioceses had been at peace for a long time; the farming freemen were loath to stand watch under arms. He ordered seagoing barks to be built in the larger rivers, and stone strongholds to be raised at strategic points like the corridor of the Rhine. But the Dane king went among the Baltic Slavs, plundering those who had sworn fidelity to the Christian emperor and aiding those who fought against him. Charlemagne's armies could not manage to come up with the raiders.

It seemed as if a new Witukind had arisen on the sea, and the omen of the dragon's head was fulfilling itself.

The monk of St. Gall, with the advantage of afterknowledge, tells a tall tale of Charlemagne's struggle with the doom from the sea. "It happened that in his wandering Charles was supping at peace in a certain town of the Narbona coast, when some Norman ships came in to make a piratical raid.

When the ships were first sighted some of the people thought them to be Jewish, and some African or British merchants. But the all-wise Charles knew them at a glance by their shape and speed, and said as follows: 'These ships are not filled with merchandise but with most fierce enemies.'

"When they heard him, the people hastened eagerly to the shore. Yet they hurried in vain for when the Northmen heard that Charles was there, they vanished in marvelously swift flight. Rising from his table, the most just and devout Charles stood looking from the eastern window, while his tears ran down and no one dared speak a word to him.

"Then he explained his tears to his nobles in these words: 'I do not fear these worthless scamps will do any harm to me. No, I am sad at heart thinking that while I live they dare intrude upon this shore, and I am torn by great sorrow foreseeing what evil they will do to my descendants.' "

The worthy monk ad-libbed upon the truth that while he lived Charlemagne contrived to defend his inland areas, although the elusive sea raiders harried his coasts, and began to take heavier toll from Britain.

Southerly his frontier held secure beyond the Pyrenees. His armed host of Aquitaine—now serving Louis, his son—had drawn into it the wily Gascons, Provençals, and the former Goths of Navarre (who paid heed to Theodulf). Over mountain villages and ravines, it thrust slowly down to the line of the Ebro, where stood Saragossa, of evil memory. Charlemagne's purpose was to gain the coast as far as Barcelona, while trying to reach a truce with the powerful emirs of Córdoba. In this he seemed to be failing.

From time to time religious zeal inflamed the Arab lords of the north and drove them against the encroaching Christians. With the departure of William of Toulouse from the world of battles, leadership lacked in Aquitaine. The devout and heedless Louis could not discipline the headstrong masters of the Pyrenees castles, and Charlemagne did not venture thither. The armed host of Christians marched to seize

Tortosa at the Ebro's mouth—marched around the city in triumph into a rock-bound valley where it was ambushed and decimated like the lost array of Roncesvalles. Charlemagne heard the tidings from Tortosa in silence and grief.

But the greatest danger from Moslem power manifested itself on the Middle Sea. There the empire now held some ports. Barcelona, Narbona, Massilia (Marseilles), and the Ligurian harbors had stagnated since the ending of Roman rule. As the monk of St. Gall relates, Jewish and Carthaginian merchant craft were putting into these ports with precious contraband cargoes. Charlemagne longed to reopen this ancient boulevard of trade, and Pepin chartered a fleet along the Ligurian coast (around Genoa).

Moorish sails flashed past these coasts; crossing the sea boldly, the fleets of Moorish Spain raided the islands, the Balearics, Corsica, Sardinia, carrying off Christians to be sold as slaves. What defense could the emperor of the Christians offer the islands?

Pepin's makeshift fleet, manned by Italians, drove the raiders once from Corsica. But other Saracens in Africa launched other fleets able to navigate across the sea. Charlemagne called for great barks to be built, with rams like the Byzantine and a power of oars like the Northmen.

Easterly lay the mass of the unknown continent. Beyond the Elbe he had taken hostages and tribute from many Slavic tribes to which he owed protection from Northmen and other pagans. Under Charles, his warrior son, the armies of the great East March were drawn continually into the wilderness to enforce the emperor's peace. Charlemagne had the wisdom to give one officer, Audulf, command of this vast frontier, as Count of the East March.

High in the mid-continent, beyond the ridge of the Böhmer Wald dwelt a silent people, the Czechs or Bohemians, who had never known the benefits of civilization.

The sagacious old man at Aix knew that if these Bohemians could be conquered, the restless Slavs and Avars could be driven farther east.

Against the Bohemians Charles was sent with triple-pronged hosts of Christian Saxons, Bavarians, and Slavs. His father had invaded Avarland in this fashion. And, like the Avars, the forest-dwelling Bohemians disappeared from their high valleys. Beyond the swift Moldau supplies failed Charles' armies. He retreated, to report that he had found only a sea of grass, "the great plain of the east."

Again Charles was sent into the Bohemian wilderness, and again Louis was given reinforcement to capture Tortosa at the Ebro's mouth. The result was the same, disappearance in one case, disaster in the other.

It seems that Charlemagne realized at last that his borders had reached the limit of advance to the north and east. For some time he had been building defensive nuclei along the Elbe—walled frontier towns, strengthened by towers, manned by garrisons always under arms. Essefeld thus stood watch against the Danes, Hohbuki up the river fronted the hostile Wilzi—then Magdeburg and Halle. There the defense line turned up the river Saale and climbed the heights to the Böhmer Wald; it circled east around the Avar settlements and dropped to Friuli and Istria (beyond Trieste), where Eric had made good the defense. To the west of this line Christian settlements studded the valleys as time went on; to the east the disorganized pagan folk ranged "the great plain." This line from the Baltic to the Adriatic stood firm.

At some points Christian missioners fared beyond it. Arno carried out his life task by thrusting his churches out to the Save and the Drave (beyond latter-day Austria). For a long time these Carolingian missions marked the limits of the Christian Church.

Beyond the frontier posts of Istria at the Adriatic's head, Charlemagne's *missi* and missioners brought the neighboring Yugoslavs into the Christian fold.

For the first time he had set limits to his domain; those

limits he prepared to defend with all his energy. Within them peace must prevail.

Then hunger returned. It appeared after a dry season and grew to famine here and there. On the heels of famine, Charlemagne knew by experience would come plague, which in turn would breed disorder and fear—as inevitably as one of the Four Horsemen of the Apocalypse followed the other.

At Aix by now he had a great treasure. He called his paladins home in readiness; out of them he formed an officers' pool, sending forth each one at need. Hard they rode when warnings came by beacon fires and homing pigeons. Of the Seneschal Eberhard he took counsel. All law matters he gave to the hearing of the Count of the Palace. Still the famine spread where his officers could not gather food stocks.

They called the Frisian fishing fleets into the mouths of the Rhine; they called out the levy of arms to guard the stacked wheat and cattle herds. Each hundred-man took account of the food left in his village. "The Evil One is afoot in the land," the villagers declared, and crowded into the church to pray, instead of carrying water to the fields. From village to village the *missi* rode, exhorting those who had stores laid by to give to those who lacked. Some obeyed them, some did not, fearing worse to come.

"Obey the messengers," Charlemagne gave command, and enforced it. In his villas he had thoroughbred cattle, and chosen horses; his managers planted new and hardy grains; they made the serfs cherish bee swarms and guard the fish in the streams. His villa farms showed others by example what could best be grown in the earth. The royal manses beyond the villas Charlemagne ordered to be opened to the families transplanted from Saxony. Landless families he sent east, to clear the Saxon forests. From Aquitaine others were led over the mountains to settle in the new Spanish borderland. Folk too sick to labor took swine herds to the forests to feed.

Early in this stress Charlemagne took thought of his own

death, and what would then befall his household and domain.

Before the end of winter, 806, he called an assembly at Theodo's Villa which was nearer the center of his rule than Aix. There he decreed the partition of the so-called empire between his sons, Charles, Pepin, and Louis. In this he followed the Merovingian custom and the example of his own father.

The vast heritage he split up into three kingdoms. After his death his sons would rule as kings where they had administered their territories as viceroys—Louis' kingdom being centered around Aquitaine, Pepin's around the ancient Lombardy, and Charles' around the Rhinelands, stretching as far south as the county of Tours. With his new care for frontiers, Charlemagne was particular in naming the borders of the three kingdoms-to-be. To Louis, moreover, he allotted a passage through the southern Alps to Italy, and gave to Charles a route from the Rhine to the pass of the Mount of Jove (Great St. Bernard). In this way he kept boulevards open by which all brothers could go to the others' aid.

The rest of his household he protected by a typical Charlemagne measure. His daughters were to possess their own estates, to be cared for by their brothers, and they were to marry, lawfully, at their own desire. No grandchild might be exiled, made captive, or harmed in any way. Peace was to be maintained within the family and its domains. Yet while he lived all authority would rest in his hands; he would receive the obedience "due from sons to their father, and from the people to their emperor."

Now this is hardly the last will of a man seeking to revive the Roman Empire, or to create any political empire. By it Charlemagne provided historians with a riddle as puzzling as that of his coronation. Did he really mean to divide up his creation in this fashion, or did he intend to name one of his sons as emperor at the last hour? Charlemagne did not say.

As to his sons, he seemed not to favor one over the others. Charles, who most resembled his father—observers censored the stalwart prince for praying with his head erect—was called upon most often in war. The pious Louis received most assistance and seemed to need every bit of it. The impetuous Pepin, jealous of Charles, disputed constantly with Leo, yet accomplished much alone against Beneventans, Avars, and even the Moslems at sea. But all three were kept within the orbits of their kingdoms-to-be.

Charlemagne provided decisively for the execution of his will. He had the lords of the assembly at Theodo's Villa swear obedience to it, and he had Einhard send a copy of it to Leo, for the Papal acquiescence.

One clue to his intention may survive. The single-minded Arnulfing appeared to be more conscious of the responsibility laid upon him, as emperor, than of any privileges that might attach to him. (He disliked to be called another Augustus, or a second Constantine the Great.) Hincmar, who wrote the chronicle of the palace, speaks of such responsibility—"the responsibility begun in the time of Constantine the Great, *who became a Christian.*"

Perhaps with Charlemagne this obligation as a Christian overrode any political scheme of things. He seemed to feel that way. By his will, did he not mean the chief beneficiary to be simply the united Christian people, kept at peace by the brother kings, guided by St. Peter? Centered upon Aix, protected by the new frontiers he had set, could not this single Christian nation of the west survive?

Such a dominion had no precedent. It was visionary, built upon hope, and sustained by Charlemagne's intense determination.

Although the famine was checked, plague swept the villages, apparently among cattle more than humans. In the north, Charles' armies were immobilized by loss of animals. As far as the Italian border, strife broke out against the Beneventans, who were accused of scattering "murder powder" among the herds. Superstition stirred up fear of strangers who might be carrying the mysterious "murder powder." Wayfarers who could not identify themselves might be tied up and thrown into rivers.

At Aix throngs pressed into the Mary Church to touch the gold reliquary holding the mantle of St. Martin.

In the summer of 807 Charlemagne was disturbed by an unheard-of happening. Few of the seigneurs summoned to the year's assembly appeared before him at Ingelheim. So few that for the first time he held no assembly. It amounted to a revolt against his authority. There could be no campaign that summer. Instead of making the year's plans with his lay and ecclesiastical lords, he sent forth his *missi* to investigate each government, to discover whether obedience was given to the local seigneur or to the distant emperor.

For the effect of his absence from the provinces was becoming apparent. At first, confining himself to Aix, he had been grateful for the convenience of keeping his treasure and records in one place, instead of carting them over roads. But now it appeared that townspeople who no longer beheld his face turned to their local lords.

The men of the armed forces, the *missi* said, remained faithful to the emperor. Yet the ranks thinned because of poverty in the homes. The building of ships and churches took labor from the fields. And small proprietors paid "to be free of the need to go forth armed."

Freemen who could not support themselves and pay the church tithe were entering the monasteries, where they would be cared for.

Charlemagne fought this spreading desertion with edicts. "Freemen are forbidden to enter clerical vocation without the consent of the emperor, since many did so to evade the levy of arms . . . public prayers may be said where famine or pestilence occurs, without royal permission . . . grain not to be sold above the ordered price . . . food necessary to life not to be exported."

Landholders who did not furnish equipment for the army

were threatened with loss of their fiefs. Those owning three manses must go into armed service; of three owners of single manses, one must serve and the two others equip and maintain him. Those who had only movable belongings must send in a third of horses, cloth, swine, or sheep—of whatever kind they had.

Something unforeseen by Charlemagne was happening. To withstand Arabs and Northmen he needed an army of trained horsemen in the field all the year. Such riders in turn needed cuirasses and helmets of precious iron, strong saddles to bear such weight, and chains of iron rings to guard the necks and reins of the war horses. To outfit and feed such a man-at-arms took the labor of five freemen in the fields. (Within three centuries this rider would become the steel-clad knight supported by peasants.)

Moreover as seigneurs and bishops became responsible—under heavy penalty—for bringing fixed numbers of men to the armed host, they tended to increase their hold upon such men. The service oath of freeman to noble, in return for the traditional coin paid him, became more binding. The word *vassal* began to appear in the records. Feudal vassalage was setting in.

At the same time, the character of the nobility was changing. The dukes and counts of old time who governed areas for the king could not serve in such long campaigns and maintain order at home. (Charlemagne allowed a count to leave four men-at-arms behind at his castle, and a bishop two at his hall.) Eric and William had passed most of their years with the armed forces. A new type of seigneur came into being, a successful or popular war leader who could rally an armed following. Charlemagne ordered that a freeman could change his service from one lord to another but might not escape service itself except for extraordinary cause. He wanted to eliminate fugitives and to check the flight of the war-weary into monasteries.

The old order of the Merovingian Franks, of the few king's

officers placed over the self-armed freemen was breaking down. Seigneurs began to lead forth small armies, devoted to them, and their power increased thereby.

This embryo of the feudal system had formed before Charlemagne but he hastened its growth and his edicts legalized it. Yet while he lived the glory of his name held men in awe and they felt their highest obligation was to him. Did not Eardulf, king of Northumbria in Britain, seek his counsel, and did not the wise lord king—his people seldom called him emperor—send the fugitive Eardulf to Leo for judgment?

Yet their lord king overruled Leo the apostolic lord. Almost as fiercely as they discussed the question of the holy images, the churches argued about the Holy Spirit itself. Did it come from God the Father alone, or from the Lord Jesus as well? At Aix, Charlemagne called a church council to make this clear, and there Theodulf the outspoken maintained that the Spirit came also from the Son, as all right-thinking men believed. What mattered the objection of the Greeks to such a truth? Charlemagne wished it to be expressed clearly and to everyone in public prayer—*"Filioque* [and from the Son]." So it became part of their prayers, and the venerable Adalhard carried the words of Aix to Rome.

More than that, said the folk, the patriarch of Jerusalem himself appealed to the unwearied Charlemagne, setting forth that lawless Beduins attacked and enslaved the worthy Christians of the Holy Land to whom Charlemagne had sent such wealth, to build their hostels and adorn their altars. Ay, the Mount of Sion and the Mount of Olives were joyful with the gifts of the most generous lord king. When he heard the plea of the unhappy patriarch, who had sent the keys of the Sepulcher to his hands, he became angered and grieved, so that he dispatched his envoys to Aaron, king of the Persians, to request, for love of him, protection for the Christian congregations in Jerusalem.

Thereupon, in truth, the kalif showed his love for the lord

king of the Christians by sending an ambassador named
Abdullah, together with the monk Felix and the abbot George
of the Mount of Olives. The Persian Abdullah brought incredible presents, a miniature elephant of ivory and a vase of
glass brightened with enamel and gold, and a pavilion large
enough to hold Charlemagne seated among all his paladins.

Furthermore the same Abdullah vowed on behalf of his
master that the will of the king emperor should be done.
Pilgrims and Christians dwelling in the holy places from St.
Sabah's in the vale of the Kedron to the Sepulcher should
be protected from robbery, and despite. As token of his
pledge the kalif rendered freely to the lord king the possession of the most holy Sepulcher.

Einhard testified to that. "Not only did the kalif, when informed of the wishes of Charlemagne, grant him all he asked
but placed in his power the very holy tomb of the Savior and
the place of Resurrection."

The tidings of Harun's grant, coming at a time of emotional
stress, caused rejoicing and grew with repetition in the western hamlets, where everything pertaining to Jerusalem held
miraculous significance. Einhard, as usual, could not resist
writing it down with a flourish.

What was the truth of the intercourse between Harun and
Charlemagne? It has become a third puzzle of the great king's
reign. The records of the Baghdad court do not mention the
name of Charlemagne, nor the sending of a state embassy to
him. Arab historians knew of the Franks—they called all
western Europeans "the Franks"—and they spoke of a king.
No mention appears of the elephant Abul Abbas. Yet trade
missions came and went between Aix and Baghdad. Only
Isaac, that remarkable interpreter who turned himself into
a one-man embassy could have explained the whole truth.

It seems as if the plea of the Palestine Christians did reach
Harun, who was less tolerant than his namesake the Harun al
Rashid of the *Thousand and One Nights*. The real Harun
granted his protection to the troubled churches and pilgrims,

and as a gesture of courtesy made gift of the traditional grave of Jesus to the petitioner from the king of the Franks.

Harun may well have bestowed the narrow crypt beneath the Sepulcher church upon the unknown king of the Franks. But there is no believing that a kalif of Islam, keeper of the shrines of Islam, would have given a strange Christian authority over any part of Jerusalem, which was *Al Kuds*—the Holy —to all Moslems. Nor did he give the Frank a protectorate over either the city, or the land of Palestine as is often said. He offered to see to the safeguarding of priests and pilgrims himself.

The uninhibited monk of St. Gall gave voice to the legend that formed around Charlemagne as the "protector of Jerusalem."

"The unwearied emperor sent to the Persian emperor gifts of horses and mules from Spain, of Frisian robes both white and red, and dogs of the greatest fierceness. The king of Persia cast a careless eye over the other presents but asked the envoys what the dogs were good at catching. . . . Those German dogs caught for him a Persian lion, and Harun understood from that slight indication how mighty was our lord king. 'Now I know,' said Harun, 'what I heard of my brother Charles is true. How can I make fit return for the honor he has bestowed on me? If I give him the land which was promised to Abraham, it is so far away he could never defend it, high-souled king though he is. But I will show my gratitude, I will give that land into his power, and I will rule it as his viceroy.'"

As the plague spread through the hamlets, Charlemagne went out on the roads again. Along the Meuse and the Rhine he showed himself, with his family following and the choir of Aix singing the Lord's mercy. Understanding that such tribulations came from the will of the Lord, Charlemagne felt that it was his task to remedy them.

At the fear of the folk he laughed; flight he forbade, and

271

idleness he mocked. "Now it is our privilege to serve the Lord with great deeds."

He told them the tale of Jerusalem and the bestowal of the Sepulcher. He showed them the Standard of Jerusalem. As visible proof of that the common folk beheld marching behind him the miraculous bulk of Abul Abbas.

With the coming of cold weather the plague lessened and disorder ceased. Rumors of good happenings spread where the lord king passed, of a truce to be had with the Saracens of Spain (Louis had just failed the second time at Tortosa). Merchants were bringing fresh goods up from Provence, where Christian ships were being launched.

Charlemagne had managed to break out of the inland isolation.

He was in touch now with the currents of the outer world, and that meant the commerce that crossed the Middle Sea. At long last he was straining to reach that sea. ("That little pool," the monk of St. Gall explained.) It had not sufficed to defend his growing coast line by motionless towers and guard posts. By gaining new trading ports, he could tap the seaborne commerce and build large vessels of his own.

True, his new fleets on the Provençal and Ligurian coasts fared badly against the swift-sailing Saracens, but there was a more vital boulevard to the east, and he had seen it.

At the harbor of Ravenna he had looked out on the dark waters of the Adriatic. There the Byzantine fleets cruised unchallenged. On the far side of the Adriatic stood the outposts of Constantinople. No Frankish army in skiffs and barks could cross that barrier of water if the Greek admirals opposed it. And of late, spurred on by Nicephorus, who had refused to greet him as *Basileus,* they had been hostile enough, here and in Sicily.

Yet above Ravenna, at the Adriatic's end, there were the ancient ports of Aquileia and Pola across upon the Istrian shore. There a bishop friendly to Charlemagne had been thrown to death from a tower by the Byzantine faction. There Fortunatus, his successor, appealed for protection to the emperor at Aix. Then, too, within the mysterious Venetian isles a merchant folk built new cargo vessels and went their own way to sea secretively. At Aix appeared two Venetian doges—as they called their dukes—beseeching alliance with Charlemagne, while endeavoring to play the land power of Aix against the sea power of Constantinople. Angered by their double-faced dealing, Charlemagne stirred up a faction of his own at the Venetian port.

Then a Byzantine fleet raided the coast near Ravenna, and the doges hastened to face toward Constantinople. Charlemagne announced that he would protect Fortunatus, and sent Pepin with the Lombard army of Italy around by land toward the Dalmatian mountains and the highway to Constantinople. On the way thither Pepin would seize the hidden, treacherous port of the Venetians.

If the Venetians were made Charlemagne's subjects, new ships could be built skilfully in their yards, to enter the sea lanes of commerce—perhaps not in his own time but in the time of his sons. Charlemagne sought to hold the Adriatic, and with that advantage, to make a firm peace with Constantinople.

The headstrong Pepin, in obeying his father, made an attempt to cross the sea to Venice; Byzantine warships turned him back, and his army forced a way along the shore to the marshy inlets and lagoons. One of the lagoons he captured by making a bridge of ships' masts. Craftily the Venetians moved their vessels and belongings out to the Deep Channel (*Rivus Altus*—the Rialto).

This Pepin besieged but could not take, lacking a fleet. Holding the land, however, with his host, he kept the sea folk penned on the great outer lagoon. When the summer's heat came and the Frankish warriors sickened, the Venetians persuaded them to take a spoken submission of the isles and the payment of thirty-six silver pounds in yearly tribute to

Charlemagne. Pepin agreed, and departed on his way east. Yet he had not captured the Venetians' port, and he had the sickness of the marshes.

(From this siege the Venetians learned a lesson, and rebuilt their port upon the Rialto site, where as the Republic of Venice, it would gain mastery of the nearer seas. And in the same decade the exiled Egbert, the West Saxon, returned to Britain from the court of Aix, and took the name of the first king of England.)

So Charlemagne heard at Aix. Rotrud, eldest of his girls, lay ill in the women's wing, where priests waited to shrive her. Yet all thought of those in the palace turned to the north, where misfortunes followed fast. The doom in the north came from the Danes who ravaged the islands and Frisian shore, taking tribute of a hundred pounds of silver as the price of their leaving—then sailing up the Elbe, assailing the castle of Hohbuki, rousing the Slavs and laying waste the Saxon towns.

With the levy of arms he had sent north to meet the danger, Charlemagne had sent his elephant. The scribes of the palace made a brief note: "The elephant that Aaron, king of the Saracens, had given him perished there by sudden death."

At the end of a day when the master of Aix was walking back through the colonnade by the statue of Theodoric, a messenger stood in his way. The man bore the marks of hard riding, and he kneeled. He asked the king's mercy before he gave out his news.

"Speak without harm," the king said impatiently.

"The words are not mine but of Godfried, the Dane king."

"I bid you tell them."

"These are his words. Godfried says the land of the Frisians and land of the Saxons lie under tribute to him. Now he takes his way hither to burn your court of Aix. By this warning, he gives you time to flee."

That night in his anger Charlemagne summoned those paladins who waited at Aix; he took with him his guards and the Meuse-Rhine freemen. Swiftly he sent advice to Charles his son to bring the army of the East March and Audulf up to the Weser. By the Rhine, and the springs of the Lippe, Charlemagne would come in haste to meet with him at the town of sore memory, Verden. They would stand between the Danes and Aix.

So at sixty-eight years of age in the early summer of 810, with Rotrud's death grieving him, Charlemagne went out to seek battle with the Northmen. It was no easy task to bring to standing battle the seafarers who could slip along the coast in their ships.

When he left his tent at the first road camp an ill thing happened that Einhard, who saw it, recked little at the time but remembered well later.

"He was leaving camp before sunrise to start the march," Einhard explains, "when he saw a ball of fire falling from the sky with a great light. It sped across the clear sky from right to left, when the horse Charles was riding gave a plunge, throwing him to the ground. He fell so heavily his cloak buckle broke and his sword belt parted. After his servants ran to him and relieved him of his arms, he could not rise without their help. The light spear he had held was found twenty feet or more from the spot."

Charlemagne had grown heavier, and he was fully armed when he fell. He limped with one leg after that.

At the time the omen did not seem to be doomful. For the Carolingians, father and son, met and waited on the Weser and their spies beheld no sign of the Northmen. Charlemagne waited there in his tent, hunting the forest. There they heard how Godfried's life had ended by assassination and his ships had sailed home to Scandia, where the new king besought a truce with Charlemagne. When he made certain that these tidings were not a lie to deceive him, he rode home himself.

Beyond Venetia, by the plague or other sickness, Pepin who ruled Italy had died. Ungovernable at times, his spirit had been the strongest among the three sons.

As soon as he reached Aix, Charlemagne summoned a man in whom he had entire faith, Adalhard. "You will go to Lombardy, you will have the tomb of my son built within the basilica of Mediolanum [Milan], for he reigned over that land. At the basilica of St. Peter you will announce that Bernard his youngling son is king of the Lombards and all others who were subject to his father."

There was more to be done by Adalhard. A *Spatharius* of Constantinople who had sought Pepin waited at Pavia. This ambassador must be honored and brought to Charlemagne at Aix instead. "For he is the link of peace between the two empires. And if the Venetian dukes are a stone in the path of that peace, let the *Spatharius* know the stone will be removed and the Venetians given over to the rule of the most gracious lord of Constantinople. Let him know that peace will be made."

The frontiers of the Christian folk must be kept secure, in spite of plague and death, and the pagans beyond the borders. So Egbert went over the sea to rule England, and the infant Venice was freed, to lie beyond the doom descending upon the empire of Charlemagne. Envoys bearing truce were on the road from Córdoba.

The stout, lame man laboring at Aix was determined to put his house in order, and by doing so for these few months he influenced the happenings in the outer world.

As the plague ended death struck its hardest blows. It took Gisela, his saintly sister at Chelles; at Prüm it carried with it his first-born, Pepin Hunchback, who had imagined once that he might hold the throne. The plague seemed to be gone when the next year ended and the Twelve Days of Christmas drew near.

For the last entry, the scribes wrote in the annals, "Charles, the eldest son of the Lord Emperor died on the second day of the Nones of December; and the Emperor stayed the winter at Aquis [Aix]."

"He was the hope of the empire," the paladins exclaimed, grieving perhaps for themselves as much as the leader of the emperor's armies.

The sense of loss struck deep into Charlemagne. He had given the hardest tasks to Charles, who had been more than a namesake. Perhaps he had driven his son too hard as a boy; Charles had not married; the boy had been betrothed to a girl of the Mercian king—as Rotrud had been pledged to the young emperor of Constantinople. Even Gisela—he barely recalled it—had once been betrothed to the royal Lombard line. He had not allowed those marriages. What if they had left him, to take distant thrones? He could not imagine that.

Now his family had changed. In the palace only the elfin Rothaid stayed, with the grandchildren and the children of those last women who had belonged to him after Liutgard, the women who took their ease in the curtained chambers, and cared nothing for evensong. They hobnobbed over their new garments of damask silk; sometimes they tried to prattle Latin to please him. Within his presence they made much of him, but he seldom saw them now, because they slipped out at night to seek their men elsewhere.

Rothaid did not like to read, even to him. Yet she would dance whenever the music played, holding up the edge of her skirt, flashing between the candle gleam and the fire.

At dawn and after dark Charlemagne would go alone in his weathered mantle and slippers from his sleeping chamber to the colonnade where the monks waited to escort him through the imperial door of his chapel church. There he made his orisons, marking the rise and fall of their chanting. . . .

For the first time when the weakness came on him after Charles and the others had gone to the mercy of God, he remembered that he could find rest. He could leave the world, by departing to the cloister of St. Arnulf, or the cell that Alcuin had craved, close to valiant St. Martin. Many of his ancestors had done that.

277

Vaguely he had thought of it, while Charles lived. In his weakness his heart labored after he mounted a horse, . . . as the heart pumped lifeblood through the limbs—Alcuin had read him that, out of Pliny's pages—a family needed some part, some person to sustain the others. Charles would have been such a life-giver to the family. And the people themselves, the idle folk of slothful minds, must have such a life-giver, or they would fall again into the despair of ignorance.

How did they name Louis, his surviving son? Louis the Gentle, Louis the Pious. Comely, sensitive, and ineffective, Louis might have found his vocation in the Church.

Ill tidings did not cease. Far in the east Nicephorus had been slain and his armed host decimated by the khan of the Bulgars. Off the Lowlands, northern sails had been sighted. From St. Peter's came fresh warnings, of Saracen fleets assailing the islands. They were not the raiders of Spain but the fleets of Moslem Africa. What would befall if the Moors and the Africans combined to invade the Christian coasts? No one army, however powerful and loyal, could march along the shore to keep pace with ships.

At Rome, Leo planned to fortify his coast. He could not wall in a coast as if it were the heart of a town . . . And Charlemagne had never mustered a powerful army; he had coaxed and driven the levies to march forth every summer except two, with banners flying and trumpets sounding.

No, there was no likelihood he could forsake the affairs of the world. The truce was sworn with the Dane king, but those warriors thought more of gain than keeping a pledge to Christians. The armies could not defend the Christian folk unless the king found a way of his own to do it——

During the winter Charlemagne kept to his hours of work, calling in those who waited in the antechamber—where no women frolicked now—to appeal to him, while he pulled on his shoes and wrapped his leg thongs. Of nights he wandered from the Treasury chambers to the Vestiary and the Library, carefully noting what wealth of his remained.

"He wished to give inheritance to his daughters," Einhard relates, "and to the children of his concubines . . . in the case of his death or withdrawal from the world."

This disposal and inventory Ercambald wrote down in grand style. "In the name of the Lord God, the Almighty Father and Son and Holy Spirit. This is the inventory and division dictated by the most glorious and most pious Lord Charles, Emperor Augustus, in the 811th year of the Incarnation of our Lord Jesus Christ, in the 43d year of his reign in Francia and 37th in Italy, the 11th of the empire and the 4th Indiction, which piety and prudence have decided him, God allowing, to make of his treasures and money known to be this day in his treasure chamber."

Of such fine phrasing the diligent Ercambald was a master. In state documents it might be necessary, yet Charlemagne had an odd fancy. From his small marble throne in the gallery of his Mary Church he could watch the lettering that gave, in red mosaics, the name of the builder as *Karolus Princeps*. He had told the mosaic masons from Sicily to put it in like that—Charles the Chieftain. It reassured him to read those simple words, so unquestionably true.

By his will, he divided his jewels, gold, regalia, coin, and valuables in three parts, which were put into three great chests. Two chests were sealed. They were to belong to his churches throughout the lands, to be received by the twenty-one archbishops of cities. This much to alms, as a Christian obligation.

The third part, in the third chest, was not sealed up. It held personal belongings as well as treasure. It could be used by him, and after his death it would belong to his family, to his servitors, and to the poor of the lands in equal parts.

Since there were bulky objects like vessels, and brasswork, precious staffs, carpets, and even arms and saddles belonging to him that would not fit into the third chest, he ordered that they be added afterward.

Then he made some special provisions. His chapel, the

Mary Church, must be left as it stood, untouched, with its ornaments.

His library of books, so carefully gathered by Alcuin, was to be sold at fair prices, and the money given to the poor.

One of his silver tables, bearing the plan of Constantinople, was to be sent to St. Peter's; the table depicting Rome—to Ravenna. The third and richest, bearing the world map, would belong to his heirs, including the poor.

So Charlemagne divided all his belongings. Among the witnesses signing the disposal document were Arno and Theodulf, and the abbots Angilbert and Fredugis.

As soon as this was arranged, in mild spring weather Charlemagne hastened down the Meuse to the coast, to speed the building of forts at Ghent, of war vessels in the rivers. On the Channel, where Northmen appeared, he inspected Boulogne, raising a lighthouse and launching ships from the ways. Wherever he went he told gladly the tidings of victory from Spain. Tortosa had fallen to the Christians, who now held the line of the far Ebro.

The proof of that was the arrival of envoys from proud Córdoba, who offered peace from Hakam the emir. Far to the south, Bernard had been crowned king of Italy, and Adalhard had reached a sworn peace with the Beneventans, who could be expected to abide by it, if Constantinople came to terms.

He *must* have alliance with Constantinople. Charlemagne thought it a sign of God's providence that the Moors should still be at the palace when the stately ambassadors came in from Constantinople. He had an hour of anxiety when he discovered they were not of the highest rank, being Michael, Metropolitan of Constantinople, the envoy of earlier years and an officer of the guards of the new emperor, Michael. But he mustered all available splendor of his own guards in bright new cloaks, of his paladins in their silk and plumes, his seigneurs in their robes. He had the banners of his twenty-one cities lining the stairs by the statue of the bear.

Charlemagne's City

When Burchard the Seneschal hastened to confide in him that the envoys of the true emperor suffered anxiety as to the Bulgar invaders, and wished no "misdeed to come between the lords of the east and the west," Charlemagne took heart before he reflected that Byzantines always began by offering compliments sweet as honey.

He ordered them to be brought, not to the great hall, which was ample enough but poorly ornamented by Byzantine standards, but to his most glorious chamber, the nave of the little Mary Church. There he sat in jeweled diadem, in his mantle of cloth of gold, with the sword of gold and jeweled hilt at his side, and the fine scepter of Tassilo in his hand.

As the envoys paced in, wearing black and gleaming purple, the chapel choir sang *Vexilla regis prodeunt*, while the organ sounded. They bent their heads, they went down on their knees, they placed in his hands a document. It was an offer of peace.

The scribes wrote down at the end: "They praised him in their Greek speech; they called him emperor and *Basileus*."

After twelve years, Charlemagne had been recognized as an emperor, equal of the *Basileus* of Constantinople.

Chapter X

GROWTH OF A LEGEND

IT CAME FIRST in quiet voices from the land. A boy picked herbs for medicine in a garden close. Bending low, he drew in the fragrance of hyssop and thyme, and he thought how when he carried the herb basket to the door where the old Benedictine waited, he would add his words, although he could not make much of a poem as yet. "Such a little gift, my father, for so great a scholar—if you were sitting here in this green darkened garden, all your boys of the school would be playing here under the apple growth. All your laughing boys of the happy school. Will you, my father, who can make a book out of thoughts, prune and shape these my words so they can be a poem?"

This boy grew up to attend the school, and he did make a poem which he called *About Gardening* and explained that it was a very poor gift from Walafrid Strabo to the venerable abbot of St. Gall.

Then, walking by the sandy bank of the Loire, Fredugis, who had taken Alcuin's place, tried to bring back the thoughts of his master, of "the field flowers yielding herbs that heal, where the birds sing together their matins, praising God who made them. Where the fragrance of apple orchards creeps into the cloisters. Like the memory of your voice, echoing within the walls."

These small voices in strained cadence bespoke, however,

a new hope and peace of mind. The boys thronging into the growing School of Tours, the books flowing from the writing chamber in the fine clear script, going on to Reims and Reichenau, where the monks painted in more lifelike saintly figures, out to the fields of Brittany and the heights of the Asturias, where artisans worked with forge and pliers to shape new lamps like the Moors of Córdoba—this quiet in labor, this articulation of joy, came out of the peace of those few brief years.

In his chamber at Orléans where a map of the world had been painted, the busy Theodulf remembered Rothaid, who had brought apples to her father, and who now "shone in royal splendor of precious metal and jewels." At St. Denis upon the highway to the obscure, overgrown island of Paris, the former Lombard, Fardulf, announced that the hostel palace he had built in gratitude awaited the arrival of Charlemagne. A sleeping chamber, kept in order for him with damask on the couch, overlooked the distant Seine. It awaited him—would he not visit it again in the Hay Month?

A stranger riding to Aix beheld these river lands and spoke of them as "Flowering Francia." They reminded him of the Florentian city in Italy.

There is no mistaking the meaning of the voices. The land was at peace. In the mind of the stripling Walafrid, and the wayfarer alike, the aspect of this land had been brought about by Charlemagne. Who else? What province or diocese of Christendom did not obey him?

"Since the beginning of the world," the Irish Dungal asked, "when has there been a king in the lands now ruled by the Franks so wise and strong as he?"

These speakers express an awareness of something taking place around them. However moved by their hopes, they sense an ending of barbarism, while a great Christian community extends as far as the outposts of the Church. Inwardly it gains understanding of itself, and it goes on its way with no other aid than religion.

In spite of Einhard's fondness for calling it a revival of Rome, few others behold in it anything to do with the empire of Rome. One or two speak vaguely of the golden time of Romulus, at the founding of the other empire. And of course, the word *Imperator* stands on the coins of new weight and fineness—like the new measures and weights for scales. Most of them, beholding the paintings covering the walls of Reims and Ingelheim, as well as the pages of the fresh Bibles, think of the domain of King David, or of Moses, leading his people away from the peril of the Red Sea crossing.

Oddly enough, there was a meeting of minds between the monks who never left their cloisters and the veterans of the wars. The old soldiers remembered how after Irminsul was overthrown the thirst of the drouth-stricken army was quenched by a miraculous torrent of rain. On the walls of Fritzlar—did not two unknown warriors in shining white appear to aid the Christian swordsmen? These twain the monks identified as Sts. Martin and Denis. To cap that, the soldiers chanted the refrain of Sigiburg—how in the shield ring of the Christians appeared two shields flaming as with living fire, frightening the pagans to their doom.

Such were the *cantilènes* that the grandsons of Kerold heard in the camps. The cause of such celestial intervention, in the minds of the old soldiers, could only have been Charlemagne. That time he fell from his horse and his spear flew twenty feet from his hand marked the almost miraculous death of his enemy, Godfried the Dane king. The spear flying away from his hand gave a sign that he would not need it. And certainly the time of the double eclipse in the sky, of the sun and moon, had been that of the deaths of his two sons, Charles and Pepin.

Thus while Charlemagne lived the semblance of the second Charlemagne, the king of legend, was forming around him. And the massive Arnulfing took pains to encourage the legend. It helped to control troops led into an Avarland, or to quiet villagers frantic with fear of the plague. Tall and impressively round in body, he rode at the head of gleaming dukes, lords, and bishops, with the standard of Jerusalem going before and a remarkable elephant following after. He sang with the chanters at the altars and the drinkers in the taverns. This combination of most potential monarch and artful comedian always pleased the crowds.

Yet he could not have anticipated the consequences of his acting an emperor in this fashion.

Being confined now to the palace at Aix, Charlemagne no longer heard the songs of the camps or the miracle tales of the monastic refectories. Because he limped heavily he wore a long mantle edged with ermine. The apple-wood stick had been discarded for a long staff of carved ivory head, the gift of Frisian seal hunters.

At his dawn rising, he allowed himself to be shaved, and even waited for the barber to brush his gray mustache out on both sides. Now that his hair had turned white as old Sturm's, he let it grow down below his ears, so that it resembled a gleaming helmet, bound by the thin gold of the diadem.

The morning that he heard about the fire, he managed to step through the chamber curtains with an even stride, bracing himself against the pain that shot through his joints.

He greeted Burchard, and Einhard the fosterling, hearing from them that Arno had sent Croat Christians to take oath to him, and that the count waited with the case of the Saxon family.

The lawmen made much of this suit of the slain Westfalian grandsire. In Witukind's day, this Saxon grandsire had been baptized. Although a Christian and a sword-bearing noble, he had been slain by mishap when Charles the king's son had ravaged the Westfalian *pagus*. Then the Saxon's son had renounced claim to a death amend by swearing loyalty to Charles. So far, it was well enough. Yet in the disorder of the last campaigns in Saxonland, this father, a free man and vassal of Charles, had been carried off into exile with his family by the dragnet that swept so many into new homes in Frankland. Now the three sons, tall youths bearing weapons, brought suit to recover their ancestral lands in Westfalia, since they were the heirs of the dead grandsire who had possessed the lands.

Being Saxons, these three appealed to Saxon law. But were they exiles or free men? In the archives at Aix they were written down as exiles. Saxon law laid down that "Only by the king's will may an exiled noble be granted possession of his property again."

The lawmen had argued the case with determination, without finding an answer. Reluctantly the Count of the Palace had granted their appeal to the lord king.

Charlemagne looked toward the three young Saxons. Straight they stood, flushed with excitement, their blue eyes reflecting awe and expectancy. At their age, they knew him only as the great king who had driven the raiding Northmen from Westfalia. They would make the best soldiers——

"I grant it," he announced. "As loyal servants, they shall inherit the property."

Burchard, making a note on his tablet, muttered something like, "And how many other thousand Saxons!"

As he passed the kneeling boys, Charlemagne could not resist glancing at their exultant faces. He looked at the Croats, dark men with white felt cloaks and silver armlets. They had brought him a rude silver processional cross, and he was glad that Burchard had selected more valuable gold arm bands as Charlemagne's gifts to them.

He progressed through the throng as far as the stairhead and was listening for the chime of the metal clock that would sound the past-noon hour when he could lead the way to the dining hall, and after staying his hunger could take off his shoes, mantle, and girdle to sleep for two hours or even three.

Then the messenger from the Rhine courier boat came

through to report the fire that destroyed the great bridge at Mainz. It had been built with massive strength, to stand forever above the flood waters. Drunken roisterers had dropped their torches into the wooden beams, instead of the river, and in three hours the charred bridge fell into the water.

"We will build it again of stone," he said curtly. But when he dozed that afternoon he could not rest in sleep for wondering how masonry could be arched between stone piers, and how any piers could be raised in midstream. The force of the river was too great.

The force of a spring storm toppled over the covered colonnade that sheltered him on the way to his church. His masons could not bind stones together like the Romans, who had raised the aqueducts. . . . How long had it taken them to build their monumental Rome? Four centuries, Einhard said. That was nonsense that Alcuin could have banished with a jest. These younglings, raised in his palace, told him the *words* of books, not the meanings. Even if those words were clearly inscribed in the new small letters, they could accomplish no more than tiny sticks laid for a fire. The mind itself had to seize on the words and kindle with understanding, as if flame had caught in the sticks.

Yet if understanding came, and the mind strove with clear purpose to achieve something, how could that something be achieved unless by the will of God, the Almighty Father?

No lawmen could answer that question. They looked to him. Burchard waited for his word to plant the new seed grain from Africa; Arno sent the Croats to him. The broken colonnade, the fallen bridge, the graves of the plague-slain and the beseeching of their thousands of sons all waited to be preserved by him. . . .

When he stirred up from his nap, the pages of the sleeping chamber found him limping in his blue mantle toward the stair that led to the church. They called Rothaid from the gossiping ladies, to tell him this was the hour when he must take his throne seat to hear the fiscal reports of the Thuringian bishops, and the codification of his judgments in law matters.

At this time in the afternoon the body fire that the physicians called fever wearied him, and confused his thoughts. Often he looked at the faces ranged around him, to remember what he must do next. Burchard urged him to send for his surviving son, by Hildegard. But Louis was on the Spanish March with the host of Aquitaine; the boy had his duties there. Charlemagne put Burchard off, and did not send for Louis.

There in the south the sea border was aflame. The Saracen fleets did not hold back for the truce signed at Córdoba. The Moors of Spain joined with their brethren from Africa; they swept over Corsica again, and Sardinia, landing on the mainland at Nicaea (Nice) and at Narbona, and the Tuscan coast. Leo's forts could not move to meet the incoming ships. One hope Charlemagne held to. A Byzantine fleet had been sighted off Sicily.

If the arm of the other emperor reached out from Constantinople to aid him, in this fashion, the two of them might keep the coasts safe, even if the isles were lost.

Charlemagne nursed that hope. He had failed to launch strong fleets; his clumsy craft of green wood had been scattered and driven as if by blasting winds. When he sat down at the silver table he studied the plan of Constantine's great city. Surely it had mighty harbors and an arsenal, with the buildings called University where—his envoys said—the Greeks made an unquenchable flame named Sea Fire, because it burned on the water. This Greek flame could destroy enemy vessels.

Who was his envoy at Constantinople? Hugo, the young count of Tours, and Amalhar the bishop. Hugo reported faithfully that the peace treaty could not be signed because the weak Michael had been exiled by a stronger soldier called the Armenian. No one could be certain of this Armenian's policy, except that he did not favor images. . . . Strange it was that Irene, a scheming woman, had been devoted to the holy images. . . . Charlemagne waited for Amalhar to return with the peace treaty signed.

Anxiety weighed on him since the loss of Charles and Pepin. Both his hands had rested on those two strong sons. Now he labored alone, using his ivory staff as if it were a new kind of scepter, walking slowly bareheaded through the broken corridor, waiting for tidings that would ease his despair.

He counted the weeks until he could put aside his staff, and robes, to mount for the hunting. When he could take the road to the Ardennes with his huntsmen, the devil of fever would leave him, and he could sleep until sunrise showed the tree branches in shadow shapes upon the tent over his head.

Before then would come the assembly of the seigneurs, and the plans for the next year. This year the assembly must be at Aix.

When he told Burchard that, the Constable nodded, in silence.

"Bernard must make the journey from Pavia to be at the gathering. Adalhard can wait at Rome."

His officer assented and said gravely that the Count of the Breton March could not leave his post, because of restlessness among the Breton folk. And the lords of the Basque mountains with the Gascons could be counted out; they had deserted the armed host of Aquitaine.

The words stirred memories in the aged king. Thirty and five years before, Roland had been the Warden of the Breton March, and the armed host had fallen before the Basques at Roncesvalles—the place no one mentioned now.

"You say the Basques have deserted?" he asked.

His sharp tone alerted his commander of the armed forces. "The report is, Lord King, they have left the standard of Louis the king, and disappeared into their mountains."

"Where—does Louis bear his standard?"

"Toward Huesca, by the Ebro."

Charlemagne had known that. He only wanted the officer to confirm it. Huesca had revolted from his rule; it lay near to Saragossa.

In memory he beheld the red heights of Spain, against the thin blue of the sky. He felt the heat of the sun striking through him at dawn. A land of treachery and hidden danger. In his mind he weighed the heedlessness of Louis, the boy's blind trust in the protection of the Lord. The Basques had vanished into their mountains. Again he searched his memory, listening to the warning of the warrior, William of Toulouse. Above the road the empty hills were a sign of danger, because the shepherds had driven off their flocks. The memories brought deep foreboding.

One son he had left to him. What his labor had created depended now on the survival of Louis, the heir. The flames of torches tossed away had destroyed his Rhine bridge, massive and enduring. How much more fragile was the rule of a dozen peoples!

"Lord Constable," he said, formally, "send at once to Louis, my son, my wish and command that he return at speed from the Ebro March. With his standard and the armed levies."

His memory quested along the valley of the Ebro, climbing to the two passes, one perilous and one safe. Burchard, surprised and attentive, waited for him to finish speaking.

"I wish the route of his return to be by Urgel, the town, and the pass of the Perch, to his city of Toulouse, then hither in his own good time."

"By Urgel and the pass of the—Perch," murmured Burchard, who had a way of repeating orders. Curiously he stared up at the old man, who seemed to be lost in brooding. Had he anything more to add?

Twisting the signet ring on his thick finger, Charlemagne roused from brooding. The summer's assembly would be festive, he said slowly, and the lay and ecclesiastical lords

290

would come not for a campaign but to render fealty to Louis, his son, as emperor. It was time that his son received the crown. (He said nothing of summoning Leo, the Pope, to bestow it.) Let the lord Seneschal prepare to entertain mighty people in all their numbers.

"For joyous tidings have come to us by land and by sea," Charlemagne informed his paladins. "Never have our land and our folk been more blessed by the mercies of the Lord God. It is fitting that in peace and glory, the Lord aiding, my son shall take the title of emperor, together with me, to be emperor alone at my death."

So great appeared his anticipation that his paladins felt relief and joy in their turn. Einhard told the physicians and they were glad that the sick man had at last called his strong son to his side.

Alone in his sleeping chamber that night, Charlemagne counted over the weeks to come, and decided that Louis would begin his journey by early Hay Month, and the coronation would be held at Second Cropping. Then, by the moon of the Vintage Month he could summon his huntsmen and take the road to the Ardennes.

The legend grew that summer. Where the lords' cavalcades filled the highroads, they held festival. Where the monastic trains of hooded folk wound down from the hills, they chanted prayers for the emperors twain. From Orléans, where Theodulf joined him, to Theodo's Villa the folk made holyday when Louis passed with the array of his kingdom. Yet when the throngs cried acclaim they shouted also for the mighty Charlemagne in his city of glory.

It was a fortunate journey, said the seigneurs of Provence, for they had come unharmed through the Pyrenees, despite the trap laid for them by the treacherous Basques, "as they are wont to do."

Although short in stature as his grandsire, Louis made a brave appearance, broad in shoulders and erect, zealous in praying at the shrines. Gentle they called him, handsome and pious.

The throngs filled the valley of the Würm, and pavilions rose on the far hills. For Charlemagne had summoned in all bishops and abbots; for weeks he held them in council "to decide among themselves all matters for the good of the empire." On the reading stand before Hildebald—who had come from the Colony to be archchaplain of Aix—lay the great Bible of Alcuin's making.

Long did these lords of the churches debate the new laws, the tithes, and benefices, while Charlemagne waited with his staff, on his field stool by the Mary Church. They went out to him with their opinions and his high voice exhorted them to greater things. "You have numbered the vices of these, my people; now list what good works you have done . . . there is no dignity save in merit of works . . . you say there is peace and accord; show me the compacts of peace you have made with my counts who accuse you of quarreling . . . for after the emperor, the duty of governing the people of God lies between you and those counts!"

Not speedily did these lords of minsters and monasteries reach agreements that pleased their emperor. The rumor of their debates passed out to the farmers and the pilgrims at evensong.

Some of the visitors noticed how beggars showed their sores at the portals of the palace; vagabonds skulked by walls to slit purses. Prostitutes rode in with the merchants' carts from Pavia and Passau. In ribbons and pheasant plumes they walked the courtyards with eyes for ermine cloaks passing and the flash of jeweled hands. For a silver solidus or whispered promise of a lusty half hour the doorkeepers let in the women. Servitors in the corridors took more money from them and snickered, whispering that the birds of finest feather nested upstairs in the royal chambers, and charged a higher price.

Bernard the young king came in from Italy with his four

half-grown sisters and knew not where to quarter them because the women's chambers babbled and reeked like a brothel. Charlemagne quartered the young girls, his grandchildren, among the girls of his concubines. Sometimes he could not remember the names of the younglings. With the elfin Rothaid, Adelinda the Saxon beauty reigned in this roost, because she was mother of Thierry, the seven-year boy, last to be born to him.

To Bernard the old emperor babbled how his enthroned son and grandson must nourish and minister to this tender brood of children.

When Louis the Pious came in, he eyed with disdain the bedizened women, thinking of the good Hildegard, his mother. He took up his residence with Hildebald, and his father allowed it.

Charlemagne greeted his son with tears of joy, for now in his weakness he wept and laughed easily. Anxiously his glance swept the faces behind Louis, recognizing with relief Bera the Visigoth. But Sancho the Wolf, hero of the Basques, was not in the king's following; Rostaing of the Gironne, who had carried the standard, had not come.

So the disloyal had deserted his son. Louis, joyful at beholding the gold dome of the Chapel, recked little of it. Yet loyalty was the first link in the chain that bound together the Christian people. Without loyalty there could be neither good will nor honesty. How many links were needed to make strong the chain? Nourishment from the harvests joined to trustworthy money, they stretched all the way to the anchor link of armed force, by sea and land. That last link he had never been able to forge. He had tempered it in the blood of his champions, of Roland and Eric, Gerold and Audulf.

Now, enthroned before the western windows, he greeted his liegemen assembled in the great hall. When he heard murmurings of evil tidings from the Campanian coast, he told his liegemen of final peace, by Adalhard's making, with the last of the Lombards, the Beneventans. The peril of the

Saracen fleets had allied together Greeks, Lombards, and Franks, to resist them. When the Count of the East reported the pressure of Slavs, he retorted that Hohbuki had been won back. If Huesca had been lost, the watch castles of the Pyrenees stood safe, owing to the merit of Louis the king, and the providence of the Lord God.

Every day he searched the faces before him for that of Amalhar the bishop, who was on the road from Constantinople. If Amalhar could arrive, to set between his hands the signed peace of the other emperor—then the coronation of Louis would be fortunate in omen.

By the dawn of the coronation day, Amalhar had not arrived. Charlemagne limped from his curtain and eased his weight down on the bench, with a grateful sigh, to be shaved and combed.

The sky over the hills seemed to be clear. Pointing at it, he said, "A good sign. Are not the storms of strife and famine ending? Never has a day come with so much of peace and charity awaiting us."

Then, feeling the iron knife edge caressing his jaw and the ivory comb stroking his head, he slumbered. The illness had taken from him the small store of strength remaining at his age of seventy-one. He had become a mask, a moving image of majesty. One step following the other, he drew himself through the ritual of ruling, sustained by a reflex of his will. He could no longer separate in his mind his brood of grandchildren, the younglings of his family, from the empire he had made. The need of the gangling bastard Thierry joined with the necessity of Amalhar's coming . . .

In the full morning of that eleventh of September, 813, he entered the nave of his church, while they sang, "The Cross of the faithful . . ." One step after the other, he passed between the dark columns toward the myriad lights of the altar. Leaning on the strong shoulder of his son, he did not need his staff. His head bore the imperial crown, on his chest a heavy chain of gold bore the regal insignia. As nearly as Charlemagne could tell, he wore the robes of the ancient emperors.

Beheld in this manner by the priesthood at either side and by the nobility in the gallery, Charlemagne towered among them in majesty. Kneeling in prayer, rising to turn at the altar, where rested the other crown, he seemed to them to be vital with hope and power. When he spoke of Louis as a true son and true servant of the Lord, they shed tears of rejoicing. When he asked if they were agreed that he should grant the crown of the empire to this son, the king of Aquitaine, they responded with one voice that it should be done, "by the will of God and the interest of the empire."

Only when Charlemagne faced his son and questioned him as to his will to carry out the duties of ruler did his voice ramble unexpectedly. After demanding of him the protection of all churches, the charity toward all in misery, Charlemagne went on, "And to be at all times merciful to your sisters, to your nephews and nieces, as well as all others of your blood."

Again he asked his son to swear to do so, and Louis gave his oath. Then Charlemagne placed the crown upon the head of his son, and prayed: "Blessed is the Lord God who gave my eyes to behold this day a son of mine upon my throne."

The throng shouted, "Long life to Louis, emperor and Augustus!"

Hildebald advanced to the altar to celebrate the Mass, and the song began, "Come Holy Spirit . . ."

To the watchers at that moment, Charlemagne was clothed in more than majesty. He stood by the altar, summoning them forward like an apostle of the old, miraculous age. The boy, Bernard, came forward for consecration as king of the Lombards.

They held festival that afternoon with high heart. For days the lords of the realm swore fealty to Louis, their co-emperor, and Charlemagne heaped upon his son the richest gifts. No one except Burchard, and Charlemagne himself, remembered that Amalhar had not returned from Constantinople.

Yet they were surprised when Charlemagne bade his son journey back to Aquitaine, where his duties awaited him. "So that," a chronicler explained, "the Lord Emperor might retain his title with accustomed honor."

The physicians and Einhard were deeply disturbed, because the ailing father had need of the son's strength. Moreover the place of an emperor of the realm was not far off, in Aquitaine. But there seemed to be no realization in Charlemagne that another could share his rule at Aix. Obediently Louis departed, leaving questioning behind him.

The vintage moon was rising. It stood over the wall of the pine trees, lighting the crowded city and the silver thread of the river. At night the cold breath of autumn came from the forest. Charlemagne counted the days until he could ride into the forest to rest.

Under the moon Aix resumed its wonted shape. The pavilions were gone from the hills. After sunset few lights showed. In the forest red sparks gleamed where leaves burned. The cattle were turned out to second-crop the garnered fields. Charlemagne summoned his four huntsmen, asking for mastiff dogs and horses to be readied. They were ready.

The physicians begged him not to go forth into the cold. He said he would not fare to the dark Ardennes but to the near preserves of Aix. He told Burchard the things to be done. Waking at night, he felt his way to the candles that burned in the Treasury and Vestiary. For a space he looked at the sealed chests. He sought out the silent Rothaid where she slept apart from other women, and bade her have care of the boy Thierry, born like herself out of wedlock.

One dawn hour he went to the private door of the Mary Church, unshaved and unrobed. He had on the sheepskin jacket and the blue mantle, and he felt at ease. After he had made his prayer, he looked over the vessels on the altar, and the lamps that he had ordered to be kept alight. Then he went out to summon the huntsmen.

296

"He set out to hunt as usual," Einhard wrote, "although weak from age. From the hunt near Aix the Chapel he returned about the first day of November. There in January he was seized with a high fever and took to his bed. He prescribed fasting for himself as he usually did with fever. Yet he suffered from a pain in the side that the Greeks call pleurisy; still he persisted in fasting, with only occasional drinks to keep up his strength. On the seventh day after he took to his bed, he died at the third hour of the morning, after partaking of the holy communion, in the seventy-second year of his age."

Charlemagne died in January 814. A few days after that Amalhar, the bishop envoy, arrived from Constantinople with the treaty of peace between the two empires signed. But Charlemagne was no longer there to enforce it and to try to join together the divided halves of Christian rule.

From the first day there was a sense of the unusual in the death of the monarch who had dominated the lives of so many people for nearly forty-six years. Louis, absent in the south, could not take over the direction. Charlemagne had neglected to tell his officers where he wished to be buried. The paladins consulted together and decided to entomb the aged body the next day in royal regalia within a marble sarcophagus beneath the altar of his basilica at Aix, the city he had created. Then, too, only young children led by Rothaid appeared in the mourning procession from the palace.

Stirred by the improvised burial, the people of Aix very quickly remembered portents of the end—how a trembling of the earth had shaken down Charlemagne's colonnade not long before, and a bolt of lightning had struck the dome of the Mary Church, knocking the gilt ball to earth.

In the chapel itself they pointed out to Einhard how the inscription on the cornice above the lower piers had changed mysteriously. In the two words *Karolus Princeps*, the red of

297

the title word had faded away until it could barely be seen. And Einhard thereupon recalled how in the earlier year of the sun's eclipse a flaming light had crossed the sky, to dash Charlemagne's spear from his hand and so forecast the approaching end of his rule.

Such portents could only mean that the hand of the Lord lay upon Frankland. What would follow, if not some change in their world? So, to the widespread sense of loss was joined fear for themselves, deprived of Charlemagne's protection. Out in the villages reassuring rumors sprang up that the great king had not actually died—he slept in his tomb, to waken again if calamity came. Yet fearful throngs of men and women deserted their homes to seek the security of the monasteries—a proceeding that would have drawn an angry tirade from the living Charlemagne.

When Louis arrived at last from Aquitaine, the young emperor proved himself both conscientious and fanatically devout. With care he carried out all his father's directions for the disposal of the palace treasure. At the same time he named four arbiters to comb out of the palace chambers the bevy of privileged women and hangers-on. Beggars and bribe-hungry doorkeepers were driven from the portals, while jugglers and dancing bears were banned as creatures of the Devil.

Louis ordered an arch of gold to be raised over the tomb with the words:

BENEATH THIS LIES THE BODY
OF CHARLES, GREAT AND DEVOUT EMPEROR,
WHO NOBLY ENLARGED THE KINGDOM OF THE FRANKS.

Very quickly, however, a change took place. Louis the Pious held himself to be a devout emperor, heir of the Roman emperors. Ruling with beneficial tolerance, he held splendid audiences and assumed the title of Emperor Augustus, which his father had avoided using. At Ingelheim's palace he ordered paintings to show on the walls the victories of Charles the Hammer, the founding of the cities of Rome and Constantinople, and the crowning of his father.

With zeal Louis undertook the duty of caring for the churches, yet he did not ride the width of the provinces and the length of the coasts. The mass of people knew him only by name, and were constrained to seek mercy and aid from their local seigneurs. Without the magic of Charlemagne's name, their loyalty turned more toward the counts and dukes. These also became more independent of the emperor at Aix.

In the family itself Louis conscientiously protected the younglings, the chance-born brood of Charlemagne. (Many of the children became noted in later years, as chroniclers like Nithard, or heads of abbeys like Thierry.) Yet in Italy Bernard, headstrong as his grandfather at that age, revolted against his imperial uncle, and Theodulf, that man of imagination, joined the revolt, which was wiped out in blood.

Lacking force to control the flux of his dominion, Louis the Pious followed the example of his ancestors in partitioning it among three sons. In his case they survived him, and his death began their struggle for mastery. A poet wrote of their battle at Fontenoy in 841:

> The cry of war is here,
> And over there fierce fighting breaks forth,
> Where brother brings down brother . . .
> Their ancient kindness forespent.

Louis had been devout. But religion alone could not hold together this nascent *imperium* of Christians. It had been fostered by the personalities of Charles the Hammer and Pepin the Short. It had been shaped and enlarged by Charlemagne. Without him, lacking racial base or lasting institutions, it ceased to be.

Oddly enough, Louis had been the first to name himself Roman emperor, when the western empire was ending and the chaos of feudal Europe beginning. Suddenly the Rhine ceased to be a mighty arterial and became an embattled barrier between the Germanic-speaking folk to the north and east, and the romance-speaking peoples of West Francia and Aquitaine—between the future Germany and France. Charlemagne's communication corridor from the Lowlands, over the Alps into Italy, was lost in the feudal kaleidoscope—except for a shadowy "Lotharingia"—and the plains of Lombardy became again a road of conquest, while isolated cities fortified themselves with higher walls, ruled by their own dukes of the palace and guilds of the market place, to become a Milan, Florence, Ferrara. And the Venetians on Rialto's isle sought their future on the sea.

Elsewhere, with the shattering of Charlemagne's *imperium,* feudal vassals clung to their fiefs, and the abbeys to their benefices. Soon they would defy the central authority of kings. Papal Rome, unable to summon the armed force of a Pepin or Charlemagne from the outside, would sink into new weakness. Some fragments of the Carolingian frontier zones would develop into new communities, in northern, Christian Spain and along the Danube, where Austria would take shape out of the East March.

But while the brief Carolingian dynasty failed and the nascent empire died, something else survived unnoticed and almost unrecorded. The Carolingian renaissance went on.

It endured through the failure of government and the wars, a fragile heritage of knowledge and hope. Charlemagne's School, Alcuin's fellowship of minds, Angilbert's half-heeded songs, Theodulf's open law courts and strong-ribbed churches were the pioneer efforts of a wider recovery. The chapel of Aix, the palace of Ingelheim, the community of St. Denis gained new, small splendors. Charlemagne's life line of the churches, from Bremen to Tortosa, did not break down entire.

The great Gregorian chants, the sacramentaries and breviaries, Alcuin's new Bible, passed outward in the silence of the monasteries. The copying of books in the clear Carolingian script went on. The verses of Virgil and the vision of St. Augustine reached greater numbers of untaught minds. They went from abbeys and palaces to the parish schools. They escaped destruction in the barbarian invasions because they could not well be looted or burned. They fled with the monks inland to the mountains, to Reichenau and the lake of Constance, where artists gained new skill in illumination.

The Carolingian writing penetrated to Italy, as far as Monte Cassino. In Anglo-Saxon England, a king of Wessex, Alfred the Great, struggling himself to keep culture alive by copying books, sent to Frankland for instructors like John the Saxon.

By then the memory of the real Charlemagne had become obscured. It appeared for the last time in many centuries when Einhard the Dwarfling retired to the Benedictine monastery that he had enriched with relics brought from Rome in his journeys. There Einhard penned his loving portrait of his great king and companion, the *Vita Karoli*. Yet to his human portrait the Dwarfling added nostalgic touches, as well as a few attributes of his other hero of imagination, Augustus Caesar. By that time, a dozen years after his death, the real Charlemagne began to assume the physical likeness of the legendary king.

The remembrance of his lust for women did not vanish without a trace. An obscure monk wrote a *Vision of Charlemagne* relating how the mighty Frank carried away a saintly virgin, one Amalberga, to his palace and in consequence now suffered the torments of purgatory. But this was a lone voice, soon lost in the chorus of *cantilènes*, folk tales, and monastic rewriting of the life and deeds of the son of Pepin the Short.

For, by some alchemy of human imagination, Charlemagne became the hero, not of court chronicles or of his own Franks but of whoever wrote, told, or sang in the new calamities of western Europe. He became, as it were, the heroic monarch of humanity at large.

Soon after Einhard the student poet Walafrid Strabo wrote a foreword to the former's *Vita Karoli*. While Strabo seemed to know the facts about the dead king, his "most glorious Emperor Charles" already showed traces of the remarkable monarch of a golden age. "... beyond all kings he was most eager in making search for wise men ... he rendered his kingdom which was dark and blind (if I may use such an expression) when God put it into his hands, radiant with the blaze of fresh learning, unknown until then in our barbarism. But now once more men turn to other interests, and the light of wisdom, less loved, is dying out in most of them."

It is not, perhaps, surprising that Charlemagne's deeds should be exaggerated in this way. But it is extraordinary that in legend he became what he had never been in life.

The real Arnulfing had been rather tall and unusually forceful, particularly in his determination, as well as shrewd in sizing up people. After three generations his wraith, the legendary Charlemagne, changed in physical semblance. It towered above other men by a head, terrifying pagans and foes by the glance of its piercing eyes. It shed the old Frankish dress for imperial robes, and wore a crown when riding to hunt. By its anger it reduced all listeners to trembling silence. Riding back to stricken Roncesvalles, it holds the sun arrested in the sky to prolong the daylight.

In life the hefty Frank had hardly been a figure of kingly dignity. His legendary self became majestic, all-wise and all-powerful. A long beard added dignity to this *aureus Karolus,* this golden Charles. Naturally the body in the tomb at Aix adjusted itself to the legend. There Charlemagne in his long sleep sat erect, a great Gospel book on his knees, his face toward the portal. Since he was not dead, his beard continued to grow, even into the cracks of the stone flagging.

About this time (885) the worthy monk of St. Gall wrote out his *Gesta Karoli*—Deeds of Charles—to depict with his "stammering and toothless tongue" the mighty events of the "golden empire of the illustrious Charles." After hearing echoes of the *cantilènes* of old soldiers, the good monk gives many a realistic twist to his anecdotes of the real, earthly and "most cunning Charles." Yet by now, in his mind, the great king has become an "iron Charles," whose people, "harder than iron themselves, paid universal honor to his hardness of iron."

So in the memory of the monk an invincible Charlemagne ruled over a warlike people during a golden age of security and peace. This is a startling metamorphosis of the Arnulfing who was no leader in battle but who led an unmilitant people out to campaigns for some two-score years.

The invasions were responsible for it.

Charlemagne had not been in his tomb a dozen years when the Northmen began to break through the sea borders. Up the Rhine and the Seine and the Loire their fleets advanced to devastate the cities. There was no longer an army to hold them off. As early as 845 a grandson of Charlemagne watched helplessly with his seigneurs and levies—who refused to attack the formidable invaders—while the Northmen gathered up eleven hundred captives from the Seine villages.

A second Godfried ascended the Loire with his long ships, to loot and burn Tours. Theodulf's Orléans fell to the sea raiders. At. St. Denis they broke open the tombs of the Arnulfings to get at the regalia on the bodies. Up the Meuse they turned to Aix, burning the Mary Church. Between raids they built themselves winter settlements along the coasts.

While the triumphant Dane-Normans ventured as far as Spain, the Moslem fleets of Andalus and North Africa possessed themselves of the western Middle Sea. From their island bases the aggressive Moslems (Abbasids uniting here with Ommayids) seized the land bridge to Italy. After capturing Malta, they concentrated along the Sicilian coast by Palermo, seizing a bridgehead near Salerno and thrusting up into the Adriatic, and the coast to Rome.

Religious zeal drove the Moslem attack forward, but the Arab admirals made use of organized shipping with high

303

technical skill. One of them, off Sicily in 837, matched the "Greek" fire of a Byzantine fleet with new naphtha flame throwers. They gained their objective, which was to pry the Byzantine navy loose from the sea lanes.

At Rome another Leo built a last-ditch defense wall around St. Peter's. Up the Volturno, Arab horsemen advanced to the rock height of Monte Cassino. Only weak resistance met them. The scattered Carolingian kings lacked ships, the Popes had no army; Benevento sought only to defend itself, Venetian warships undertook little so long as their haven at Rialto was safe; the Byzantine navy fought only to keep open the channels of trade.

Constantinople itself, instead of joining forces with this Christian west, withdrew into new isolation. Flotillas from the Russian rivers, led by Scandinavians, plagued the queen city, while the powerful Bulgars gained mastery in the Balkan hinterland and the Dalmatian coast.

Beyond the Bulgars a greater peril appeared from the "great plain of the east." Savage Magyars drove up the Danube into the Bavarian valleys; their horsemen broke through Charlemagne's East March, skirting the Venetian isles, dividing devastated Aix hopelessly from beleaguered Constantinople. Trade of the outer world no longer penetrated to the remnants of Frankland, which were driven inland as they had been before the rise of the first Arnulfings.

Again the surviving Franks were thrown on their bodily resources. A terrible migration began, away from the coasts, the river routes, and fertile valleys, toward safety in the mountains. It turned east. Fugitives took their herds across the Rhine into the Saxon wilderness. They sought refuge in the hilltop castles of strong, fighting seigneurs. Again they were isolated from the boulevards of the sea.

Inertia set in. Except in northern Italy (the old Lombardy) urban life ceased. In Rome, they say that from the year 870 to 1000 no new building was raised or old one repaired. The island of Paris was besieged and sacked by the methodical and militant Northmen. There was no longer any force to protect the Christian people.

Surviving congregations looked for salvation only after death. In the general despair it seemed as if the familiar world were moving toward its end at the year 1000 of salvation——

Through this breakdown of government and interregnum of thought the memory of Charlemagne lingered, and changed. The image of the "unwearied king" who had never despaired merged into that of the lord of Christianity—*sire de la créstienté*—who preserved his people. By comparison his age seemed to be one of enlightened peace.

More than that, by some transmutation of longing, the name of Charlemagne became the hope of the varied Christian peoples. As their sufferings increased, so grew the poignancy of their lost hope.

Something very unusual happened to the memory of Charlemagne as the ninth century ended. Because the civil strife and barbarian invasions devastated so much of his ancestral Frankland, from the Loire to the Rhine, much of the records, the building, the very objects, and local traditions of his time was lost. Teachers and the "hooded folk" fled from the ancient Roman river towns easterly into the mountains. Ironically, many Frankish nobles migrated across the Rhine into the security of the former Saxonland. Monastic settlements of the old East March, from Fulda to St. Gall, became the new survival centers.

The effect of this exodus on the memory of Charlemagne was decisive. Traces of the actual man largely vanished. Tales of the legendary king went with the migrants into new territory. Precious books and relics salvaged from the menaced Rhine valley became the evidence elsewhere of the idealized lord of Christianity.

During the ensuing catastrophic generations little was written of Charlemagne. His memory went, as it were, underground. But it endured. It passed on by travelers' tales and it crept into songs. Monks of Fulda, observing the stars, called the guide stars of the great Bear the *Karlswagen*. Hostel keepers of the Pyrenees pointed out a cross of stone as Charlemagne's. Hunters in the Alps told how a white hart had appeared, to show Charlemagne the road to the east.

At Venice, which he had attempted to master, he became in memory the inspired prophet of the city's preservation. They said there he passed by, and cast a heavy spear into the deepest green water, declaring, "As surely as no one of us will ever see that spear again, your enemies will always be defeated by God's anger."

Dispersed in this fashion by legend tellers, the memory of Charlemagne took root in many lands. Transplanted, it tended to become the image of a universal benevolent monarch. In Saxonland, now the rallying point of Germanic strength, it went through rather remarkable evolution. Tenth-century Teutons seemed to remember him at first as a maker of laws, and then as the king missionary who had brought Christianity to them. Did not his manifold fine wooden churches prove that beyond a doubt?

Did not the illuminated books, the goldwork, and rare ivory carvings at Fulda and Reichenau testify to the splendor of his day? When these East Germans began to offer real resistance both to Northmen and Magyars, their new kings, the Ottos, arose in Saxony with mixed conceptions of Charlemagne. They could not wholly claim him but they could not manage without him. So they claimed him as the first emperor of their *imperium Teutonici*. The first Otto imitated Charlemagne's festivals and had himself crowned in the rebuilt chapel at Aix. The third Otto sought coronation farther afield in Rome, as restorer, after Charlemagne, of the Roman Empire. (The one thing Charlemagne had not sought to restore.)

After revering him as a missionary monarch, and honoring him as the founder of their "empire" (soon to be entitled the meaningless Holy Roman Empire) the Germans began to conceive of Charlemagne as saintly, keeping in touch with heaven through the services of the Angel Gabriel as messenger.

By then the legendary Charlemagne became a force in the minds of men.

The world, although stricken, did not end in the year 1000. New vitality came to Christian Europe, and the legendary Charlemagne also gained new life.

Like a wraith invisible he accompanied pilgrims journeying to shrines. Along the pilgrim routes, monasteries and hostels naturally desired to gain credit, by miracles and relics. What miracle drew such crowds as that of the *sire de la créstienté* prophesying about the place? What relic would be more coveted than a scrap of writing or shred of cloth "truly of Charlemagne himself?"

The road across the Pyrenees became known as the "road of the Franks." (Actually this pilgrim route did not pass through the rather shallow valley called Roncesvalles.) Each halting place revived feverishly the memory of Charlemagne as the purest of the pilgrims, the mightiest of monarchs. All the way to the edge of the fearful western ocean the memory went, to the shrine of St. James of Compostela. Had not Charlemagne been there when he conquered all of Spain, except Saragossa, from the paynim Saracens? True, that great wayfarer had not been able to cross the barrier of ocean. (The remembrance that his course had been checked by the sea persisted for a long time.)

On the roads of Burgundy, the churches cherished priceless relics, drops of the sacred blood bestowed, they said, upon Charlemagne by the patriarch of Jerusalem. (There was still doubt whether Charlemagne had reached Jerusalem himself, but it seemed that he had fared east to Constantinople to advise the lord emperor of the East how to defend himself against the pagans.)

When the poets of Provence found their songs, they delighted hearers with the deeds of Charlemagne, the king and champion of the Lord. And their audiences demanded still more tales of him. On the island of Paris they sang how he had held his court by the rock of Montparnasse, and had blessed the church of St. Geneviève.

When the songs rose into the great *chansons* of a new France, Charlemagne emerged in them, joyful as the monarch of that sweetest land—*"un roi en France de moult grant seignorie."* Had he not devoted himself to good St. Denis from his boyhood? All his life he had labored for the *dolce France.* In his day they were certain their sweet France had extended far indeed, beyond the dark Ardennes, beyond the Alps of the snowy passes, and the land of the Huns, to far Cathay.

With this beginning of feudal life, the image of Charlemagne assumed the attributes of a feudal monarch. Mighty vassals served him—twenty dukes carried the plates to his table. Four kings attended him, and the Pope chanted the Mass for him. At the crowning of his son, Louis, however something unexpected happened that the psychologists of history might trace back to the reality of the coronation at Aix. To Charlemagne's great anger, Louis was afraid to come forward to take the crown!

With the advent of knighthood and the singing of prowess in single combat, the image of Charlemagne—as the champion of sweet France—fell easily into this new mold. The man who had been such a consummate strategist and prime mover of peoples in real life became a warrior king in the new style, capable of splitting an armored foeman apart from helm to saddle with one blow of his sword. The man who had tried to keep his Franks out of ranged battle now decided wars by a single triumphant onset and onfray of lances. His iron broadsword—which the records of his time mention only during ceremonies—also gained new personality. *Joyuese* by name, forged of the finest steel, it bore within its hilt the most precious of relics, a fragment of the Sacred Lance. Since minstrels of this later day turned quickly to the love interests of their heroes, Charlemagne also fared forth on behalf of a matchless damsel who was usually the daughter of the Saracen monarch of Spain, converted by Charlemagne from the devil worship of "Mahom" to Christianity. His brood of lusty daughters vanished into the person of a single, virtuous, lily-white and rose-red *Bellisent*.

Nothing that appealed to the popular fancy was denied this "first king of France, crowned by God while the angels sang." Even at the advanced age of two hundred years, he rises from his ivory throne and summons his failing strength to go to their aid, with the cry "Barons of France—to horse and to arms!" Mothers in the cottages consoled their children in hardship by repeating, "When Charlemagne beheld our misery he shed tears from his eyes that ran down his long nose, and all down his white beard and fell to the neck of his horse."

Jealously the imagination of the French nation claimed the Charlemagne of legend as its own. At the same time the aspect of the sleeper in the tomb at Aix changed to conform to the legend. From the diadem of gold, a veil descended over his face. His gloved left hand supported the gold-bound Gospel on his knees, while his right hand held erect his bared sword "drawn for ever against his enemies."

This ghost of the Arnulfing very soon became visible to the eyes of the curious. Illuminators of the manuscripts of his legend painted him aroused from sleep by good St. James, or riding into Constantinople; woven into tapestries, he bore the regalia of later-day majesty, ermine and velvet, on his body, orb and scepter in his hands. Goldworkers shaped reliquaries for his bones or belongings (his body had been exhumed, to be clad in, among other things, a mantle of purple Byzantine silk, adorned with elephants). When stained glass gave splendor to churches, the Charlemagne of fable stood revealed to the congregations.

To these convincing pictures there was soon added a biography. A monk of Châlons wishing to honor his patron saint, James of Compostela, gathered out of the legends a really marvelous life of Charlemagne for the instruction of future generations.

With that the image of Charlemagne became, after more than three centuries, monarch of a world of wish fulfillment in which Normans were driven into the sea, and Saracens expelled from Christendom, and the aid of the Lord brought to sorrowing human beings.

Perhaps only in such an age of growing faith and vitality could a legend leave its imprint on royal courts, national institutions, laws and monastic life, as well as popular literature and arts. But the legendary Charlemagne did that.

A real mystery of his lifetime overshadowed medieval Europe. What, exactly, had been the empire of Charlemagne? Was it the *imperium Christianum*? Men of the churches argued so. Was it the *Imperium Romanorum*? The Papal court maintained so, arguing that it possessed still the authority by which Leo had crowned Charlemagne emperor in Rome. Was it the *imperium Francorum*? The newly risen German monarchs claimed that Charlemagne had founded their Germanic empire. One of them contrived to have him canonized, locally, to begin the cult of Charlemagne. All three concepts were denied by the French, who claimed him as their first king.

So began the long disputation of the powers and principalities of the western, Christian Europe that Charlemagne had tried in vain to gather into a whole. Monarchs of the Holy Roman Empire—which never united Europe—looked back to Charlemagne. Frederick Barbarossa invoked his deeds as precedents for his own ambition; Frederick II staged anew the exhumation of the skeleton, to wrap a new mantle over the elephant shroud, and in our modern age Napoleon Bonaparte, calling himself emperor of the French, invoked the memory of "our predecessor, Charlemagne." But all that lies within the record of history, not of the legend.

It refused to die. It could not be localized. At Aix-la-Chapelle they said that the church bells rang without human touch when Charlemagne died. In the mountains of Bavaria they said that Charlemagne waited there, within a cavern. In the Rhineland they said that when Charlemagne's beard grew three times around his tomb, the end of the world would come.

When the Christians of Spain began their long struggle for freedom with the kalifs of Córdoba, their minstrels told how Charlemagne had gone that way before them, with Roland. The memory of his paladins changed into the Twelve Peers, heroes of other legends, now serving Charlemagne—Oliver, and Ogier the Dane, brave Duke Naimes of Bavaria, and the valiant archbishop Turpin.

When Gascons and Provençals rode to this war they carried the banner of Charlemagne, the standard of Jerusalem, now the oriflamme of France.

Around them the immortal *Song of Roland* took shape, with its burden of courage and death.

When men in the west, from England to the Rhineland, left their homes to journey forth on the first crusade, there was a lifting of spirits, a sense of a new horizon to be found, that had not been felt since the time of Charlemagne.

To the crusaders on ship or shore minstrels sang how Charlemagne had gained Jerusalem before them from the Saracen Harun. He had voyaged to Jerusalem, to the land of the apostles, to guard the Sepulcher itself.

So the image of Charlemagne remained a force in the minds of humanity at large, summoning them forth from their homes. It went with wayfarers as far as the roads led.

The barbarian Arnulfing who built his city in the forest and raised the small gray Mary Church had become a memory jealously possessed, striding over Europe—a memory of a day now vanished when Christians had somehow gathered together to seek their Lord.

AUTHOR'S NOTE

IN THIS EFFORT to tell a life story of Charles the Great, I am deeply indebted to the work of Arthur Kleinclausz of the Faculty of Letters, Lyon. His volumes on Charlemagne, Alcuin, and the rise of the Carolingian empire have served as a guide.

This narrative of the human Charlemagne is based on the sources of that time, and laid against the setting of his Frankland as well as I could reconstruct it. In it rivers almost always have their modern names. So do the cities, except for those important then and little known today, as with Theodo's Villa for Thionville. Titles and ranks are given in the simpler, later medieval form—seigneurs for *seniores*, and Seneschal for the rather odd Latin-Teutonic blend of *Seni-Skalkoz*, Eldest of the Servants.

All people in this book lived as they are depicted; their names are given in the most familiar form, regardless of language. Often, to escape the bare narrative of events in the chronicles, bits of letters or tradition are developed into brief scenes of living persons. Some details and incidents have been drawn from the notorious monk of St. Gall, who seemed to know much of the habits and nature of his great king.

There has been a great amount of history written about Charlemagne, and his legend as it affected literature and events after him, yet the life of the human being who was Charlemagne seems to have escaped the written record.

In writing this book for the general reader—and my own satis-

Author's Note

faction—it struck me that too much emphasis had been laid on what survived of his realm and how it affected the nations of western Europe. Perhaps the most important thing died with him. That was his purpose, his dream, if you will. Kleinclausz calls it, as in the case of Justinian, his ideal and moral aim rather than material accomplishment. And the French master adds: "*Sur la géographie politique singulièrement confuse de l'Europe occidentale et centrale à son avènement, il a projeté une soudaine clarté.*"

It was like the flash of a lighthouse beacon through the murk of Europe, and it did not appear again until the crusades. This narrative tries to tell about that, not so much of his success as of his vital failure.

INDEX

Index

Aucher, Duke, 15–18, 40, 48–49, 62

Audulf, Count, 143, 150, 258, 262

Augustine's *The City of God*, 86–87

Austrasian Franks, 33

Avars, 60, 103, 211; alliance with Bavarians, 136–37, 149, 160–61; attack on Italy, 166; campaigns against, 176, 182–86, 197–99; negotiations with, 194

Baghdad, 217–18

Balearics, seized by Arabs and retaken by Franks, 225, 227

Barcelona, envoy from, 218

Basques, desertion of, 289–90; massacre of Franks by, 94–95; subjected by Moslems, 96

Bavarians, brought under rule of Charlemagne, 149–65; resistance to Pepin, 35–36

Benevento, Italy, 61, 66, 71, 110, 152–55, 163–65, 293–94

Bernard, nephew of Charlemagne, king of Lombards, 276, 280, 289, 292–93, 295, 299

Bernard, uncle of Charlemagne, 20–21, 48–49, 57–60, 62, 85

Bertha, daughter of Charlemagne, 126, 146–48, 179, 213

Bertha (Bertrada), mother of Charlemagne, 23–26, 31, 38, 115, 131; policy and influence of, as queen mother, 40–43, 46–47

Bible prepared by Alcuin for king, 220, 224–25, 247

Bohemia, expedition through, 185

Bohemians, expeditions against, 262–63

Bologna, Italy, 165

Books, copying of, 246–47, 300–1; development of Carolingian script, 251–53; *see also* Bible; Library of Charlemagne

Bremen (Brema), cathedral of, 161

Bretons, revolt of, 136, 143

Breviary prepared by Alcuin, 246

Bridge across Rhine, 190, 210, 287

Britain, commerce with, 146–47

Bulgars, 278, 304

Burchard, Seneschal, 281, 285–90

Byzantine Empire. *See* Eastern Roman Empire

Canal between Rhine and Danube, efforts to dig, 199, 212, 215–17

Capua, Charlemagne at, 154–55

Carcassonne, Aquitaine, battle with Moors at, 187

Carloman, brother of Charlemagne, 23, 26, 30; conflict with Charlemagne, 40–42; death of, 48; half of kingdom inherited by, 39–40

Carolingian Books, 206, 223

Carolingian dynasty, establishment of, 19

Carolingian Renaissance, 245–51, 253, 282–84, 300–1

Carolingian script, development of, 251–53

Carrier pigeons, use of, 129

Charlemagne, anointed by Pope as king's son, 22–27; Bavaria brought under rule of, 149–65; campaigns against Aquitaine, 40–41; campaigns against Saxons, 52–53, 78–83, 102–9, 131–41; conquest of Italy, 54–71, 154–55; crowned emperor of Western Roman Empire, 231–38; division of empire between three sons, 265–66; invasion of Spain, 85–96; legend of, 301–3, 305–11; legend of, during lifetime, 282–85; marriages of, 31, 42–47, 51, 131, 196–97; named king of all Frankland, 48–51; named king of half Frankland, 39–40; as temporal ruler of Italy, 109–14, 165–66; tomb of, 297–98, 309; will of, 279–80

Charles, son of Charlemagne, 100, 125, 135, 139, 166, 179, 194, 209, 262–63, 265–66, 276–77

Charles the Hammer (Martel), 19, 24, 34, 38

Childerich III, last Meroving king of Franks, 19

Christianity, ambition of Charlemagne to unite nations under, 84, 86, 167; conversion of Saxons to, 78–83, 134–35, 140–41, 207–10; *see also* Church of St. Peter

Church, Byzantine. *See* Eastern Roman Empire

Church of St. Peter (Roman), 35; assisted by Pepin, 18, 27, 42;

315

Index

Index